Poor Relief and Charity 1869–1945

Also by Robert Humphreys

SIN, ORGANISED CHARITY AND THE POOR LAW IN VICTORIAN ENGLAND

NO FIXED ABODE: A History of Responses to the Roofless and the Rootless in Britain

Poor Relief and Charity 1869–1945

The London Charity Organization Society

Robert Humphreys
Department of Economic History
The London School of Economics and Political Science

First published 2001 by
PALGRAVE
Houndmills, Basingstoke, Hampshire RG21 6XS and
175 Fifth Avenue, New York, N.Y. 10010
Companies and representatives throughout the world

PALGRAVE is the new global academic imprint of
St. Martin's Press LLC Scholarly and Reference Division and
Palgrave Publishers Ltd (formerly Macmillan Press Ltd).

ISBN 0–333–96839–5

This book is printed on paper suitable for recycling and made from fully managed and sustained forest sources.

A catalogue record for this book is available from the British Library.

Library of Congress Cataloging-in-Publication Data
Humphreys, Robert, 1928–
    Poor relief and charity, 1869–1945: the London Charity
    Organization Society/Robert Humphreys.
        p. cm.
    Includes bibliographical references and index.
    ISBN 0–333–96839–5 (cloth)
    1. Charity Organization Society (London, England)—History.
    2. Charities—England—London—History. 3. Public welfare–
    –England—London—History. 4. Poor—Services for—England–
    –London. I. Title.

HV250.L8 H85 2001
361.8'0941—dc21

                                                              2001046003

10   9   8   7   6   5   4   3   2   1
10 09 08 07 06 05 04 03 02 01

Printed and bound in Great Britain by
Antony Rowe Ltd, Chippenham, Wiltshire

To Trish

Contents

List of Figures

List of Tables

Acknowledgements

The research and presentation of this work would not have been possible without the supportive friendliness of my colleagues in the Department of Economic History at the LSE. The mental stimulation and spirit of good-will gained during my many enjoyable and ever helpful discussions within the Department have been essential. At a time when so many establishments are staffed by people wracked with acute emotional stress I recognize my good fortune in being surrounded by hard-working colleagues who so willingly find the time to help others.

I am also indebted to the invariably helpful members of the various libraries and other custodians of source material; especially to those in the British Library of Political and Economic Science and to those in Goldsmith's Library, Senate House.

I am also most appreciative of the wonderfully loyal support of my friends and family. To Paul and Adrienne, my thanks for time in their busy lives in commenting so constructively on various draft chapters. In particular, I thank Trish for her invaluable comments, corrections and organization of the script. Also for always being there with her calm dependability whenever my spirits seemed to be flagging.

I am entirely responsible for any remaining errors.

List of Abbreviations

AAOC	American Association for Organizing Charities
AICP	Association for Improving the Condition of the Poor
AR	Annual Report
c	by command
CAB	Citizens Advice Bureaux
CAD	Central Aid Society
COQuarterly	*Charity Organisation Quarterly*
COR	*Charity Organisation Reporter*
COReview	*Charity Organisation Review*
COS	Charity Organization Society or, more fully, The Society for Organizing Charitable Relief and Repressing Mendicity and later titular nuances. The acronym COS refers overwhelmingly to the activities and principles initiated by their Council in London. Occasionally, where an action or statement is attributable to a specific COS District Committee in London, a provincial COS in Britain or an overseas COS, this is made clear in the text.
CRS	Central Relief Society (Liverpool)
DC	District Committee
DPS	District Provident Society (Manchester and Salford)
DVS	District Visiting Society
ed.	Editor
edn	Edition
FWA	The Family Welfare Association
GH	Guilds of Help
LGB	Local Government Board
NCCC	National Conference of Charities and Correction
NCSS	National Council of Social Service
PLB	Poor Law Board
PLC	Poor Law Commissioners
PP	Parliamentary Papers
SWA	Social Welfare Association
£	Pound sterling = twenty shillings
s or /-	Shilling = twelve (old) pennies
d	(old) penny

1
Beginnings of the London Charity Organization Society

The charity organization movement emerged around 1870 from a number of similarly motivated groups and rapidly succeeded in spreading its gospel around the world. In London, where the organizationist spark burst into flame, it was an association of gentlemen aided and abetted by the nobility and royalty. They transmitted the belief that it was the responsibility of the better-off to protect and develop the character of the poorer elements of society. This, they said, would best be achieved by halting the prevalent irresponsible haphazard provision of relief to the impoverished. Instead, the veracity and background of each impoverished applicant would first be methodically investigated. Individuals they judged to be deserving of, and likely to benefit from, assistance would be directed to the most appropriate charitable agency to develop their rehabilitation into society. Those pronounced as being unworthy or unsuitable for voluntary assistance were despatched to the Poor Law authorities; these 'undeserving or ineligible cases' included the indolent, the sick and the aged.

The concept of charity organization had immediate attractions for gentlemen of independent means and their female counterparts with time on their hands; especially if they had a twinge of conscience telling them that they should employ a few of their spare hours amongst the poor. What was more, the principle of applying 'scientific' methodology to expose the cunning of the slothful poor and help rectify their immorality, fitted snugly with contemporary individualist ideas. Not surprisingly, the London Charity Organization Society (COS), established in 1869, rapidly attracted the rich and famous. District offices were opened swiftly throughout the metropolis.

Associated COSs mushroomed across Britain and around the globe. Throughout the late-nineteenth century and the early decades of the twentieth, London COS proudly published, annually, the names and addresses of hundreds of overseas Societies practising their principles. Most of Europe and Britain's major colonies rushed to participate in the 'science' of charity organization. But it was in the USA that COS social strategies became most robust and extensive. No USA city was without a Society claiming to practice the principles originating from London COS. During the 1920s there were over 350 American towns represented on the London COS annual list.

Charity organization was heralded throughout the world as being the solution to the growing problem of improving the condition of the urban poor. There seemed to be nothing that could undermine the unbounded confidence of the London COS hierarchy. With the support of the Establishment, they commanded a position of omnipotence on all social matters. How and why their seemingly impenetrable self-assurance was gradually eroded is the main theme of this volume.

Social and economic background

The nineteenth century served to confirm Britain's Greatness to the nation's Establishment. They disseminated the realization that Queen Victoria came to the throne as Queen of the most extensive and powerful Empire known to man. She was titular head of the world's first industrial nation, one that had become by far the most influential in trade, finance, economics and politics. There had been a setback when the recalcitrant American colonists declared their independence back in July 1776 but Britain's leaders interpreted this as little more than a blip in a whole succession of events confirming their nation's global dominance. Wellington's final defeat of Napoleon Bonaparte at Waterloo in June 1815 ended his Hundred Day's adventure and was further confirmation of Britain's incontestable strength and justifiable confidence.[1]

The most obvious reason for the advance in Britain's fortunes was believed to be the exceptional character of its people. Its sons had led the way in showing how science could effectively be harnessed to the good of mankind. Thomas Savery, Thomas Newcomen and James Watt were a few of a whole succession of inventors who successfully developed the steam engine as the vital link in the industrial revolution. By 1787 the introduction of a centrifugal governor, which regulated engine speed predictably so that it could drive wheels throughout industry, meant that steam power was no longer restricted largely to pumping operations. Steam could now drive the wheels in textile and flour-mills, breweries, potteries, the chemical industry – as well as nurturing the development of other manufactures. The introduction of steam meant that industry was freed locationally, no longer confined to being adjacent to a river or other water source. Of course, the steam engine was but one of many inventions contributing to Britain's industrial power; others were the massive improvements in engineering and production techniques that were experienced elsewhere in the industries mentioned above as well as in transport, iron and steel, coal, machine tools and agriculture.

Probably of even greater importance than the improved production methods themselves were the complementary organizational structures. These developed with the economies of scale achieved by transforming small-scale domestic production into processes benefiting from large-scale production in factories. The wealth of those families who had been 'landed' before the industrial era was greatly enhanced by the growth in national wealth, without the family members themselves ever needing to become involved in what most of them saw as the demeaning manufacturing trades. Those sons of 'gentlemanly' families who had the urge to take up a profession went into the church, the army, the law or became associated with the City through banking. Even here the benefit of taking advantage of scale economies was not overlooked. The issue of currency notes was restricted to the Banks of England and Scotland and as the century progressed a limited number of joint stock banks gradually absorbed many smaller private and country banks. Changes in company law encouraged the formation of institutions big enough to finance seemingly massive commercial, infrastructure and manufacturing developments both at home and overseas. Throughout the nineteenth century the City of London became and remained the world's unchallenged financial and commercial centre.

Contemporary ideas on the condition of the poor

Britain's organizational improvements in industry, commerce and banking were consciously stimulated by the essential change in the late-eighteenth century from the restrictive environment of mercantilism to the openness of free trade. During the mercantilist epoch, governments were not prepared to allow merchants to trade where they chose in case they drained the nation's gold supply. Tariffs and other trade barriers were the order of the day. These were becoming increasingly frustrating to British commerce when, in 1776, Adam Smith famously berated the restrictions. He claimed that they prevented the natural expansion of wealth since the entrepreneur is only at his best when he fears competition.[2] Others, like the Rev. Thomas Malthus, Ricardo, Bentham and the Mills, developed Smith's economic format. Jeremy Bentham and John Stuart Mill becoming particularly influential with their application of the principle of 'utility' to all bodies and institutions, requiring them to function on the basis of fulfilling the 'equal claim of everybody to happiness' and their '*right* to equality of treatment'.[3]

The resultant creed of 'Utilitarianism' had immense impact on the Victorians. This was partly because it could be selectively interpreted for popular consumption in emphasizing that personal success came only from individual diligence and application. Samuel Smiles was prominent among those who popularized the individual aspects of the *laissez-faire* ideal that 'national progress is the sum of individual industry, energy and uprightness, as national decay is of individual idleness, selfishness and vice'. Smiles pushed the idea that 'the spirit of self-help, as exhibited in the energetic action of individuals, has in all times been a marked feature in the English character and furnishes the true measure as a nation'. Smiles alleged that all Englishmen possessed equal opportunity to succeed and described how, regardless of external factors, destitute people could improve themselves. This claimed improvement was adopted by Smiles as being confirmation that 'the extremest poverty has been no obstacle in the way of men devoted to the duty of self-culture'.[4] It suited the spirit of the time that there should be this emphasis on the dominant role of character in individual progression and that a person's quality was fashioned by morality, diligence, discipline and deference. The logical extension to this hypothesis was that the extremely poor had only themselves to blame. Indolence, drunkenness, depravity and lack of interest in improving personal respectability were the culprits of indigence. Thrift and virtue were synonymous, as were extravagance and sin. Those who were in such a miserable condition as to have to plead for relief demonstrably lacked character and needed to be reformed under the watchful guidance of their betters. Any disequilibrium of socio-economic structures was not considered to play much part in the condition of the poor.

Although individualism remained dominant, the Utilitarian message contained clear challenges to unbridled *laissez-faire* concepts. John Stuart Mill recognized in *On Liberty* that the untrammelled freedoms of a privileged few were very different from those of the majority whose only liberty was to sell their labour or to starve. Another mitigating gloss to the harsher facets of *laissez-faire* teaching came from the Revs Frederick Denison Maurice and Charles Kingsley who were among those advocating 'Christian Socialism'. The spiritual development of the individual and an association with his fellows in co-operative production was intended to improve their social condition. They hoped that this would be achieved in those cases where political channels had failed to bring social improvements for labour. The practical successes attained by Christian Socialism were limited, but its principles attracted an influential group of newly graduated University men including Thomas Huxley, John Ruskin and D.G. Rossetti. Each was willing to spend time in the East End of London to apply their own superior social and economic background for the benefit of the labouring classes. The Working Men's College, established by Maurice in 1854, was one of their successes. Ruskin attacked the contemporary science of political economy with *Unto This Last*, first published in 1862. He argued that the 'let alone' principle failed to recognize that 'work is the nation's wealth' and that all persons who work '*are* the wealth', not just a limited few. 'The true veins of wealth are purple – and not in Rock, but in Flesh – perhaps even that the final outcome and consummation of all wealth is in the producing as many as possible full-breathed, bright eyed, and happy-hearted human creatures'.[5] Nevertheless, Ruskin kept within the traditional ethos whereby 'wealth' was a fundamental concept governed by inviolable 'natural laws' outside the power of man and beyond his conscience.[6] When the organizers of charity emerged in the late 1860s, he joined their Council.

Although during the 1860s and 1870s these reformers were to effect little change in public opinion, there were other theorists building on the earlier ideas so as to make inroads into *laissez-faire* doctrines. Prominent were the Idealist economists within academia who were engaged in methodically eroding utilitarian doctrines. They claimed that utilitarianism had taken the individual for granted since adherents approached the problems of democracy as superior persons and thus the inadequacy of their psychology proved self-defeating. Thomas Hill Green at Oxford with Henry Sidgwick and Alfred Marshall at Cambridge were conspicuous among those redrafting the role of liberalism in a modern industrial society. They argued that there were logical reasons why the state should intervene selectively in social matters to protect individualistic principles for the 'common good'. But in spite of Green's inspirational and general directional qualities to Oxford undergraduates his messages were also tainted with imprecision. This was nowhere more so than on the crucial question of how far individualism should succumb to interventionist actions. Not until the later decades of the century did a broad consensus formed about what had been Idealism's practical intentions. Meanwhile, COS stalwarts Charles Loch and Bernard Bosanquet, both of whom had been closely associated with Green at Oxford, ploughed what increasingly became a lonely furrow by rigorously shunning state involvement outside the stigmatized Poor Law. COS supporters continued unflaggingly in their efforts to convince others that it had never been their mentor's intention for there to be more than the absolute minimum of intervention of any kind. Even then, it should only be after the individual's character had been thoroughly investigated and confirmed as being morally sound. How this COS obsession contributed to their eventual downfall is discussed later in the book and particularly in Chapter 6.

The increased involvement of the state

The Poor Law in Britain had been fashioned by the Tudors. During the succeeding centuries it was honed into a framework that provided the basic human right for the indigent to receive relief against starvation. It compared well with similar systems on the continent. Prior to 1834, an essential characteristic was its great reliance on the parish as a unit of administration. However, the 15 000 or so parishes in England and Wales were often small in size, feebly funded and with variable response by part-time amateurish administrators. Elizabeth I's Poor Law of 1597–1601 had possessed the underlying government motive of providing social stability by the alleviation of discontent. Each parish was made responsible for the maintenance of their own poor through annually elected overseers who worked with churchwardens in levying a poor-rate upon the inhabitants. Parishes had responsibility for relieving the sick and aged, apprenticing poor children and putting the able-bodied unemployed to work. Most parishes accepted their obligations in principle but the way they were put into practice varied enormously. If they were lucky, the sick were cared for by a contract through a local doctor. Or, like the aged, they were sometimes supported in the parish Poor House, a place often nothing more than the most rudimentary protection from the elements and a source of squalor.[6] More often, outdoor relief was provided to pay the cottager's rent with additional minimal allowances towards food, fuel and clothes.

Although parish support hovered close to subsistence level, in rural areas it was usually just sufficient to keep body and soul together when augmented by crumbs from the better-off table. In the expanding towns this was less so. When trade was bad, adequate parish relief became impossible. The rejected unemployed attempted to hang on to a wretched life in derelict unsanitary tenements, courts and alleys, by begging or doing unpopular odd jobs, but many failed. Urban death from starvation was commonplace when the economy slumped. Dorothy George claimed that at one such time, more than 20 people in London died weekly of hunger.[7] There was an attempt at rationalization with Gilbert's Act (1782). Contiguous parishes were encouraged to marshal their resources by constructing workhouses for joint use. However, by 1801 there were still around 4000 miscellaneous Poor Houses scattered around the country.

In stagnant economic periods, the growth of population caused downward pressure on wages. When this was coupled with bad harvests and higher bread prices times got unbearably tough for the labouring poor. Local solutions based on providing outdoor relief to supplement wages were applied. The most famous of these was the Speenhamland system by which the supplementation was based on variations in the price of bread and family size.[8] Nationally, the cost of parish relief had risen rapidly through the eighteenth century. The total cost of £400 000 in 1700 had rocketed to nearly ten times that figure before the century ended.

The Napoleonic wars brought further poor-rate increases as wheat prices edged upwards. However, post-war there was a reduction in gross national poor-rate expenditure when excellent harvests helped to lower bread prices. Nevertheless, the anti-Poor Law lobby still complained in 1832 that total poor relief expenditure had grown to around £7 m compared with just over £4 m 30 years earlier. They chose not to dwell on the fact that over the same period the population had increased from around 9.13 million to well over 14 million which suggests that during the early decades of the nineteenth century the poor relief expenditure per head of population had shown only marginal change.[9] Despite this, more than 60 years later, William Chance, a prominent COS member, claimed that because of the increase in poor-rates prior to the appointment of the 1832–34 Royal Commission on the Poor Laws, it was 'no exaggeration to say that the country was in danger of being consumed by its own children'.[10] One of the main issues causing officials concern was the immorality allegedly encouraged amongst the labouring classes by profligate outdoor relief. In spite of these worries, many parishes frustrated the intentions of the central authorities by continuing to assist poor people in their own home rather than forcing them to become Poor House inmates. The 1834 Report of the Commissioners claimed that 'the most pressing of the evils' besetting the nation were those 'connected with relief of the able-bodied'.[11] There was dismay at the whole question of augmenting wages with outdoor relief. The Commissioners saw it as being morally destructive and sabotaging any ambition the recipient may have had for better-paid employment. They alleged that outdoor relief would inevitably lead to a deterioration of all working people and eventual collapse of the nation. It was also claimed that the whole economy suffered disequilibrium from the illegally supported low wages disturbing the natural freedom of the labour market. With these powerful, if inaccurate economic guidelines, the Poor Law Commissioners recommended that administration be rationalized nationally. To replace the existing heterogeneous facilities scattered across England and Wales, administrative power would be concentrated in fewer than 650 unions. These larger units aimed at achieving national conformity through adherence to uniform building specifications, improved workhouse management and standard accounting procedures. The upkeep of the union workhouses would be from individual parish contributions calculated in proportion to poor-relief expenses.

To achieve the necessary 'well regulated' workhouse premises it was usually necessary either to construct a new larger centrally located building in the old parish network or to radically extend existing premises. Segregation was seen to be the essential element of the modern workhouses, to 'avoid the extension of vicious connections between inmates'. Various categories of pauper were to be housed in separate sections of the building, namely: the aged and the 'really' impotent, children, able-bodied females, able-bodied males, the sick and vagrants. Each family member was assigned to their appropriate section of the institution.[12] With the intended abandonment of outdoor relief and by making the union facilities unwelcoming through the principle of 'less eligibility', the 'offer of the House' would test whether or not the supplicant was 'deserving'. If workhouse internment was not accepted, local Poor Law officials were to presume that the applicant had gone on his way and devised a plan for personal recovery using principles of self-help.

By 1836 there were signs that the Poor Law Commissioners were not satisfied with merely curtailing out-relief for the able-bodied and broadened their attack by including other categories of outdoor pauper. They emphasized that the responsibility of providing for infirmity and old age lay with each individual and his family.[13] They announced later that more than one-third of the aged and infirm outdoor paupers were 'partially able to work' as were many widows in the habit of receiving outdoor benefit. Again, the central authorities raised alarm with the allegation that outdoor relief to such cases led to a general reduction in wages, just as certainly as they believed it did to the able-bodied. Thus, by 'fraudulently' burdening the country with relief costs, all outdoor relief subjected the 'independent poor' to 'unfair competition'.[14]

But the Commissioners had to recognize that while they could disseminate central edicts on such matters they had little chance of tightening constraints uniformly across the country until parishes had been rationalized into the new unions, each with the requisite amount of segregated accommodation.[15] They remained confident that when the construction and refurbishment of all union premises had eventually been completed, the resulting network of workhouses would allow them to exert a near dictatorial influence on local affairs. Such ambitions were to remain unfilled largely because of guardians failing to implement rigorous action against outdoor relief. It was to be more than 30 years before legal and social circumstances nationally had crystallized sufficiently to put Whitehall in a strong enough position to direct a strategy which would have much hope of eliminating outdoor relief.

Notwithstanding local obstructionism, the central authorities never lost sight of their primary objective of drastically restricting outdoor relief. They maintained what pressure they could, over the years, by issuing a number of restrictive Orders. For example, when by 1844 most urban unions had developed 'well regulated' workhouses, they took the opportunity of sending rural unions an Outdoor Relief Prohibitory Order. It aimed to prevent assistance to the able-bodied or to their families other than as workhouse inmates. But the rigorous veneer of the Order was not matched by its substance. Sufficient cracks were found in its drafting for guardians to develop many 'exceptions' to the order when it so suited. In practical terms the Order was most effective in tightening constraints against able-bodied men.[16] Eight years later there was a similar attempt to stiffen the urban rules. The resulting 1852 Outdoor Relief Regulation Order lacked even the surface stringency of the earlier legislation and allowed local officials to manipulate their affairs as it suited them. This meant that while a few guardians provided next to no outdoor relief, by far the majority continued to supply outdoor relief much as before.

Most guardians were not greatly impressed by the central hypothesis that applicants refused outdoor relief would be saved from idleness by being forced to transform themselves into independent thriving members of society. Guardians usually found it more attractive to be influenced by another aspect of *laissez-faire* principles encouraging them to shun bureaucratic interference. Two other factors prompted the guardians' attitude; one political and the other compassionate. First was the voting popularity they gained from maintaining low poor rates. Local opinion usually supported the provision of a few shillings in out-relief rather than the unpopular and costly alternative of work-house internment. The second reason was that out-relief caused less local emotional distress. Even with the larger, less personal union system it remained the case that the individual circumstances of most supplicants were known to at least one guardian or relieving officer.

The Poor Law Board (PLB), which replaced the Poor Law Commission in 1847, eventually recognized that before they could orchestrate a successful general assault against outdoor relief it would be advantageous to first stimulate greater awareness in rating procedures and in local Poor Law expenditure. The PLB, under the Presidency of Charles Buller, repeatedly emphasized the greater fairness and general advantages in poor rates were they to be freed from the restrictions of being centred on the parish. Reforms of this nature were consistently stonewalled by landed interests. But gradually, across the country, there was greater exposure to the social stresses caused by the darker sides of industrialization. In addition, an urban situation developed which had parallels with the rural open:close parish disparities in that poor rates in working class industrial parishes were often higher than in middle-class ones. By early 1861, the transition of parliamentary voting power away from the landed aristocracy had been sufficient to allow C.P. Villiers to unfold his important Irremovable Poor Bill. This improved the opportunity for labourers to seek employment away from their parish of birth and at the same time required union common funds to be created on the basis of the rateable value of each parish rather than on the amount of pauperism.[17] The Parochial Assessment Bill (1862) and the Union Chargeability Act (1865) were then introduced to (a) lubricate worker mobility further; (b) to make accurate rating assessments possible without undue local interference from entrenched interests; and (c) to make the Poor Law union the sole area of local administration. The central authorities now considered themselves to be in a much stronger position to launch a successful drive against outdoor relief when the time was ripe. Such an opportunity occurred in London towards the end of the decade when troughs in economic cycles and adverse weather had brought increased demands for outdoor relief on East End unions, see Figure 1.1. The PLB

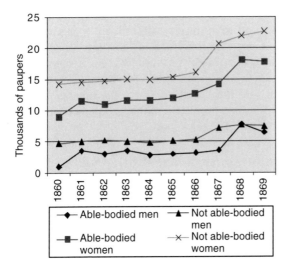

Figure 1.1 Metropolitan outdoor male and female paupers (1860–69)

Sources: Data extracted from annual reports of the Poor Law Board are the average of the daily counts taken 1st January and 1st July 1860–69. Data are exclusive of lunatics, the insane, etc.

claimed that London's outdoor pauperism had shown such dramatic growth as to make it necessary to 'guard against any alarm which might arise on the part of the public'.[18]

The PLB ignored the fact that London's population had also grown rapidly with a decadal increase of 16 per cent by 1871. When this was taken into account the rate of pauperism was scarcely changed and the jump in the numbers of outdoor applicants during 1866–67 could reasonably be attributed to the current downturn in trade and the associated massive unemployment among East-End weavers, dockers, shipbuilders and ancillary trades dependent on riverside activity.[19] As far as the PLB was concerned, now that the worker had legally been granted more mobility as a result of Villiers' Acts, the conditions were propitious for the effective implementation of their long-standing theories about the moral, economic and social advantages of housing paupers in workhouses practising the principle of 'less eligibility'. To that end, the Poor Law Board President, George J. (later Lord) Goschen, circulated a Minute to metropolitan guardians on 20 November 1869. It warned of the dangers inherent in outdoor relief and particularly of double distribution between the statutory authorities and the voluntary sector. Goschen argued that there should be 'opportunity for every agency, official or private, engaged in relieving the poor to know fully and accurately the details of the work performed by all similarly engaged'. He was also clear that the necessary rationalization of relief was a task for the voluntary sector and not central government.[20] This requirement, specified by Goschen, was most encouraging for the recently formed London Charity Organization Society (COS). Whether by accident or design, only a few months previously they had assigned to themselves precisely the same co-ordinating role.

Early attempts to encourage thrift, organize charity and repress mendicity

Before discussing how the London COS leapt enthusiastically to fulfil Goschen's specification, it should be said that there was little that was novel about the specific concepts of charity investigation, selection, the deterrence of mendicity or the encouragement of thrift featured in the armoury of the Charity Organization Society. What the COS was to attempt, in addition, was a collective methodology whereby the activities of all charities would be marshalled so that their efforts could be directed cohesively but selectively towards the poor. Half a century earlier, William Davis published 'hints for philanthropists' in 1821 as to how best people of goodwill might organize themselves to avoid the poor becoming 'bereft of all manly spirit and independent principle' so that they sank into a 'state of moral and intellectual degradation'. He alleged that by 'abandoning themselves to habits of idleness and vice' the poor frequently tended towards the 'commission of crime'.[21] Around the same time, periodicals such as *The Philanthropist* had focused on the benefits to the nation should people in superior stations of life succeed in developing providence among the poor. Readers were provided with 'Reflections on the Expediency of forming Parochial Institutions for promoting Habits of Industry, Prudence, and Economy, among the Labouring Poor, by assisting them to adapt the Income of the Year to its Expenditure, so that the Surplus of one Season should be preserved to supply the Deficiencies of another'.[22] A correspondent to *The Philanthropist* explained how one class of poor were 'peculiarly deserving of consideration'. They were those among the labouring classes who had no surplus annual income to invest in 'Banks for Savings' but at certain seasons of the year had 'surplus earnings which, if husbanded and protected, would amply provide for the deficiencies of the remainder, without any aid from charity or recourse to the parish poor rates. The Dorking Provident Institution was one such Society encouraging poor people in the 1820s to deposit with them weekly during the months of most productive employment. Depositors' savings were then returned, with generous interest, during the season of the year when work was scarce and provisions costly.

One of the earliest charities subsequently recognized as bearing some of the characteristics adopted by the COS was the Society for Bettering the Condition and Improving the Comforts of the Poor (SBCP) launched in 1795 by Thomas Bernard, William Wilberforce and Shute Barrington. It was designed as an umbrella organization, publicizing benevolent experimentation and the latest scientific charitable techniques. It dedicated itself to putting philanthropy on an exact and rational basis (much as the London COS was to attempt nearly three-quarters of a century later). Charity would give the rich the power to influence and educate 'the wilful and ignorant poor into becoming providential, self-regarding and morally responsible adult citizens'.[23] Like the later COS, steps were taken by the SBCP to make sure the poor remained acutely aware of the favours they were being granted and of their temporary nature. There were also differences between the two Societies, instanced by the SBCP's strong belief in the benefits of soup kitchens. Nor, unlike the COS, did the SBCP overtly claim the right to organize the activities of existing charities.

Among provincial Societies combining the principles of providence and charity was one formed at Brighton in 1820. It aimed to encourage thrift and self-sufficiency among the labouring classes while securing them a 'supply of Food, Fuel, and Clothing during the Winter Season'.[24] The Brighton Provident and District Society investigated the needs of applicants and urged residents and visitors to 'withhold promiscuous charity'. For poor savers, the Society guaranteed an added premium of 12.5 per cent on deposits provided the accumulated sum was not touched 'until the winter months'.[25] Two of the more important Societies formed to encourage thrift among the poor both happened to be formed in 1833. One was the Liverpool Provident District Society which 30 years later formed a constituent of the emergent Central Relief Society (CRS).[26] The other was the Manchester and Salford District Provident Society (DPS).[27] Both of these prestigious provincial provident Societies were later to become associated with the London COS.

In the 1860s, the tenacity of beggars, shown by their presence in the street and by their appealing letters, was of recurring disturbance to the tranquillity of the leisured classes. These annoyances were not confined to London. Anti-mendicity Societies had long been established provincially with the objective of (a) investigating the veracity of the beggar's case; (b) encouraging the police into action when appropriate; and (c) generally persuading people not to provide money but instead a ticket entitling the recipient to food and possibly shelter under controlled conditions. An Oxford group founded in 1827 by Archbishop Whatley was itself a re-birth of the 'Society for the Relief of Distressed Travellers and Others' started in 1814.[28] Another, the 'Society for the Suppression of Public Begging' was founded in Edinburgh in 1812.

The London Mendicity Society (LMS), founded in 1818, has been seen as another forerunner of the COS. The LMS attempted to apply the uniform enforcement of the rule 'no relief without enquiry' across metropolitan London. In theory, this common centralized system was to be operated by gentlemen volunteers who alone would decide whether or not an applicant was deserving of support, which if granted, was usually in the form of tickets entitling the recipient to a food order or a meal. Applicants found to be 'undeserving', by which was meant the impotent poor, including the elderly, sick, the mentally unstable, the single mother or widow with young children, were despatched to the Poor Law authorities. Much as the COS was to find later in the century, the commitment and practical expertise of their gentlemanly volunteers rarely fulfilled the needs of the theoretical model. Within a few years, most day-to-day business activities had to be transferred to a salaried full-time 'assistant manager'. W.H. Bodkin, the man first appointed to this post, was the very gentleman whose advertisement had been basic to the launch of the 'voluntary' LMS. *The Times* claimed at the time that Bodkin's salary was sufficient to relieve 750 mendicants at the LMS's current rates.[29] Outside London, in localities such as Ayr, Clackmannan, Dorset, Gloucestershire, Hereford, Wiltshire and Worcestershire, there were mendicity societies bearing a variety of titles, indicative of their main objective, the suppression of vagrancy.[30]

In spite of these various earlier British attempts to repress mendicity and to generally encourage the development of self-help among the poor, it was mainly to two particular experiments that the COS was to turn regularly to justify the soundness of its principles. One was the activity of Thomas Chalmers, a clergyman and moral philosopher, who in the early 1820s allegedly produced dramatic improvement in the condition of the poor in a Glasgow parish. The other was the structured system of social control practised at Elberfeld (now Wuppertal), a textile manufacturing centre in the Ruhr where responsibly minded townsfolk were said to have voluntarily become involved in caring for the poor with extraordinarily beneficial results. Convincing evidence, summarized briefly in the paragraphs that follow, suggests that neither of these ideological bedrocks was quite what the COS and its acolytes made them appear.

The Rev. Dr Thomas Chalmers came from a middle-class Scottish family. He expounded his philosophy on how effective relief to the poor could be achieved with economy to the rich and moral benefit to others. His conviction was that 'to make almsgiving and religion go hand in hand was injurious to both'.[31] Chalmers attempted to apply his theories when given charge of a new, but poor, parish of St John, Tron, Glasgow. He stipulated to church elders that he should have full control over the administration of church poor relief collections and be allowed to distribute them at his discretion. Chalmers phased out the traditional relief activities and gave the responsibility for dealing with new supplicants to deacons, each responsible for the condition of the poor in a specific area of the parish. Deacons would generally not be parishioners but volunteers drawn from wealthier neighbourhoods outside St John's. A marked difference in social status between the dispenser of alms and the recipient was seen as being essential. Chalmers believed that the superiority of one man to another was natural and that the respectful consideration in which 'occupiers of the higher state' were held by more lowly people enhanced the quality of the gift and the recipient's appreciation of it.[32] A thorough investigation of a poor person's means was fundamental to the procedure.

From autumn 1819, Chalmers applied his regime at St John's for over three years. He claimed that both the parish economy and the improved condition of the St John poor had outstripped his own expectations. In later years, reading, digesting and attempting to apply Chalmers' ideas, became a basic need for those wishing to become proficient in charity organization.[33] His claims provided eternal proof to the COS that, given the opportunity, its simulated methodology would improve the condition of London's poor. COS members were to venerate Chalmers and his system of 'social economy' whereby the deserving poor should be 'taken in hand entirely by charity, not miscellaneous pauperizing charity,...but a wise, discriminating charity, salutary charity,...sweetened and permeated by kind and thoughtful intercourse'.[34]

Chalmers' supporters were 'stunned' when he resigned his living to return to the University of St Andrews. Brown has suggested that although his departure was supposedly influenced by exhaustion and illness, 'perhaps the most important reason' was weariness about the 'continuing attacks upon his poor-relief programme from the Glasgow

press'.[35] Kirkham Gray has pointed out that Chalmers' 'brutal optimism' was not universally approved of by his contemporaries.[36] More
analytically, after 'closer scrutiny into the figures', Checkland has questioned the veracity of Chalmers' financial assertions. She criticized his
'curious accounting' procedures and recommended that the COS
'might usefully have enquired more closely into the figures which supporters of Chalmers so readily quoted'.[37] Furgol maintains that
Chalmers' refusal to 'even consider that he might be mistaken led him
to ignore any unsatisfactory evidence' so that he 'manipulated statistics' to 'prove' his theories. She asserts that Chalmers' 'practical experiment in poor relief in St John's failed unequivocally as did its
imitators', so that the 'ideal small community he envisaged' and which
has so often been extolled, never actually materialized.[38]

The other much quoted lynch-pin of COS activities was the experiment carried out at Elberfeld in northern Germany. From 1853, the
municipal council set up a poor relief scheme based on 'volunteer' visitor almoners, each personally responsible for the well-being of about
four poor families in a predetermined small section of the town.
Grisewood claimed half a century later that the city of 163 000 inhabitants had 585 visitor/almoners operating under municipal regulations.
Each visitor was 'supposed to have no more than two dependent cases
in hand at any one time'.[39] Changes in the circumstances of cases were
reported by the visitor to their district supervisor and each recorded in
what had become a case-paper dossier. Key to the scheme was the close
personal supervision expected of the visitor befriending each case and
by the visitor's personal pressure which was designed to develop independent character in their charge. Prior to this treatment, each supplicant was closely interrogated about their circumstances, their ability to
work and whether relatives could help. Elberfeld was held by the COS
to be a great success as measured by the reduced number of cases
applying for relief and by the resultant smaller overall cost.[40]

The structural similarity of the Ruhr-based venture with Chalmers'
project at St John's was clear. Both seemed to confirm the universal
validity of principles which were to be slavishly praised by the would-be
charity organizers who followed. For decades, Elberfeld was to become
a Mecca for charity reformers with its relief methods an ever-recurring
subject for glorification at Poor Law Conferences and COS seminars.
Equally, as with the Rev. Chalmers' activities, the Elberfeld scheme has
not lacked adverse criticism. The frequently repeated idea of it being
illustrative of genuine voluntary effort and a high level of personal
commitment has been found to be particularly questionable.

Col Granville Browne reported that at Elberfeld 'the duties of overseers and visitors are compulsory and unpaid'.[41] Others have recorded how each 'volunteer' was actually recruited by the threatened loss of franchise rights.[42] The reported sympathetic personal relationships between rich and poor were ridiculed by William Chance. In 1897, he pointed out that critics of the English Poor Law system were 'apt to forget' that the conditions of obtaining relief at Elberfeld were relatively 'harsh and oppressively rigorous'.[43] But these later pilgrims to Elberfeld should not have been surprised by what they found. Way back in 1871, the Local Government Board's (LGB's) Andrew Doyle had himself reported from the site that 'the applicant for relief is subjected to an examination so close and searching, so absolutely inquisitorial, that no man who could possibly escape from it would submit to it'.[44] Information forthcoming at the fiftieth anniversary celebrations of the 'Elberfeld Poor Law' left no doubt that the administration of the much vaunted system of charitable distribution was directly associated with the municipal authorities, both as regards funding and the visitors' need to fulfil statutory demands. There were also indications that by the twentieth century the Elberfeld administrators had become more religiously inclined.[45]

With strong encouragement from the LGB and their new-found ally the London COS, the Elberfeld system was attempted experimentally at a few provincial centres in Britain. None were successful for long. For example, in 1872, the LGB considered Macclesfield was 'of all places the one best suited for the experiment'. They proposed to recruit 'a corps of 100 volunteer assistant guardians' to share equally the problems of the 400 relief cases. The local Mayor was confident that the town's worthies would be wholeheartedly supportive. Among those said to be willing to serve as assistant guardians was Mr Brocklehurst, MP, and 'several working men'.[46] The COS detected early signs of the experiment being carried on 'with a good promise of success' whereas the *Macclesfield Courier* believed that the early sharp fall in the number of outdoor relief cases was 'primarily due to the increase in trade'. Mr May, Clerk to the Macclesfield guardians, focused on how the new system of enquiry had led to many more parents and children being made to contribute to the repayment of relief 'to an extent never known before'. The main stumbling-block, Mr May explained, was in 'obtaining the services of assistant-guardians' in sufficient number.[47] Within a few weeks, general disquiet about the novel system was registered by Joseph Chapman, Secretary of the Silk Weavers' Association. In particular, he provided details of three cases claiming that each had been treated unfairly.

Mr Heathcote, relieving officer of the Poor Law Union, accepted that mistakes may have occurred but in mitigation pointed out that it was not possible to reduce the local outdoor relief total from £126 weekly down to £68 weekly 'without committing some errors for want of information'. Even the COS conceded that Mr Chapman's 'fair criticisms, and the publicity given to them' would further test the Macclesfield experiment. They regretted that Mr Chapman and 'others of his class did not accede to the urgent appeal made to them to become assistant-guardians'.[48] The Macclesfield scheme failed to become a long-term feature.

Argument about COS beginnings

A major influence leading to the formation of the COS was the establishment of the Society for the Relief of Distress (SRD) during the exceptional distress experienced by Londoners during the late 1860s. In letters to *The Times*, Mr Davenport-Bromley and others centred on the needs of the poor and the inadequacies of existing charitable agencies to deal with them. Other SRD members included G.M. Hicks, the Rev. John Richard Green and Edward Denison. From the beginning, SRD members bickered amongst themselves. Hicks expressed dissatisfaction about the Society's methods and circulated a four-point action plan for future progress, namely (1) relief of temporary distress rather than permanent; (2) almoners or visitors to be appointed to specified districts; (3) investigation of relief applicants at local offices; and (4) co-operation with existing charities and Poor Law authorities. The sub-committee which followed developed these recommendations and drew up guidelines for the district visitors. In the following years, Hicks continued to place particular emphasis on the need to conserve charitable alms so that after investigation they might be directed to deserving cases.

Edward Denison, one of the other prominent SRD founders, was soon to die from tuberculosis when only 30 years of age. His name was to be retained in favourable memory by COS members in future years. Denison was the son of the Bishop of Salisbury, a nephew of the Speaker of the Commons and an MP himself for a short while. His reputation had been consolidated by his determination to live amongst the poor in Philpot Street, Mile End Road, Stepney for eight months in the late 1860s to prove the benefits of personal involvement in teaching the poor to be 'frugal and thrifty'.[49] Denison condemned the absence of the leisured classes from the East End. He was convinced that the presence locally of people prepared to give some time and energy to guide lesser mortals, would result in most labouring families being saved from pauperism. He abhorred the irresponsibility of charitable bodies who provided haphazard relief and advocated close co-operation between Mile End charities and the local Poor Law authorities. Denison's researches on continental relief methods and persuasive letters to influential friends were quoted repeatedly in later years as being inspirational for COS members.[50] In the twentieth century, London COS Secretary the Rev. John Christian Pringle, referred to Denison as, 'Our Patron Saint'. Many years after his death, Denison's name was chosen for the address of the new COS headquarters. It was considered as symbolic of all that was good in charity organization.

In spite of the SRD's efforts, London's charities showed no improvement – or, using the expression current at the time – were in a state of eleemosynary confusion. Co-operative action between charities became recognized as a paramount need among other philanthropic gentlemen, including a number of local clergymen. Concerned individuals gave papers and lectures on the condition of the poor and how to improve it. Two papers presented to the Society of Arts during 1868 were among the more important. First was one in June of that year by the Rev. Henry Solly on *How to Deal with the Unemployed Poor of London and with its Roughs and Criminal Classes*. Second was Dr Thomas Hawksley's *Charities of London and Some Errors of their Administration* presented in December 1868.[51]

Solly was the energetic, imaginative son of a Baltic timber merchant and a well-known figure in the East End among groups endeavouring to improve the condition of the poor. He took an active part in the founding of the Working Men's Club and Institute Union in 1862 and was its Secretary for some years. Later in his life Solly was keenly involved in the concept of industrial villages. He died in 1903, aged 90.[52] Thomas Hawksley, who remained throughout his life steadfastly loyal to Solly's claim to be the COS founder, was a hugely successful physician with practices in London and Brighton. He was also consultant at Margaret Street Consumption and Chest Diseases Hospital and founded the Destitute Boys National School of Handicrafts at Chertsey in 1885.[53] Hawksley had practised medicine for years in the East End of London. The experience had lead him to believe in a system of central and district offices for organizing charity, each based on the location of metropolitan Poor Law unions, He explained that this 'would constitute in effect a "police of charity"' and recommended that each London charity pay one per cent of its income into a common fund to meet his estimated annual cost of £40 000.[54] This calculation was used, optimistically, by the COS in its early financial deliberations and has also been severely criticised.[55] Even among contemporaries, Hawksley's proposal was not well received. W.M. Wilkinson, a few years later, recalled the adverse response of the audience to Hawksley's theme. It 'created great discouragement amongst some of us, for not only had the meeting manifested such signs of impatience that Dr Hawksley was obliged to cease speaking before he had nearly finished, but almost all the speakers were strongly opposed to his whole plan and refused altogether to have their charities organised'.[56]

There was a great deal of activity during the six months between the Solly and Hawksley papers and this resulted in the establishment of what was initially called the 'Society for the Prevention of Pauperism and Crime' (SPPC). The title was modified during this gestation period to that of 'The Association for the Prevention of Pauperism and Crime in the Metropolis' (LAPPC), an association which formed a strong Council of interested individuals, as will be discussed Further in Chapter 2. On 29 April 1869 there was agreement between the LAPPC Council, together with others, to form 'The Society for Organizing Charitable Relief and Repressing Mendicity' or, more colloquially, the London Charity Organization Society, (COS), the main focus of this volume.

Just how much credit the various precursor Societies and individuals should be accorded in contributing to the formation of what eventually became the COS remains debatable. For years there was rancorous correspondence between Henry Solly and others in which he explained why, as a relatively impecunious cleric and family man, he needed to be remunerated. His claim was that fellow founder SPPC members had persuaded him to largely give up his living as a Unitarian Minister to concentrate on the development of concepts he had proposed. Solly's intriguing letters about his parlous finances were largely directed towards the Earl of Lichfield who shortly was to appear on the scene as a major COS benefactor.[57] Throughout their correspondence Solly staunchly maintained his claim that, aided and abetted by others, he was, on account of his creative initiative, the initiator of the Charity Organization Society. He returned repeatedly to the presentation of the two papers to the Society of Arts during 1868 – those of himself and Hawksley – as being the essential precursors of the COS. Solly's distinctive contribution had been his plea for the bringing together of 'secular agencies, *all of which must be combined if* we would carry the war effectively' (orginal italics). Solly had urged 'that our benevolent Societies should form or co-operate with this joint Committee for deliberation and collecting the materials for future action'.[58]

As an indication that the subject of charity organization was being quite widely debated as the 1860s proceeded, it is helpful to recall that, C.B.P. Bosanquet, the first salaried Secretary of the COS, had himself outlined a scheme for co-ordinating the charitably inclined of London.[59] He wrote in 1868 'surely some attempt at permanent combination, or concerted action, amongst volunteers will be made ere long…our need in London is so evident and so great that we cannot afford to ignore their experience…if competent leaders can be found I am confident that followers will be forthcoming'.[60] Solly contended that what uniquely distinguished his own contribution to the formation of the COS from others was that he was the prime mover in actually forming an organizing Society as distinct from others who merely talked about the possibility.

There has been much written about the turbulent formative COS days and there is not the space or need to repeat again the intrigues in more detail. Sufficient to emphasize how these frequently conflicting accounts illustrate the ways in which a number of individuals claimed, or were acclaimed by others, to be the major COS progenitor. Other interested bodies were angered by some of these assertions and by their own deletion from the COS Halls of Fame. These fractious debates raged for decades both within the Society itself and by external commentators. They make fascinating reading. A list of the essential papers and letters published (mainly by the COS) on this subject are provided below. Many other pertinent sources of information for those wanting to delve further into this subject are included within these references:

1. C.B.P. Bosanquet, 'The History and Mode of Operation of the Charity Organisation Society' (1874).
2. Thomas Hawksley, 'Objections to "The History" of the Society published by the Authority of Council' (1875).
3. 'History of the Society', *COR* (27 January 1875), p. 14.
4. W.M. Wilkinson, 'A Contribution towards the History of the origin of the Charity Organisation Society' (1875).
5. G.M. Hicks, 'A Contribution towards the History of the Origin of the Charity Organisation Society, with Suggestions on the Reports, Balance Sheets and Audit of Charity Accounts' (1875).
6. Sartor Minor, 'Philanthropic Tailoring and Historical Cobbling', Dedicated to the Council and Members of the Charity Organisation Society' (1875).
7. C.B.P. Bosanquet, letter to *COReview* following the death of the Earl of Lichfield (February 1892) pp. 45–6.

8. Lynedoch Gardiner, letter to *COReview* following the death of Earl of Lichfield (February 1892), pp. 46–7.
9. W.M. Williamson (misprint for Wilkinson), *COReview* (February 1892), p. 60.
10. W.M. Wilkinson, letter to *COReview* (April 1892), pp. 121–2.
11. C.J. Ribton Turner, letter to *COReview* (April 1892), pp. 122–3.
12. Editorial Note, *COReview* (May 1892), p. 190.
13. 'The Origin of the London Charity Organisation Society', *COReview* (October–November 1892), pp. 355–72.[61]
14. 'The Origin of the C.O.S'. *COReview* (February 1893), pp. 51–2.[62]
15. There are also more recent books and articles providing descriptions of aspects of the Charity Organization Society's formation and these are well worth perusal.[63]

The chapter that follows will examine how London COS quickly spread itself across the metropolis and how, within the space of a couple of years, a district office network was established to remain its *modus operandi* for generations. In later chapters, discussion centres on how the charity organization concept, spawned in London, took root in the provinces and overseas. Long after the London COS had itself lost much of its early sparkle, its methodology continued to mesmerize adherents abroad. In particular, annual national USA Conferences early in the twentieth century consistently featured London COS devotees among their principal speakers.

2
The First Five Years

The first Council of 'The Association for the Prevention of Pauperism and Crime in the Metropolis' (LAPPC), formed during 1868, was 23 strong and was an important precursor of the COS. It met at 1 James's Street, Adelphi, London WC and included a number of personalities who were soon to become prominent propagandists for charity organization. Among them were; General Cavenagh, Francis Fuller, Thomas Hawksley, Archbishop Manning, Col Maude, Capt. Maxse, John Ruskin, Rev. Henry Solly and Thomas Webster. Between then and the formation of the London 'Society for Organising Charitable Relief and Repressing Mendicity' (COS) on 29 April 1869, they arranged a number of 'Conferences of Charities'. These were not as well attended as had been anticipated. Despite this lukewarm response from the general public, the fraternity of would-be charity organizers were successful in attracting a formidable collection of socially prominent recruits. Probably the most important was the Earl of Lichfield who, for the early years, was to become the COS's main financial backer. Before agreeing to participate in their activities, Lichfield insisted that the LAPPC should abandon its wider interests, including a 'Waste Land' scheme of Thomas Webster and Francis Fuller. Lichfield's demand did not come as a surprise to the LAPPC Council. Already, on 30 November 1868, Henry Solly had circulated a strongly worded protest against the 'composite and unwieldy character of their prospectus' as it then stood. He claimed that any proposal to combine other schemes with his own ideas of charity rationalization was 'hopeless'.[1] Lichfield accepted the invitation to chair a LAPPC meeting on 18 March 1869 where it was agreed to integrate the Council of the Association with its executive committee. The combined body, shortly to emerge as the COS, had full powers to pursue their objectives – which were expected to focus mainly on securing mutual co-operation between a wide range of charities and the Poor Law authorities. Within a matter of weeks, Lichfield funded the transfer of COS operations to 15 Buckingham Street, Adelphi, WC which for many years was to remain the fulcrum of its activities.[2]

The newly formed would-be charity organizers received an enormous boost when in November 1869, whether by design or co-incidence, the government signalled their whole-hearted support for the idea that the activities of the many disparate charities in London should be co-ordinated so as to work effectively with the local Poor Law authorities in improving the condition of the poor. As mentioned in the previous chapter, a Minute circulated to all metropolitan guardians by George Goschen, the PLB President, pointed to the need for separate functional limits to be agreed between the statutory Poor Law and those of voluntary charity so that they were operationally combined to maximum effect. Goschen's message was to remain a favourable point of reference for many years, both in the COS's own Conferences and in those held by Poor Law officials. Goschen accepted that responsibility for the destitute must remain with government but argued that all other help to the poor should be provided through the charitable sector. He was concerned that without carefully controlled organization of the separate functions to prevent overlapping, both between and within them, there would be unacceptable waste, both moral and financial.[3] His recommendation was that there should be a 'public registering office' in every district, in order that every agency, public or charitable, should be aware of what others were doing. Goschen's proposal was to be heralded repeatedly as an official guide and endorsement of COS principles. Within the space of about 12 months there were 16 District Committees (DCs) across the metropolis. Five were chaired by noblemen, six by clergymen, and three by gentlemen retired as senior officers from the armed forces.[4] Goschen, together with Parliamentary colleagues including William Gladstone and Lord George Hamilton, were among early COS Vice-Presidents.

The first COS District Office had opened for business in St Marylebone during October 1869. With the Earl of Lichfield as Chairman, it attracted some formidable local individuals, not least of whom were the Rev. Samuel Barnett and his wife Henrietta (prior to their pastoral living being transferred to St Jude's, Whitechapel), Octavia Hill and, crucially, a number of sympathetic local Poor Law guardians including General Sir Lynedoch Gardiner who became COS District Hon. Sec. With these connections, the St Marylebone COS Committee was able to attract, for a few years, some co-operation from local relief agencies. Miss Hill, the granddaughter of Dr Southwood Smith who had been associated with Edwin Chadwick at the beginning of the public health movement earlier in the century, had, not surprisingly, become influenced by the Christian Socialist movement. She established a worthwhile body of COS visitors in St Marylebone, peaking in number at 35. It was claimed that for a while the parish achieved a social structure similar to what Thomas Chalmers had aspired to in Glasgow during the 1820s. Like Chalmers' experiment, the one in St Marylebone lasted for only a few years, seemingly lapsing after 1875.[5]

The second district to hoist the COS flag was St George's, Hanover Square. It was in areas such as this 'where rich and poor lived near each other and where sources of charity were most numerous' that the Council found the need for the organization of charity 'most obvious'.[6] With the support of Lord Grosvenor, a sub-committee of local luminaries had been formed during the middle months of 1869. The search for suitable office accommodation took some months but on the 13 December of that year COS activities started. When compared with most districts, they fared well in the recruitment of influential supporters who had both spare time and money. The emergent St George's clique quickly made their presence felt within the COS Council, particularly as regards questions of finance. An example was when a cheque for £50 intended for the Council found its way to the St George's Committee. This roughened further the friction which had already prompted those in Buckingham Street to specifically request St George's to describe itself as a local COS committee when appealing publicly for money. The prestigious Hanover Square faction did not take kindly to such instruction. Helen Bosanquet describes how they despatched a letter shortly afterwards admonishing the COS Council in which were detailed 'several grounds for dissatisfaction', including their opinion that they had not received as much benefit as they had hoped from the conferences at Buckingham Street.[7] Later, St George's attacked the Council about their intention to pay 'a large sum to one or more of their secretaries'.

The essence of the arguments between the COS in wealthier districts and others in the Council was that the former were very much against any idea of centralizing COS fund-raising and expenditure structures. On the contrary, the richer districts advocated repeatedly that the Council should be reconstructed so as to consist entirely of District Committee (DC) representatives and should be funded by each district paying a small percentage on their receipts to defray central office expenses. This, it was argued, would prevent the need for the Council to canvass directly for expenses. To demonstrate their zeal and influence, the St George's COS members established parochial councils in the Hanover Square locality to create the 'proper management' of the poor from a charitable foundation. The parochial councils were expected to take up 'sanitary questions, including the improvement of the dwellings of the poor', etc.[8] In reality, the parochial councils involved themselves in little other than relief work.[9]

During the early 1870s, other individuals became involved in organizing the new campaign against profligate and irresponsible charity. Among them was W.M. Wilkinson, a solicitor and historian of the Society's early years whose faith and commitment to the COS cause never foundered up to his death in 1897. Other important early activists included General Orfeur Cavenagh who joined the Society in 1869 after a distinguished career in India. He became Chairman of London COS Council in 1884–85 and was a vociferous contributor to Council debates over many years. In much the same vein was Sir Charles Trevelyan, a retired senior servant, who joined the Society's Council in 1870 and participated actively in Council work until ill-health brought his retirement in 1883. Alsager Hay Hill was one of the Society's earliest joint Hon. Secretaries.

The inaugural COS Central Office manual 'earnestly requested' the 'intelligent co-operation' of all interested in the welfare of the poor of London in the Society's 'difficult undertaking'. It described 'the main object of the Society' as being the improvement of the condition of the poor. This, it was said, would be achieved by; '(1) bringing about co-operation between the Charities and the Poor Law, and amongst the Charities; (2) securing due investigation and fitting action in all cases; and (3) repressing mendicity'. The Charity Organization Society was described as consisting of a Federation of Committees within the metropolis. It was anticipated by the COS that each would be aligned functionally with the nearby Board of Guardians responsible for a local Poor Law union. The COS manual described how these Committees would contain representatives of the local Board and of all Charities in the Poor Law district. They were expected to raise and expend their own funds. Their methodology was allegedly based on the desire to bring about a 'division of cases between the Poor Law and Charities, and also among the various Charities'. Cases of temporary distress, where there was evidence of good character, were to be looked upon by COS Committees as deserving of private charity. It was confidently expected that the diverse charities already existing in the locality would be able to afford 'the requisite assistance' to these deserving individuals. Should the COS District Committee occasionally find themselves having to consider use of funds entrusted to them, they were told in no uncertain terms that they must never even contemplate undertaking 'to find the pensions which chronic cases need'. Small regular weekly doles of food or money should be avoided because these undermined the independence of the recipient much as they alleged was the case with outdoor relief. However, in suitable cases, the COS Committees were encouraged to 'willingly' give assistance in 'the forms of loans with proper security for repayment'. Loans were recognized as the one relief method sure to build strength of character among the poor. The COS manual concluded with the homily that to benefit the poor of London permanently, the main factors required of the public were thought and personal exertion.[10] S. Morley, Esq., MP, who was 'perfectly in accord' with COS principles, explained that before being converted to charity organization he had found it hard to believe in the 'unwisdom' of giving money in the streets. Now he had proved it for himself by taking beggars to a baker's shop and 'purchasing them a wholesome stale loaf, for which he had been soundly abused by them'.[11]

The COS District Committee was intended to be the local decision-making forum. Although keen to attract clerics to their colours, the COS studiously avoided being associated with any particular religious denomination. They made a point of being 'perfectly unsectarian' with the wish 'to blend all creeds in a crusade against pauperism and benefit the really deserving poor'.[12] Each DC had a Chairman, at least one Honorary Secretary and an Honorary Treasurer. Some districts delegated facets of their work to sub-committees. One might focus on finance, another on administrative matters, while in wealthier districts 'working' committees might meet weekly on prearranged days to decide the fate of applicants. District Offices aimed to be open to the public for around three to four hours daily, typically from 10.00 am to noon and from 3.00 to 5.00 pm.

The first annual report of the COS Council announced its determination to augment the statutory efforts of the workhouse by establishing a Charity Office in each London Poor Law division. This was to be managed by a COS Committee which, it was hoped, would include representation from all local charitable agencies. The Charity Office was intended to form the front line contact with the needy. Each district would employ the services of a waged Agent paid around 30s a week. Where funds would permit, the local Committee could decide to engage other employees carrying the self-explanatory titles of Collector or Enquirer to assist an overworked Agent. It was expected that the latter would communicate regularly with the local Poor Law Relieving Officer, with the clergy, and with representatives of a whole gamut of local charities. The Charity Offices would hopefully become recognized as the centres for all charitable disbursements across the capital.

Another element of the original charity organization concept was that COS tickets would be circulated directing those who were appealing for relief to the local Charity Office. The COS was confident that potential benefactors would recognize a clear social advantage in offering tickets to supplicants rather than doling out their traditional unplanned charity. On submitting a ticket to the Charity Office the supplicant would undergo a searching personal investigation, often by the Agent. The latter was expected to unearth details of: the applicant's previous job, their past and present addresses, the names and whereabouts of relatives, club membership, state of health, accommodation rent and the value of any articles currently lodged with the pawnbroker. The printed form used by the COS in their investigations included space for replies gathered by their Agent during his subsequent enquiries to confirm details about the applicant's previous employers, clergy and school teachers. His home would be the Agent's next port of call to check the correctness of what had been claimed by the applicant about his domestic circumstances. All the collected data would then be transcribed to the 'Applicant and Decision Book' prior to consideration by the DC or by its 'decision sub-committee'. It was they who decided whether the applicant should be (a) rejected; (b) referred to another agency; or (c) when other help was not available, should receive some direct COS assistance.[13] Referral or direct assistance was to subsequently involve repeated COS visits to the family home until the householder had been restored to independence or until the COS had decided to abandon their attempt to instil individual responsibility. In the latter case, failure was blamed on the person's own inadequacy of response to the corrective treatment. District Committees were encouraged to supply the confidential details they had unearthed about the applicant to the charitable person who had initially distributed the COS ticket to them. The receipt of this information was expected to illustrate to a grateful patron how thoughtless profligacy had been avoided and how, when the applicant had been judged deserving, relief had been prescribed scientifically by the COS.[14]

There were early signs that the direct involvement of COS volunteers in investigating new applicants was producing unreliable results. The Council alleged that volunteers were foolishly becoming sympathetic and succumbing to misplaced emotions about the plight of applicants. COS Agents were believed to be much less likely to fall into this trap and could be depended upon to carry out investigation rigorously. The Council therefore resolved that while they valued 'very highly the active co-operation of volunteers in the executive work of the District Committees', it was advisable that the 'primary investigation in all cases should rest with the Charity Agents'.[15] This advice upset some districts, including the COS flagship at St Marylebone, where they claimed volunteers were examining applicants successfully. Generally, regardless of whether investigation was by amateur or wage-earner, unacceptable problems developed that had no easy solution. Not only was the COS curbing relief to worthless applicants, it was also causing unwarranted delays in supplying its scientifically measured help to deserving cases. Col Lynedoch Gardiner found it 'most unpleasant' after having himself fully investigated and personally visiting deserving cases to face their 'constant disappointment' at being told that nothing could be done for them 'beyond writing their names in a book'. As applicants had 'commonly expressed it', they were being 'made fools of'.[16]

COS self-delusion and its attempt to confuse outsiders surfaced in its pride at finding a reduction in numbers applying for relief at St Saviour's COS, Southwark. The District Committee's report, in 1873–74, explained that the decrease was probably related to the poor having 'found from experience that their characters will not stand investigation by the Inquiry Officer'. The COS chose not to recognize that their perceived hard-heartedness not only deterred needy applicants for relief but also discouraged potential benefactors of the Society. As regards the fading support from the latter group, the St Saviour's Committee blithely regretted that the 'diminution of the subscriptions' locally had prevented them 'from carrying out to the full extent the objects of the Society'. They had to acknowledge that COS activities in Southwark 'must have come to an untimely end had it not been for support afforded to it by the Central Committee' of a £50 grant to see them through the year.[17] The COS Council in 1874 revealed serious administrative inadequacies in many districts. Of the 36 offices investigated; 13 were found to be 'occasionally deficient in important particulars', six were 'frequently deficient' and at two offices the investigation of applicants for relief was 'very nearly nil in almost all the cases examined'. The survey also exposed the fact that several cases referred elsewhere by COS districts were 'clearly made in error'. Some districts apparently had no clear idea of what was the intended COS meaning of the word 'referred'.[18]

From its beginning there was a transparent social status distinction adopted by the COS regarding their waged employees and other members. When DC publications named the Agent he was allocated the prefix 'Mr' to mark him out as a working-class waged person. This contrasted with the names of other male COS members who were accorded the suffix 'Esq.'. This distinction was allegedly made because the latter were subscribers to the Society. Annual subscription lists indicate that some gave no more than a few shillings. Social class differences were maintained by continuing to accord the names of 'Honorary' Secretaries with the suffix 'Esq.' even when they had to be provided with a salary to retain their continued COS involvement.[19] On the other hand, when occasionally an artisan was persuaded to join a COS District Committee, he was pointedly referred to in print as 'Mr'. It was not surprising that when, intermittently, the occasional tradesman was persuaded to join a COS Committee they soon became disillusioned and resigned. From time to time the advantages of recruiting working-class men to join the Society was debated in Council but with negligible long-term success.[20]

COS Council business was conducted from hand to mouth initially, with expenditure running ahead of income. Special donations from Lord Lichfield and G.M. Hicks kept the Society afloat during the formative months before an Appeal for public subscriptions and donations launched in October 1869 managed to almost match the Society's needs up to 6 December 1869 which were:

Rent	80
Assistant Secretary	140
Clerk	52
Boy	13
Office	110
Total	£395

The central expenses budgeted by the COS as being 'really necessary' for the following year 1870 were:

Rent	80
Secretary	250
Clerk	100
Boy	26
Unallocated Offices Expenses	150
Total	£606
Query	95
	£701

Appended to the above estimate was the recommendation that C.J. Ribton Turner should be appointed COS Organizing Secretary 'at such salary as the funds of the Society may justify'.[21] His appointment was confirmed rapidly. Ribton Turner contributed much of the energy and administrative skill needed to create the COS District Committee network across London. The difficulties of funding and of recruiting COS supporters in poorer parts of London is illustrated by the sizeable amount of Council time given to debating the problems of the Kilburn Committee during 1871. The central COS Administrative Committee advised their Council that 'while fully recognising the zeal and energy with which the affairs of the Kilburn Committee had been conducted by Col Strange' they should not assist in paying Kilburn Committee's debts. This advice was supported by the Secretary to the Council C.B.P. Bosanquet. He explained that there were 'many other districts which had a much stronger claim for assistance' and that the funds of the Council and of the Districts were 'quite distinct'. Ribton Turner also agreed, pointing out that he had 'repeatedly stated that the number of applicants at Kilburn was too small to justify an expenditure of £150 a year' and yet the local Committee had not devised worthwhile cost savings. A minority of Council members, including Sir Charles Trevelyan, sympathized with Kilburn's precarious situation. This was mainly because, as individuals, the Committee members would face debts on the COS venture should it be abandoned. Nevertheless, the Administrative Committee's resolution not to assist Kilburn was carried.[22]

By the third annual meeting of the Society the galaxy of distinguished persons seemingly adding their weight to the charity organization venture gave an illusion of strength and stability. Even then, the Earl of Lichfield urged the public to consider the great need for funds if COS endeavours were to be carried out successfully. He was 'perfectly aware' of the misleading accusations being made against the Society concerning the spending of an 'enormous amount upon organisation and very little in actual relief'. The Earl saw no reason for apologies and was adamant about the need for adequate investigation. He had no hesitation in saying that for every £15 spent on relief he 'would gladly give another £5 to see it properly expended'.[23] The ratio between administrative expenditure and relief mentioned by Lichfield, partly for dramatic effect, was already being exceeded regularly by COS District Committees throughout London. H.J. Bristow, of the newly formed Deptford Committee, said it was 'perfectly correct' that it had cost his Committee £102 to give away £183 but that they could still 'with pleasure point to the strict economy which characterised the management of their Society'. With the exception of 'a moderate percentage necessary for the expense of properly investigating all cases submitted to them, every penny of the money subscribed is applied to the relief of the deserving poor'. Deptford COS claimed to have recruited the services of a 'most intelligent and trustworthy charity officer who thoroughly investigated all cases coming before them'. Allegedly, his diligence had repressed mendicity with the result that whereas '242 professional mendicants' had applied for relief during the winter of 1869–70 only 62 had approached them during the following winter and the 'number now applying would exhibit a still further reduction'.[24]

A COS Sub-Committee (hereinafter the 'Relationship Committee'), was appointed on the 17 October 1871 to consider the relationship between the Council and the 'present state of the various Committees'. It was also to advise on how: (a) the District Committees may be strengthened; (b) a more perfect organization could be promoted; and (c) a greater uniformity might be obtained in carrying out the principles of the Society.[25] The Relationship Committee consisted of Lord Lichfield, Willis Bund, Hornsby Wright and the Secretaries with 'the advantage' of Sir Charles Trevelyan's and Col Freemantle's assistance for their later meetings. The COS Council could already detect uncomfortable similarities between themselves and the Poor Law authorities regarding the identical problem of combining the 'principle of self-government and self-support' with the amount of centralization and mutual assistance needed to create an essential unity of purpose. Even after the appointment of Howgrave Graham as Assistant Organizing Secretary, the Council continued to feel there was 'great need of more personal communication between the different Committees and also between the Committees and themselves'.[26]

The Relationship Committee revealed that the standard of 'investigation and reporting was not as high as they would wish to see it'. They called the attention of each district to the 'importance of receiving *ex parte* statements with great caution'. Persons whose character may be tainted by such statements must be given 'an opportunity of clearing themselves'. They recognized that the co-operation COS District Committees were obtaining from other 'local charitable agencies' was 'by no means satisfactory'. As a result, they had not been 'able to get or give relief for many of the cases which they would wish to assist'. Much harm was said to have been caused, 'both with the public and their own Committee men'. The Relationship Committee announced that 'hardly any Committee would seem to have made much progress towards becoming a local Council with representatives of most of the district charities upon it'. Therefore they had not been able to become a 'real centre of charitable organisation' for their district. They concluded that a basic reason why the COS had been so unsuccessful in gaining representation from other charities was 'the want of leisure' among gentlemen on the COS Committees. The Relationship Committee 'did not want to close its eyes to the fact' that the evidence they had collected revealed 'a position of affairs requiring serious consideration and one for which it is not easy to find an adequate remedy'.[27]

Maj. General Cavenagh addressed the COS Conference on Charity and the Poor Law held on 21 March 1872 in Exeter Hall, London. He proposed that whereas 'it was essential to the proper treatment of the poor that there should be thorough and cordial co-operation between Poor Law Guardians and Charity Committees', it was 'inexpedient' to attempt to define by 'arbitrary rules' the exact nature of the cases to be dealt with by the statutory and voluntary sector respectively.[28] Col West recognized that this underlined the need for the closest relations to be created between Guardians and Charity Committees. He recommended that as a first step, as many people as possible should serve on both bodies simultaneously. Whereas Alsager Hill was anxious to be associated with much of what Cavenagh had said, he could not endorse the 'principle that poverty was an ineradicable heritage of human nature'. Hill believed that 'no social science could be progressive that did not recognise that the whole aim of humanity was to eradicate both poverty and suffering'.[29]

Two years later, in 1874, the Council 'especially' pleaded with the public to provide their most direct and valuable form of co-operation, that of 'personal service'. This included the assisting in and the 'superintending of office details', the taking part 'in the deliberations of District Committees', the visiting of the poor in their homes and the promotion of their welfare. The COS emphasized that the services of a larger number of 'judicious volunteer workers' were essential, especially in the 'poorer parts of London, to make the machinery work smoothly and effectually'. Active volunteers were at a premium.[30] The Earl of Lichfield admitted, yet again, that 'one of the great defects in the Society' remained their failure to create 'satisfactory organisation in some of the poorer districts of London'. There was still considerable difficulty in 'obtaining funds sufficient for the payment of office expenses' with financial deficiencies needing to be rectified from Buckingham Street.[31] Wealthier districts of London had been able to cope markedly better with COS administrative needs. The Marquis of Westminster's great concern about the better-off areas was that COS members were continually having to cope with 'the warm hearts and open hands of the metropolis which indulged in the great evil of indiscriminate almsgiving'.[32] A COS general meeting cheered the Marquis when he 'desired to bear testimony to the noble work done around St George's, Hanover Square for the Society by the young Officers of the Guards'.[33] Within a few months, urgent public appeals were being made for volunteers since 'through the exigencies of service' the St George's Committee had lost some of its 'energetic and valuable members' with Col Fletcher, Col Freemantle, Col West and Captain Fitzroy having been called away.[34]

17 January 1872 had seen the launch of the weekly *Charity Organisation Reporter (COR)*. It laid no claim to being a newspaper but served as the propagandist mouthpiece of the Charity Organization Society. *COR* was also intended to collate information relating to the 'removal of causes of pauperism and bearing on the elevation of the poorer classes'. The first issue showed how the Executive COS Council, operating on a weekly basis, was shorn of the names of many of the aristocrats, nobility and other eminent figures featured in the published *List of Council*. Even then, those who attended weekly at Buckingham Street were themselves a formidable array. The Earl of Lichfield, as Chairman of the Council, attended fairly regularly and on the occasions where he did not attend, significant matters arising in Council were reported back to him by Ribton Turner, his confidante and private secretary. Other regular attenders were mainly gentlemen (and the occasional lady) of leisure and those with experience in one of the established professions, often clergymen, lawyers or retired Officers from Her Majesty's armed forces. Most members represented a particular COS District Committee as either their Chairman or Hon. Secretary. A flavour of personnel attending a weekly Council meeting is available from the one held on 15 January 1872:

Present were:- Maj Gen Cavenagh (in the Chair); W. Wynyard, Esq, *Kensington*; J.R. Hollond, Esq, *Paddington*; Capt. Boyce R.N., Miss Courtenay, R.A. Aspinall, Esq, W.S. Seton-Karr, Esq, *Chelsea*; Lieut-Col H.C. Fletcher, Capt C. Fitzroy, *St George's*; Sir Charles Jackson, Miss Octavia Hill, *St Marylebone*; Rev H.F. Mallet, G. Harris Lea, Esq, *Hampstead*; Professor Willis-Bund, *St Pancras*; F. Burdett Roberts, Esq, *Islington*; E.C. Grey, Esq, Lightly Simpson, Esq, Jun., *St Giles and Bloomsbury*; Rev R.J. Simpson, *Strand*; L.T. Cave, Esq, *Southwark*; Rev A.T. Edwards, Jun., T.T. Powell, Esq, R. Simpson, Esq, *Lambeth*; T. Galabin, Esq, *Camberwell*; Capt. G.H. Gardiner, R.N., *Lewisham*;

E.W. Hollond, Esq, *Inquiry Committee for East London*, Sir C.E. Trevelyan, K.C.B., Rev C.L. Butler, H.J. Cameron, Esq, G.M. Hicks, Esq, Alsager Hay Hill, Esq, *Additional Members of the Council*; C.B.P. Bosanquet, Esq, *Secretary*; C.J. Ribton Turner, Esq, *Organising Secretary*; T.Ll. Murray Browne, Esq, H.H. Graham, Esq, *Visitors*.

The foregoing relatively trim working group contrasts the much weightier 'List of Council' which was published annually as part of the 'Society's method and its strength'.[35] Queen Victoria was persuaded to be the Society's patron as early as 1872. Sir Charles Trevelyan took the names of the 'distinguished men' who presided over their annual meetings as proof that the Society had made 'satisfactory progress'.[36] The Council List published with their fourth annual report is replicated in Table 2.1.

Concerns about the wide disparity in population density across London were shared by the Earls of Lichfield and of Shaftesbury. The latter pointed to how the 'enormous masses' which came to London as part of the national trend to urbanization had not been absorbed satisfactorily. Newcomers were compounding the 'conglomerations of poverty' existing in the East End and immediately along the south side of the Thames. Shaftesbury was concerned that in marked contrast to the inward flow of working-class people, every person in London earning upwards of £200 a year was moving out of the urbanized area with their nights and Sundays being spent in the country.[37] The demographic pressures had been confirmed by the 1871 census. It showed the population of the metropolitan registration division to be 3 251 804 (3 254 260 when revised). In 1801, the population had been only 958 863. The mean density of population by 1871 over the 122 square miles of the metropolis was 42 persons per acre. It was the great inequality in population density which caused most concern. There were 150 persons per acre in the central districts, 107 in the east, 56 in the north, 52 in the west and only 21 in the southern districts which accounted for considerably more than half the entire area of London.[38] Disturbing changes in the density of population had occurred in some areas during the previous decade. For example, in the ten years from 1861, the number of Battersea residents had advanced from 19 600 to 54 016, an increase of 176 per cent.[39]

Until mid-1872, the Society had little presence in the densely populated East End of London apart from in Shoreditch, Bethnal Green and the COS East London Inquiry Office. A preliminary meeting was called on 2 May 1872 to develop COS representation at St George's in the East

Table 2.1   Charity Organization Society Council, 1872

LIST OF COUNCIL
PATRON: THE QUEEN
PRESIDENT: THE LORD BISHOP OF LONDON
VICE-PRESIDENTS

THE DUKE OF NORFOLK	REV DR BARRY
THE DUKE OF NORTHUMBERLAND	B. BOND GABBELL, ESQ
THE MARQUIS OF CAMDEN	GEORGE CUBITT, ESQ, MP
THE MARQUIS OF LANSDOWNE	C.J. FREAKE, ESQ
THE MARQUIS OF SALISBURY	RT HON W.E. GLADSTONE, MP
THE MARQUIS OF WESTMINSTER, KG	RT HON G.J. GOSCHEN, MP
THE EARL OF DERBY	R.S. HOLFORD,ESQ, MP
THE EARL NELSON	ANDREW JOHNSTONE ESQ, MP
THE EARL OF SHAFTESBURY, KG	F.D. MOCATTA, ESQ
LORD LEIGH	HODGSON PRATT, ESQ
LORD VERNON	JOHN RUSKIN ESQ
THE BISHOP OF WINCHESTER	W.H. SMITH, ESQ, MP
ARCHBISHOP MANNING	RT HON J. STANSFELD, MP
LORD GEORGE HAMILTON, MP	RT HON W.F. COWPER-TEMPLE, MP
SIR DUDLEY C. MARJORIBANKS, Bt	W.M. WILKINSON, ESQ

COUNCIL
Chairman – THE EARL OF LICHFIELD
Vice Chairman – MAJOR GENERAL CAVENAGH, ALSAGER H. HILL ESQ
Treasurer – H.B. PRAED, ESQ

SIR RUTHERFORD ALCOCK, KCB	J.R. HOLLOND, ESQ
REV B.H. ALFORD	T.R. HUNTLEY, ESQ
DR ANDERSON	REV J. JEAKES
MAJOR GEN. BAINBRIGGE	A.H.H. JESSE, ESQ
E. BEEDELL ESQ	T.J. PHILLIPS JODRELL, ESQ
MAJOR BELL	LLOYD JONES, ESQ
J.H.W. BISHOP ESQ	HON E.F. KENYON
GEORGE BLOUNT, ESQ	H. KIMBER ,ESQ
MAJOR GEN. BLUNT	REV W.H. LANGHORNE
REV F.W.A. BOWYER	G. HARRIS LEA, ESQ
CAPT. BOYCE, RN	COLONEL LYON-FREMANTLE
J.BRYCE, ESQ	REV H.F. MALLET
J.W.WILLIS BUND, ESQ	REV C.J. MEADE
REV C.L. BUTLER	R.W. MERRINGTON, ESQ
H.J. CAMERON, ESQ	C.A. MINER ESQ
F. CLEEVE, ESQ, CB	MAJOR R. OLDFIELD, RA
I.H. COLE, ESQ	E.L. O'MALLEY, ESQ
HON REGINALD CAPEL	GEORGE PARKER, ESQ, JP
VERY REV R.W. CHURCH	MAJOR L. PRENDERGAST
REV G.T. COTHAM	T.P. PRICE, ESQ
MISS COURTENAY	REV J. PULLING

Table 2.1 Continued

REV H.I. CUMMINS	GEN. H. RIVERS, RE
W. DAY, ESQ	A. RIVINGTON, ESQ
REV A. EDWARDS, SEN.	F.B. ROBERTS, ESQ
S. ETCHES, ESQ	T. RUDD, ESQ
J.T.G. FAUSSETT, ESQ	J. SAPSFORD, ESQ
C.W. FREMANTLE, ESQ	G.B. SIMPSON, ESQ
STEPHEN FULLER ESQ	D.R. SMITH, ESQ
CAPT. G.H. GARDNER, RN	STEPHEN SMITH, ESQ
E.D. HACON, ESQ	EDWARD THORNTON, ESQ
SIR J. HARINGTON, Bt	SIR C.E. TREVELYAN, KCB
T. HAWKSLEY, ESQ, MD	E. WALLER, ESQ
REV H.G. HENDERSON	W. H. WILLANS, ESQ
R.M. HENSLEY, ESQ	REV J. WILSON
G.M. HICKS, ESQ	W.W. WOOD, ESQ
A.H. HILL, ESQ	W. WYNYARD, ESQ
MISS O. HILL	MAJOR YARD
T. HILTON ESQ	

Secretary – C.B.P. BOSANQUET, ESQ
Organising Secretary – C.J. RIBTON TURNER, ESQ
Assistant Organising Secretary – H. HOWGROVE GRAHAM, ESQ
Bankers – MESSRS COUTTS & CO, 59 Strand, WC
***The Chairman and Hon Secs of each District Committee are
ex-officio **Members of the Council**

and Whitechapel. Ribton Turner acknowledged the great difficulty of establishing COS Committees where there were large numbers of poor and a 'small number of residents with time to spare'. The Rev. S. Bardsley, Vicar of Christ Church, Spitalfields, supported the idea because of the 'compelling need' for stricter investigation to root out crooked charitable bodies. In contrast, the Rev. G. Davenport, Vicar of St Mark, Whitechapel, was 'much opposed to the scheme'. E.W. Hollond, representing the COS Inquiry Office for East London, while not wishing 'to throw water on the idea', thought it 'useless' unless there was a 'fair and reasonable chance of it being able to commence and continue a useful existence'. The Rev. D. Greatorex, Vicar of St Paul's, Whitechapel, 'feared the difficulty' facing the COS in any attempt to recruit people willing to provide 'personal service on Committee'. He recounted the problems he himself had encountered when attempting to persuade West End friends to serve on his Whitechapel School Committees.[40] Later in 1872 a DC was established at Whitechapel and St George's in the East.

On 5 June 1872, a high-powered meeting in the Mansion House attempted to launch a COS District Committee in the City. When the Lord Mayor asked Lord Lichfield to explain the Society's objectives he focused directly on their regrettable lack of funds which, he alleged, was why the COS had not yet managed to establish across London 'an organisation as it desired to see'. Lichfield again had to accept that 'one of the strongest of several objections which had been raised against the Society' was that such a 'very small proportion of their income went to relieve poverty'. He explained that few among the general public recognized this was because it was never the 'primary object of the Society to give money in relief'. Lichfield asserted that 'as was well known', the total amount of money collected and distributed for charitable purposes in London was 'more than amply sufficient' to supply all the wants of the 'poorest inhabitants' in the metropolis 'if properly administered'.[41]

The unsolicited vetting of other charities and philanthropic bodies was adopted eagerly by COS activists. They saw it as being pivotal in their attempts to rationalize the voluntary sector and rid it of individuals and institutions not meeting with their approval.[42] The COS Council recommended that the DCs should investigate 'all appeals issuing through the public press, whether by advertisement or otherwise'. Others who were generally in favour of the idea believed that when the 'reference was a professional man of high standing' they should hesitate about making any enquiries. A.H. Hill dismissed this hesitancy. He argued that even men of the 'highest integrity' might be assisted by the experience and information already in possession of the COS.[43] It was eventually agreed that COS District Committees would send details of imposition cases they investigated to Buckingham Street for inclusion in a London-wide register aimed at warning the public against 'fraudulent charities'.[44] Well-known charities taken to court by the COS in their early days included the 'Free Dormitory Association' and 'The National Bible and Clothing Society'. As regards dishonest individuals, the 'scale or character' of the 'impositions' attempted by the likes of Messrs Carden, Taylor, Dorrington, Guazzaroni and Sullivan made the COS decide as a 'matter of public importance that their career should be arrested'. Each was prosecuted by the Society during 1872.[45] The fact that many of these bodies were well-intentioned but because they were irregular in structure and slapdash in method made them easy prey for COS zealots. This facility initially made favourable headlines for the COS but also carried dangers of tarnishing their own public image still further. Prominent COS members became disturbed about unwelcome publicity as eager volunteers applied unwarranted malevolence against those they merely suspected of deception. The Earl of Shaftesbury was totally supportive of the 'most ruthless severity in every case of fraudulent imposture' but he begged COS members to proceed prudently. He advised them to deal 'very gently' with the 'hundreds of thousands' in London who had to look for their living 'day by day and hour by hour'. Shaftesbury sustained the opinion that before these 'little trades' could be disapproved of by COS members, 'some other means must be devised to improve the condition of such people'.[46]

In spite of the problems encountered from hostile public opinion, the uncompromising efforts of Ribton Turner and Howgrave Graham succeeded in establishing COS representation across most of London, even though it was tilted disproportionately and grotesquely in favour of the wealthier districts. An impression of how the COS District Committee network expanded can be gauged from Tables 2.2 and 2.3. Once established, only minor changes occurred in the following decades and then they usually involved either the division or the combination of districts. Even when the Council felt able to commend the perseverance by 'a comparatively small number of persons' in impoverished districts, they admitted that 'it must not be supposed that these Committees have been able as yet to make any material impression on the large poor populations amongst which they are working'.[47] COS expansion in the East End continued to be hampered by the difficulty of finding 'volunteers either resident in the districts or willing to go to them with sufficient regularity to carry on the work of committeemen'.[48] The COS in Battersea had needed resuscitation after the forced closure of an office in December 1872.[49] An early group operating in the district had failed to appoint representatives to the COS Council who, as a consequence, had disowned them. At Deptford, one group of gentlemen had evaded involvement with the COS, explaining that they had formed themselves for the relief of distress and not for organizing charity.

Alsager Hay Hill feared that several District Committees remained in a 'position of some financial difficulty'. Others had so few 'decided cases' to include in the weekly returns 'it was clear that they had not yet thoroughly won the confidence of their districts'.[50] Of the 34 District Committees shown in Table 2.2, no returns had been submitted by six of them and among the remainder, 16 had investigated fewer than ten cases in the week.[51] Of the total of 276 cases investigated across London, 76 had been dismissed, 73 referred elsewhere and 127 assisted either by a grant, a loan, a letter to a hospital or by inclusion on the COS labour register. This latter innovation, launched in April 1870 at

Table 2.2 The Charity Organization Society's London District Returns of the number of applicants for assistance during the week ending 1st June 1872

Return of cases decided by the District Committees for week ending Saturday 1 June 1872	Class 1. Dismissed as					Class II. Referred to					Class III. Assisted by						Grand total
	Not requiring relief	Ineligible	Undeserving	Giving false address	Class total	The poor law	District agencies	Private persons	Charitable institutions	Class total	Grants	Loans	Employment	Letter to hospitals	Labour register	Class total	
Kensington	4	2	4		10	3	4	2	2	11	6	1		1	1	9	30
Fulham			1		1						2					2	3
Paddington	3	1	1	1	6	3			2	5	4	3	3	1	3	14	25
Chelsea	1		1		2				1	1	4					4	7
St George's Mount Street			1		1	1		2		3	4					4	8
James Street	3	5		3	11	4				4	7	1	1	3		12	27
Westminster St James's		1			1						1			1		2	3
St Marylebone		2			2	4	5	4	2	15	4	2		3		9	26
Hampstead*																	0
St Pancras: North+South				1	1	4	4		2	10					2	2	13
Islington*																	0
Hackney*																	0

	18	32	20	6	76	28	19	14	12	73	70	24	8	9	16	127	276
St Giles's and Bloomsbury	1	1			2	2				2	5	1				6	10
Strand	1	2	1		6			1	1	2		1				1	9
Holbom	2	1			4			2	2	3	1				4	10
Shoreditch*																	0
Bethnal Green*																	0
East London Inquiry Office	1				1	1			1		1				1	2
St Saviour's		1	1		1	1			1			1			1	3
St Olave's	2	1		3	1				1			1			1	5
Newington	6	2		8	1		1	2	7	5	6	2		20	30
Lambeth	2	1		3	2			7	3	3			7	3	13
Wandsworth and Putney	1	1		2		5			1	1			1	3
Battersea*																0
Clapham									3	3	1		4	4
Camberwell: Grove Lane	4			4					6	6			6	10
Peckham			2		2			2	4	3	1		4	6
Greenwich	2	1		3	4			4	4	3	1		4	11
Deptford								4	1	1		6	6
Woolwich	1			1						2	1		3	4
Lewisham	2		2		1			1	2		1	2	5
Blackheath		1	1											1
Eltham														0
Sydenham									2			2	2
Sub-class Total	18	32	20	6	76	28	19	14	12	73	70	24	8	9	16	127	276

Non-resident applications at offices: 256 *No returns from these committees. Tabulated data are as published in *COR*, 12 June 1872, p. 106.

Table 2.3   Number and value of grants and loans provided by COS District Committees between 1st October and 30th September in each of the financial years 1872–3 and 1873–4

| | 1872–3 | | | | 1873–4 | | | |
| | Grants | | Loans | | Grants | | Loans | |
	Number	Total value £	Number	Total value £	Number	Total value £	Number	Total value £
WEST DISTRICTS								
Kensington	286	337	62	195	174	193	35	125
Fulham & Hammersmith	81	65	10	25	71	56	22	28
Paddington	229	216	60	87	227	214	71	93
Chelsea	81	57	28	?	88	53	30	?
St George's (Hanover Sq)	478	438	124	221	433	487	122	243
Westminster (St James')	59	57	22	50	42	36	10	21
NORTH DISTRICTS								
St Marylebone	164	173	115	171	111	90	73	246
Hampstead	7	6	7	14	10	13	11	20
St Pancras (North+South)	21	68	35	17	66	137	59	166
Islington	5	27	9	2	56	69	7	5
Hackney	52	50	15	29				
CENTRAL DISTRICTS								
St Giles & St Geo. (Blooms)	123	109	43	88	91	117	48	88
Strand	11	10	46	78	14	16	27	43
Holborn	24	13	10	16	40	33	18	34
City	4	10	3	18	8	10	7	31
EAST DISTRICTS								
Shoreditch	43	26	33	30	63	78	33	44
Bethnal Green	61	40	21	21	56	40	37	30
Whitechapel+ St Geo. (East)	9	12	22	38	15	13	29	66
Stepney, Mile End	–	–	–	–	19	25	14	62
Poplar, Bow, Bromley	1	2	2	7				
SOUTH DISTRICTS								
St Saviour's (Southwark)	82	48	27	23	58	39	12	15
St Olave's (Southwark)	26	14	30	24	29	21	19	35
Lambeth	203	253	22	48	134	140	38	53

Table 2.3 Continued

| | 1872–3 | | | | 1873–4 | | | |
| | Grants | | Loans | | Grants | | Loans | |
	Number	Total value £	Number	Total value £	Number	Total value £	Number	Total value £
Wandsworth & Putney	39	35	19	65	41	41	29	91
Camberwell	517	96	23	60	245	77	44	64
Greenwich	30	16	132	116	29	20	140	136
Woolwich	–	–	–	–	13	12	21	40
Lewisham & Blackheath	49	34	10	35	71	36	16	42
Newington	117	64	95	37	–	–	–	–
Battersea	52	71	24	35	86	131	47	92
Clapham	80	28	10	48	59	25	11	23
Deptford	335	121	23	30	71	55	10	11
Eltham and Mottingham	–	–	–	–	2	2	2	2
Sydenham and Forest Hill	117*	100	?	38	155*	?	–	–

Sources: Annual Reports of the various COS District Committees. *Notes*: (a) Values are rounded to nearest £; (b) In addition to the tabled grants and loans most District Committees provided 'letters to hospitals', helped in the obtaining of jobs and placed names of selected applicants on a labour register. Broad indication of the extent of this assistance can be gained from Table 2.7. (c) *These applicants were said to be helped 'permanently', the division of the total provision between grants and loans not available.

59 Greek Street, Soho by Hay Hill was a precursor of the present-day Job Centre. It had a primary purpose of assisting the migration of unemployed workers to flourishing Northern industrial centres.

As an indication of how difficult it was to market the COS concept in London's distressed localities, Henry Juela, Chairman of Deptford COS Committee, regretted they had been able to collect a mere £156 9s 6d from 'upwards of 450 subscribers' during the 12 months ending September 1871. Doorstep visits by the local COS collector had yielded little. Juela complained that only 'about fifty out of the thousands in these vast parishes had given above 10s, about 140 gave 5s, the rest being made up of trifles under 2s'.[52] The meeting at the Milton Hall, Camden Town in September 1872 to support the north London COS District of St Pancras confirmed yet again the chronic dearth of COS volunteers. The Rev. Bartlett described how the COS Committee had been 'very badly attended and the work had fallen upon four or five gentlemen'. How much time these gentlemen devoted to COS matters was not stated but some measure of their input may be assumed from

Bartlett's personal offer to 'attend once a week for a month'. He asked that if 'others would give the like small sacrifice of time – for only one hour a week was required'. Bartlett was convinced that with this amount of effort 'the work could be efficiently and well carried out, and the whole of the parish could thus be covered'.[53]

Throughout the formative years, the weekly Council meetings were regularly consumed with debate as to what should be the precise relationship between COS District Committees and the Central Office. For example, at the Council meeting on the 29 April 1872, the Rev. R.J. Simpson of the Strand COS District Committee unsuccessfully moved the resolution:

> That the District Committees be requested to report every week, or fortnight, to the Council, in the form of a tabular statement, particulars of the cases of application made to and decided upon by them, especially with a view to the prevention of an overlapping of relief, or assistance, and the detection of imposture, by supplying information to every District Committee as such undeserving cases and cases of imposture, as may be deemed expedient.[54]

Dr Hawksley was concerned about the administrative burden this might incur locally. He feared some districts had such a shortage of executive capacity that they 'would find it difficult to send even lists of names'. Sir Charles Trevelyan concurred. He remained vehemently opposed to more centralized control and thought it 'clear that such work as the Society had in hand could only be done by localisation'. Others were more sympathetic to Simpson's proposal and considered that the prime need of the Society was uniformity of action. E.W. Hollond instanced cases where COS District Committees had annoyed employers by a number of them requesting identical information about the same applicant. He moved successfully that in future no enquiries should be made by Committees in the districts of other Committees 'except through the medium of such Committees'.[55] Some months later, Simpson repeated his proposal that regular tabular applicant data from the local COS Committees should be submitted to the Council. Again he encountered opposition from Council members who doubted whether the Committee system was sufficiently advanced to allow such information to be forthcoming. Trevelyan remained adamantly opposed to Simpson's ideas as it would create 'over-administration to have a detailed statement of all cases, good and bad' causing a 'heavy burden on the Central Office, as well as on the weaker Committees'.[56] After robust discussion, Simpson's resolution was again laid aside only to be raised and debated with renewed vigour the following week. By then forces had been rallied opposed to the Council's power being increased. They included J.R. Hollond who argued that such a register would be superfluous. He predicted that Agents would rely on a 'great central index' and would become 'content with slovenly investigation'. Trevelyan weighed in with the ominous claim that other 'Societies had split on the rock of over-centralisation'. Eventually, a much watered-down amendment by Sir Charles was carried whereby District Committees were merely requested 'to furnish particulars of detected impostors and of persons who gave false addresses'.[57]

The Earl of Lichfield never tired of focusing on the shortage of funds needed in poorer districts to provide the COS with 'an efficient machinery for obtaining information'. Lichfield was 'perfectly certain' that it was essential for help to be recruited from wealthier localities.[58] He proposed that equity between what were currently disturbingly disparate districts could best be achieved by all appeals being directed from Buckingham Street. He ridiculed the continued reliance on the Guarantee Fund established in 1870 as a temporary expedient to aid the Council in their endeavours towards financial stability across the metropolis. Lichfield's proposal for centralized fund-raising was defeated in Council by those including Sir Charles Trevelyan who believed such a decision 'would entirely change the basis of the Society'. Most Council members supported the belief that they could attract more subscriptions in their district than would be achieved from the centre. Bizarre claims were made about how easy it would be for districts to amass revenue. The Rev. Septimus Hansard of the Bethnal Green Committee talked airily about sums like £70000 being raised in his locality by an unnamed clergyman. Another man of the cloth in the Bethnal Green area was said to have raised £4000 in two months. Hansard recommended that local financial appeals be launched and implied that the sums he had revealed should form the bases of targets at which all local COS District Committees might aim with confidence. The annual report of the COS Bethnal Green Committee for the year in question showed that the total donations and subscriptions actually collected by them for the 12 months was £73 10s 6d.[59]

George M. Hicks felt that the Earl of Lichfield's concept of centralized fund collection deserved further consideration. He pointed to how in 1872 the seven richest COS districts had received £7474 whereas the 14 poorest, where the most needy people tended to live had attracted only £2753. While the seven richest districts had spent £2454 on grants and loans, the fourteen poorest could muster only a total of £804 to disburse. Hicks believed that Council members 'hardly realised the great difference that existed between the different classes of Committees'.[60] In spite of Hicks' plea, centralized collection of funds was again rejected. The Rev. W.H. Langhorne was another who expressed frustration about the huge revenue inequalities between East and West London districts. During 1874 he compared recent difficulties encountered by the COS in London's East End, by which he meant the area covered by the seven Poor Law divisions, Shoreditch, Bethnal Green, Whitechapel, St George's East, Stepney, Mile End Old Town and Poplar. He contrasted these with the affluent West End comprising Kensington, Paddington, Chelsea, St George's Hanover Square and Westminster Unions. Langhorne claimed it was ethically wrong that the COS did 'about five times as much work in the West as in the East' and had totally failed to bring their principles before the large employers of labour in the East End. He alleged that this also meant failure to improve the moral and material condition of the poor.[61]

Table 2.3, above, summarizes details of grants and loans as related to the various COS District Committees during each of the two financial years 1872–73 and 1873–74. It highlights distinct disparities in both number and value of the COS grants and loans provided by a few wealthy West End COS districts like Kensington, Paddington and St George's Hanover Square as compared with COS Committees in poorer districts. It should also be remembered that although the attempts of the District Committee Aid Fund (DCAF) to provide financial support to the worse-off districts was limited they went some way to disguising the gulf between the districts. Donations to the DCAF during 1873 totalled £1510. This included amounts from the COS Committees at St George's (Hanover Square) (£1100), Kensington (£100), Paddington (£50) and from individuals, including Lord Overstone (£100), G.A. Crowder (£50), and Pandeli Ralli (£50).[62] The underlying inability for COS Committees in poorer districts to raise adequate funds locally remained. During the 1872–73 financial year, the total receipts of Shoreditch COS Committee of £185 included £75 in grants from the DCAF, Bethnal Green's gross revenue of £124 included £49, Whitechapel's £191 included £50 and Poplar's total income of £62 included £45 from the Fund. Some time later, the Right Honourable W.E. Forster remained concerned about how COS operations in the populous poorer districts of London had been 'hindered' through lack of money. He was also convinced that the one thing the COS needed even more than money was persons from the wealthier districts 'to go down and assist them'.[63] The DCAF was found to be inadequate as a means of achieving district equality and by 1875 was itself in an 'impoverished condition'.[64]

Of fundamental concern for the whole COS movement was how they were cold-shouldered by most other relief agencies. Even districts like the Strand which faired relatively well in terms of COS Committee membership, if only because of colleagues in nearby Buckingham Street, there were worries about the lack of recognition from other relief agencies.[65] The COS Strand Committee appealed forlornly 'to the clergy, the police, magistrates and the trustees of local charities to co-operate with them'.[66] The COS founding fathers had been amazed by the unfavourable response as they had confidently assumed that representatives from all local charitable agencies would clamour for the opportunity to participate in the new science of philanthropy. When their original assumption was seen to have been hopelessly ill-founded, the Council recommended a more positive approach whereby 'members of the District Committees should go to the charities' and put themselves in 'communication with all relief agencies in fixed sub-divisions'.[67]

The manner in which the COS had to eventually retreat from their adoption of loans rather than other relief methods further indicates their misjudgement of public response. In the early years, to dampen internal criticism about the very possibility that the COS would be involved directly in relief provision, they made extravagant claims about the Society's ability to lend money on a strictly returnable basis rather than providing traditional grants or doles. Allegedly, loans possessed the inestimable advantage of making the recipient acutely aware of his personal responsibility to repay on schedule. The Rev. F.S. Clark 'heartily approved of the system of loans' because it inculcated thrift and strengthened character.[68] The 1872 COS Council report described how they 'continued to make loans in suitable cases with great success'. It was claimed to be 'a part of their work which hardly any other charitable associations, and still less charitable individuals, are (were) able to equal'. The Holland Street Loan Society (HSLS) which worked closely 'in connection' with the Kensington COS typified the COS approach to loan provision. Unlike Provident Societies active earlier in the century which provided generous interest rates to encourage thrift among poor borrowers, the COS version levied a charge on money repaid so as to make their scheme 'self-supporting'.[69] The COS claimed that any success of their loans could be attributed to them being 'conducted on strict business principles and the repayment legally enforced in case of need'. According to the COS, their experience in metropolitan districts by 1874 had shown that 'punctual repayment by instalments can, with care, be obtained, and the loss may be less than one per cent'.[70] An appropriate surety for each loan was considered to be the essence of their success. Persons standing surety should be 'nearly the same station or level as the borrower' and 'no District Visitor, Scripture reader, or near relative, should be accepted'. In the event of non-payment, the surety 'must be applied to at once'. If the guarantor refused to pay 'he must be summoned, to show that none are excused, except in the case of death'.[71] Major-General Bainbrigge claimed that because COS loans were mainly repaid '(except £1 per annum for casualties)', the same capital could be used repeatedly and 'thus great good is effected with a very small capital'.[72] Evidence published by the HSLS contradicts Bainbrigge's claim. Of the total of 96 loans they provided during 1873 and 1874, six cases ended in court proceedings. Over the two-year period £329 7s had been lent of which only £262 3s 6d had been recovered, a shortfall of £67 3s 6d, which was in excess of 20 per cent of the amount loaned.[73]

Mounting evidence about COS loans suggested that their practice did not match their rhetoric. District Committees were not only providing increasing numbers of small doles against COS principles but were using them to partially relieve destitute cases by the supplementation of Poor Law outdoor relief.[74] Comparison between the various COS benefits provided during the years 1872 and 1873, prepared by Major-General Bainbrigge, shows how they had paid lip-service to COS principles on loans, see Table 2.4. Bainbrigge was dismayed that while there had been an increase of more than 17 per cent in the number of COS grants over the two years, loans had increased by less than 5 per cent. Each district had, on average, provided less than one loan per week. In spite of evidence of this type indicating that in practice their District Committees were not favouring loans, the Council continued to extol them lavishly with the claim that they were what the COS did 'uniquely well'.

Table 2.4 Summary comparison of annual returns of COS London District Committees for 1872 and 1873

	Dismissed total	Referred total	Grants provided	Loans	Employ-ment	Hospital letters	Total decided	Home less	Labour register
1872	4910	4684	3292	1039	391	435	14751	12512	623
1873	4835	4350	3868	1086	332	420	14891	13322	376
Increase			+576	+47				+810	
Decrease	−75	−334			−59	−25	−140		−247

Source: extract from tabular comparison, *COR*, 11 February 1874, p. 205.

As regards the information disseminated locally by the DCs, they tended to follow the example set by the COS Council in passing resolutions alleging that their operations had brought great benefits to their locality despite evidence to the contrary.[75] In an attempt to ameliorate negative public response, Ribton Turner toured London claiming that the Society was supplying a 'great want in a great city'.[76] Most of the Society's propaganda fell on stony ground but some bore fruit. Lord Wharncliffe was so hooked on to the Society's storyline as to believe in 1873 that charity organization required 'very little advocacy to recommend it to the public'.[77] In reality the COS were failing to gain either wide popularity or even acceptance among the very social groups they had felt totally confident about influencing favourably. Their public rejection was interpreted by the COS with a perverse pride. For example, the 1874 annual report of the COS in St Marylebone recognized that many considered their opinions 'harsh and unsympathising' while others regarded the Society as 'consisting of theorising, scientific humanitarians'. They 'guaranteed' that attendance by the public at COS meetings would 'dispel such illusions'. The Stepney Committee were also well aware of the public having a 'great deal of misapprehension' about the COS and at Shoreditch they recorded their knowledge of widespread public 'objections' to COS principles.[78]

One way by which the COS activists hoped to have an important influence on the actions of other relief agencies was to join them as members so as to propagate their organizing principles from within. This tactic was most frequently applied by DC members getting themselves elected to the local Board of Guardians. As an example, Col Lyon Fremantle, who as well as being a serving Guard's Officer and COS Council member, was also a Poor Law guardian in the Hanover Square Union. He was adversely critical of the lax performance of his guardian colleagues with what he saw as their profligate provision of outdoor relief. Fremantle attracted their attention to how in the large populous poor district around Whitechapel and Stepney Unions, including the parish of St George in the East, for 'the week ended 4 September 1875, there were only 262 children on the outdoor relief list'. In contrast, within their own union of St George's (Hanover Square), which was comparatively wealthy and not so populous, there were 744 outdoor pauper children. Data compiled by Fremantle highlights the dramatic reduction in outdoor relief expenditure over a number of years achieved by the Whitechapel guardians where the majority were devoted to COS principles and to the LGB crusade against outdoor relief, see Table 2.5. Fremantle pointed to the comparison of how outdoor relief at Hanover Square had remained at an unsatisfactorily high level over the same period.[79]

The 'social state of applicants', their weekly earnings and their ages were analyzed by the Fulham and Hammersmith COS District Committee in their second annual report. The data, reproduced in Table 2.6, indicates that most applicants were either married couples (56 per cent) or widows (29 per cent). By combining data from Tables 2.3 and 2.6 it can be estimated that the total grants during the same 12 months period from Fulham and Hammersmith COS grants was valued at £65 and that this was shared between around 362 persons, adult or child.[80] The implication here is that the average grant per person over the year was worth 3s 8d. This compares with a typical *weekly* outdoor Poor Law dole of 3s for each adult and 1s or 1s 6d per child. Poor Law doles of this value were persistently derided by the COS as being insufficient to provide any real hope for the development of independent individual character. The foregoing discussion refers only to COS grants. To complete the 12-month picture of relief provision by the Fulham and Hammersmith Committee it should be noted that they also arranged 10 loans with a total value of around £25, see Table 2.3, above.

COS District Committees attempted to gain converts by publishing 'specimens' of case-work information together with their responses.

Table 2.5 Comparison between the financial amount and the changes in outdoor relief at St George's, Hanover Square and Whitechapel Poor Law Unions between 1870 and 1871

Union	Year	In-door paupers relieved	Out-door paupers relieved	Total No. paupers relieved	% In-door paupers	% Out-door paupers	Cost of out-door relief
	1871	2230	5454	7684	29	71	£394 4s 4d
	1872	1880	4085	5965	32	68	£298 0s 2d
Hanover Sq.	1873	2113	3582	5695	37	63	£269 8s 1d
	1874	1963	3182	5145	38	62	£240 13 4d
	1875	1856	2647	4503	41	59	£218 12 7d
	1870	1419	5339	6758	21	79	£168 17 4d
	1871	1219	2568	3787	32	68	£120 14 3d
Whitechapel	1872	1000	1568	2568	39	61	£ 75 18 7d
	1873	1163	845	2008	58	42	£ 50 4 5d
	1874	1154	609	1763		35	£ 36 11 1d
	1875	1170	346	1516	77	23	£ 22 9 0d

Source: *COR*, 3 November 1875, p. 31.

Table 2.6 'Social State', earnings per week and ages of applicants to Fulham and Hammersmith COS District (1872–3)

Social state of applicants in **191** cases*

Description	Without children	Applicants having the following number of children									
		1	*2*	*3*	*4*	*5*	*6*	*7*	*8*	*9*	*10*
Married couples	11	8	14	24	26	10	7		3	2	2
Deserted wives		1	1	2	1	2	1				
Widowers	2	2	2	1	1						
Widows	14	5	8	10	7	8	1	2	1		
Single men	3										
Single women	8	1									
Total	38	17	25	37	35	20	9	2	4	2	2

Earnings per week of **191** applicants when in full work*

	Under 10s	10s– 15s	15s– 20s	20s – 25s	25s– 30s	30s– 35s	35s– 40s	40s– 50s	50s– 70s	70s– 100s
Males	8	6	22	35	14	19	9	2	1	2
Females	52	17	2			2				
Total	60	23	24	35	14	21	9	2	1	1

Ages of applicants in **209** cases*

	Under 20	20– 25	25– 30	30– 35	35– 40	40– 50	50– 60	60– 70	70– 80	80– 90
Males	20	7	15	18	14	30	16	13	2	1
Females	2		3	13	12	18	9	9	7	
Total	22	7	18	31	26	48	25	22	9	1

*There were 216 resident applications during the year but the books kept by the late Agent do not give particulars in a greater number of cases than above. *Source*: 2nd Annual Report of Fulham and Hammersmith COS District Committee (1872–3), p. 27.

The following sample cases provide a flavour of factors likely to lead the COS to either dismiss applicants as being 'undeserving', prompt their 'referral' elsewhere and justify the Society to assist them directly.

1. A married woman, at Battersea, applied to a City firm for a loan of £2 to redeem a sewing machine and he requested Committee to make enquiries. It was found that her husband was in good work, and earning 25s per week and he was very angry to find his wife had solicited help, she having given away to improvident habits.[81]

2. A tradesman and family, through illness, had fallen into debt and difficulties. (City) Committee, under special circumstances, granted loan of £10. He has punctually repaid instalments and has successfully maintained and supported himself and family.[82]

3. Widow, aged 35, formerly in affluent circumstances, applied for assistance to obtain clothing, so as to enable her to obtain situation. (City) Committee made a grant of £2. She has obtained a situation and has since supported herself.[83]

4. E.N., married woman, age 66, was found begging in the street, and was referred to this office. She said her husband was paralysed and unable to work. It was ascertained her statement was untrue and that she was already receiving relief from the Parish and her husband was able to work but had been discharged through neglect of his duty and idleness.[84]

5. C.W., widow, age 63, needlewoman, in consequence of paralysis, was unable to work and had fallen into debt; (City) Committee granted loan of £4, by which she was enabled to get out of her difficulties and the loan has since been repaid, and applicant, partly by her own work and also some assistance from her daughters, has been kept off the rates.[85]

6. A man aged 49, a painter, earning 30s a week; wife aged 45, a needlewoman, earning 4s a week; eight children, five only at home dependent upon their parents; applied for help to purchase a pair of Surgical Boots, value £2.10s, for the child aged 9, of which amount the parents had paid 10s. Inquiry showed that the family were of good character and the man almost in constant work. Another 10s had been paid since the application was made. The (Paddington) Committee granted a Loan of 30s, the balance due. The Loan is now in course of repayment.[86]

7. A man, giving an address in Kensington, applied to a lady for assistance and stated that he was formerly a cabman but was incapacitated by an injury to his hand and he wished to *set up a little shop for the sale of cutlery – his wife being a native of Sheffield*. Inquiry showed that the applicant was not known at the address given and that he assumes various names – Lawrence, Dickson, Metcalfe and Watson, among others.[87]

8. O.W., a general servant, aged 53, a widow with no children, applied for money to purchase clothing to enable her to take a situation which she had obtained. Enquiries were made and it appeared that she was in the habit of dawdling about the streets during the day and that she was lodging with a man and his wife

who were drunkards. While the enquiries were being made she went to her situation and she called at the office and stated that her mistress would discharge her unless she had the clothes at once. Her mistress was communicated with, who expressed herself perfectly satisfied and said that the woman had plenty of clothes.[88]

9. W.L., a widower, aged 75, shoemaker, unable to work for the last twelve months on account of illness; one son, aged 16, a printer's boy; wages 8s. Stated to be paying 2s a week rent. It appeared that they were living with a son who keeps a dining room but with very little business attached. During the wife's lifetime she managed to keep him but he was now unfit for work. He bore a very good character. Referred to the 'Poor Law'.[89]

10. J.V., aged 39, a boot-maker, with a wife and six children applied for a loan of 30s It appeared that the man kept a little shop and had been ill for some months during which time he had been unable to work, and had been compelled to live on the stock. Enquiry was made and it was found the man's statement was perfectly true and he bore an excellent character for sobriety and honesty etc. It was also shown that he had some orders which he could not execute on account of his having no leather etc. A loan of 30s was made and the man regularly repaid that amount.[90]

11. A widow with one child stated that she was quite destitute and asked for immediate assistance. Applicant not known at the address given. Dismissed.[91]

12. A man, single, deaf and dumb (a clerk), asked for assistance and employment. Inquiry proved the man to be a drunkard. Had lost several situations through drink; lately lived by begging. Undeserving.[92]

13. A woman and four children; application for a loan to buy a mangle. This was found to be a deserving case and a loan of £4 was granted by the Bethnal Green Committee.[93]

14. This applicant applied to the sitting magistrate at Worship Street for help. He was a foreigner of genteel appearance and respectably clad. The case was sent for inquiry to the office and found to be deserving of assistance. The request was sent to the magistrate who referred it back to the Hon Sec and left the amount of assistance to his discretion. The sum for present necessity was stated to be £2, which was immediately granted and the further consideration of the man's distress and the best way of enabling him to gain a livelihood are now kept in view by the Committee. P.S. – He has since been received into the Jewish Converts Operative Institution in Palestine Place.[94]

15. S.K., a widow, with a daughter aged 18, assumed to be born in lawful wedlock, had for years received large sums in charity. In one of our principal watering places, where the clergyman, at the instance of the lady visitor had headed a petition in her favour, a considerable sum had been collected. The Committee, on the case being referred to them, discovered that the daughter had been born some year's after the husband's decease and that the father, a *married* man at the time, had all along been both able and willing to maintain and educate his child, but the applicant would not consent to part with her. This illustrated the need for inquiry before relieving.[95]

16. E.F., aged 39, left a widow with six children, the eldest 14, applied for help to purchase a mangle. The application was referred to the Committee who satisfied themselves that the case was deserving but that a sewing machine was preferable. The requisite amount was raised, the Committee helping both by grant and by loan.[96]

17. J.P., a vendor in sawdust, saved money and bought a donkey which turned out badly, he sold at a loss of 30s; next he tried his luck with a pony, getting it with harness for £5 10s. The Society for Prevention of Cruelty to Animals interfered and, on the advice of a veterinary surgeon, the pony was killed and the carcass sold for 33s In despair he asked help of the Society, and received it partly by grant and partly by loan and is now doing well.[97]

18. A.M., a machinist with four children, applied for a loan of £4 to pay arrears due on the hire of sewing-machines; she stated that she had four, two of which were paid for and two on hire. Enquiry proved that she had three machines, all on hire, for which she owed £13 5s. She offered no security. Undeserving.[98]

19. M.D., homeless, applied for assistance but would not say where she lived last. Stated she had stopped in Whitechapel where she had paid 1s 6d a week. Her statement was so rambling that but little value could be attached to it. On enquiry at the place where applicant slept on the previous night it was ascertained she was a beggar.[99]

20. Mrs B. had, by the death of her husband, a warehouseman, been left with six children and no means whatever of subsistence. All her relations could do for her was to grant 24s a month, which was not sufficient to keep the family off the parish. Nearly £20 had been subscribed for her by friends of her late husband but this alone would only have staved off the evil day for a short time. The Committee in concert with her friends determined to set her up a lodging-housekeeper; one of their number advanced £20 to which a loan of £10 was added from the funds of the Society; this, with the sums subscribed as before stated, was sufficient for the purpose. The

requisite aid to support her family while the plan was maturing, was also granted by this Society and she now has every prospect of succeeding in her undertaking.[100]

Development of the COS District Committee network up to 1875 is summarized in Table 2.7. Whereas the number of offices had multiplied from 22 in 1871 to 35 by 1875, the total number of applicants between 1872 and 1875 had remained more or less constant. As a consequence the average number of cases investigated by each office during a 12-month period had fallen from 568 in 1871 to 427 in 1875, partly as a result of trade improvements. There were minor fluctuations in the proportion of applicants dismissed, referred or assisted over the five years 1871–75 inclusive but the data imply that the ratio between the three categories hovered around 35:30:35 respectively. Of those dismissed (or unfavourably reported on) by far the largest reason given by the COS for their rejection was that they had given a false address or

Table 2.7 Summary of the activities of the COS District Committees in London over the period 1871–5 inclusive

	1871	1872	1873	1874	1875
No. of DCs/divisions supplying data	22	32	34	33	35
Total Number of cases decided	12506	15374	14891	12656	14946
Total dismissed (or unfavourably reported on):	4237	4910	4835	4738	5758
Not requiring relief	818	1037	1108	1158	1525
Undeserving	1150	1240	941	956	1186
Giving false address or o/wise ineligible	2274	2633	2786	2624	3047
Total referred to:	3909	4684	4350	3163	4677
The guardians	1482	1413	1148	555	300
Institutions or local agencies	1657	2114	2076	1531	3360
Private persons	770	1157	1126	1077	1017
Total assisted:	4360	5780	5706	4755	4511
Grants	2446	3292	3855	2712	2172
Loans	828	1039	1086	1049	1040
Employment or placing on labour register	728	1014	345	401	388
Letters for hospitals	358	435	420	593	911
Average number of cases decided upon during the year by each district committee	568	480	438	383	427
Vagrants dealt with in addition	3267	12512	13322	6885	4855

were 'otherwise ineligible'. The latter phrase covered a multitude of eventualities including: applications for loans being turned down because of inadequate security, application being withdrawn and, rather less commonly, being 'found dead from the effects of drink'.[101] Referrals to Poor Law guardians across London had dropped dramatically over the five-year period from a total of 1482 in 1871 to only 300 in 1875. On the other hand referrals to 'institutions or local agencies' had more than doubled from 1657 to 3360, see Table 2.7, above.

In spite of COS unanimity about the benefits of loans over other relief methods, in no year between 1871–75 did the Society provide more than 1086 loans across London as a whole. Major-General Bainbrigge's earlier concerns about the number of grants rocketing out of hand proved unfounded over the first five years of COS activity. After the peak of 3868 grants in 1873 the total number across London had dropped to 2178 by 1875. In addition, fewer applicants were being assisted in finding employment whereas the number given a letter for hospital access had more than doubled to a total of 911 by 1875. In addition to local supplicants, the COS Districts also 'dealt with' a substantial number of vagrants. The annual number was greatly influenced by the state of trade. During the economically depressed year of 1873 they totalled 13 322 but, helped by business growth, had dropped to 4855 by 1875, Table 2.7, above.

Up to 1875, the parlous financial position of the COS, both as regards its overall inability to attract funds needed to fulfil the metropolitan aims of the Society and the persistent imbalances between the various districts, remained cause for rancorous Council debates. A letter in the morning papers on 14 May 1874 signed jointly by the Bishop of London as COS President and the Earl of Lichfield as Chairman of the COS Council appealed for the 'considerable funds' required by the COS, particularly in the poorer districts of London. The letter claimed that there was now agreement that 'appeals to the general public should be made by the Council only'. It asked for contributions to be directed to the COS Central Office or to Messrs Coutts and Co. their bankers.[102]

During 1876 the Chairman Lord Lichfield had to remind the Council that the financial position of the Society had deteriorated markedly from what was already a precarious situation. In May 1875 the COS General Fund had stood at a modest £1095 and the District Committee Aid Fund at a mere £264. Since then the General Fund had dwindled close to zero while the total balance of the DCAF was only £15. Lichfield threw down the gauntlet to those wealthy COS districts opposed to change. He recommended the unacceptable 'financial position of the Society to the very serious consideration of those members of the Council who felt satisfied with the present mode of collecting funds'.[103] Inadequacies in fund-raising and related financial problems continued to dominate succeeding weekly meetings. W.M. Wilkinson emphasized that 'want of both sufficient means and of effi- ciently trained workers, unpaid and paid', had made it impossible for the COS to carry out its original programme. Like many before him, Wilkinson stressed how problems were particularly acute in the poorer districts where there were insufficient resources to continue, even at their present low level, without help from richer districts. To make the working of the Society 'efficient in all parts of the metropolis', twice the current £15 000 annual revenue was needed.[104] Wilkinson con- curred with Lichfield about the ineffective nature of present fund-rais- ing methods and agreed that a centralized procedure would be greatly preferable. Entrenched positions were adopted in subsequent Council debates. Sir Charles Trevelyan remained vociferously against central- ized finance. He claimed that grants made to poorer COS Committees had 'sapped their independence' so that during 1874–75 they had together collected £580 less than in the previous year.[105] Tension was stoked by a Sub-Committee Report recommending continuation of the existing method of district collection of funds. Lichfield was so exasperated that he 'could not agree with any portion of the Report' which in, spite of the dire financial plight of the Society, failed to rec- ommend meaningful change. He proposed that the Sub-Committee's conclusions were unsatisfactory and could not be adopted. Lichfield's recommendation that all COS funds should be centralized in the hands of the Council was defeated in Council.[106] Further acrimonious debate on COS finances followed in subsequent Council meetings. Lichfield's supporters demanding centralized fund-raising were ranged against those in agreement with the richer Committees. Lichfield was scathing about the self-centredness of the latter who, he alleged, were bent on perpetuating a system whereby weaker Committees may be maintained with the crumbs they deigned to let drop from their table. In June 1876, Lord Lichfield launched yet another forceful diatribe, including a survey of what he believed had always been the founding aims of the Society. He concluded with the threat that he 'saw no course before him' but to resign his Chairmanship should the Council not move to centralized fund-raising.[107] Further disputes led to Lichfield submitting 'compromise' amendments. Trevelyan denounced them as being 'the most stringent and subversive expres- sion of the centralized principle which had yet been enunciated'.[108]

The Council attempted the following compromise resolution in July 1876 regarding the Society's financial procedures:

> That within a month after the 30th September of each year, estimates of the probable expenses of each Committee for the ensuing year, together with the balance-sheet for the past year, be sent to the Secretary of the Council, to be laid before the Quarterly Finance Sub-Committee, in order that they may as soon as possible have the means of framing the estimates for the District Committees Aid fund.[109]

This failed to satisfy Lichfield. He emphasized that the 'much more important matter' was how the Society's funds were distributed across London as compared with how they were collected. Lichfield's enthusiasm for COS affairs had been permanently dampened. It was not long before he carried out his threat by resigning from the Chair of the Council. Lynedoch Gardiner later recalled that Lichfield's resignation 'was in consequence of the bitter disappointment he experienced when he realized how imperfectly the principles which he had set his heart were being carried out'.[110] Lichfield was induced to continue the nominal Chairmanship of the St Marylebone DC, the aspect of the work of which he continued to approve. Although Octavia Hill had attended many of the heated Council meetings on COS financial structures, she had contributed relatively little to the debates. Nevertheless she was so disturbed about the likely continuing precarious position of London's poorer districts as to put the following resolution before the Council:

> That, considering the needs of the poor Committees and to avoid catastrophe when most persons interested in the subject are out of town, it is desirable that every member of the Council should endeavour to give or collect either £5 or £10 each, or more if possible, before they leave town, quite irrespective of what they may have given or collected before.

When Miss Hill explained that the purpose of her motion had been to 'obviate the difficulties that must inevitably have arisen had the want of funds continued' she was eventually placated and assured that sufficient funds would be made available to satisfy the needs of each district.[111] Discussion in the later chapters of this volume equip us to judge whether the assurances given to Miss Hill were justified.

Before moving to later periods, it is important to record the London COS Council's decision on Monday 15 November 1875 to appoint

Charles Stewart Loch as their Secretary. For nearly 40 years Loch was to be identified as the personification of COS principles. He developed into being a prominent public figure used by Whitehall as a sounding board for a wide range of matters concerning the condition of the poor. Loch wrote prolifically, lectured widely, had a knighthood conferred and served famously on a number of Royal Commissions. Probably the most important of these was that on The Poor Laws, 1905–9. This appointment can be seen as being the apogee of an illustrious career and the turning point of his own physical well-being. Loch never fully recovered from the bitter realization that he and his fellow COS Commissioners could not persuade either the Liberal government or a vociferous minority of fellow Royal Commissioners to the COS way of addressing social matters. The onset of more serious illness in 1913 led to Loch's retirement from active participation in the COS the following year.

In summary, by 1875, the COS had managed to attract the support of royalty, the peerage, church leaders, Members of Parliament, the City, high-flying professionals, civil servants and senior military men. It had gained the respect of national governments as it spread across London with close to 40 District Committees. But there were also deeply disquieting signs. The difficulties of gaining grassroots support in many London districts remained unresolved. The Society continued to be rejected by many of those it was purporting to help. There was the realization that it was being ignored and even ridiculed by other charitable bodies as well as by Poor Law guardians. Perhaps the most disturbing reality facing many COS members was the glaring irrationalities across London within their own establishment. It was now obvious that COS Committees in poorer Districts were unable to provide a comparable service to the needy as could their peers in wealthier parts of London. The chapter that follows discusses the further trends in these COS successes and failures during the quarter century from 1876.

3
Developments by the Turn of the Century[1]

By 1876, London COS members had made sufficient impact with people of authority to remain confident that eventually they would convince non-believers about the correctness of their scientific methodology as applied to the condition of the poor. A powerful and influential COS Council was packed with names that demanded public respect. A formidable network of COS District Offices had been created across London, each adjacent to a Poor Law workhouse in accord with their founding plans. The Society had pushed itself into public awareness even though it had failed to gain the public's confidence. Members saw themselves as representing the voluntary sector's arm of the government's crusade against Poor Law outdoor relief. London COS believed that Smilesian moral values should be perpetuated, not only because they were ethically correct but also because they reduced the burden on ratepayers. COS members believed that in their appointment of C.S. Loch as their Secretary they had chosen a person of exceptional skill and with the determination to propagate their organizational doctrines. The COS had 'no doubt, that the poverty of the working classes in England was due, not 'to their circumstance...but to their own improvident habits and thriftlessness'.[2] If the poor were ever to be prosperous, argued the COS, it must be through self-denial, discipline, responsibility, hard-work, thrift, temperance and forethought. Dependence on others was 'a moral disease and must be eradicated', according to COS stalwart, Sir Charles Trevelyan. He regarded 'deaths by starvation as a discipline, a painful one admittedly, but nevertheless a discipline'.[3] But by the mid 1870s, COS confidence, as indicated by their ever-ready public pronouncements on social matters, was tinged with the more private doubts of some senior members of the organization. Influential sections of the public and press branded them mean and hard-hearted. Adverse criticism had reached such a pitch that the Society had been forced to argue (perversely) that the mounting public antagonism merely confirmed a deplorable widespread inability to appreciate the value of the COS's scientifically constructed social theories. Some prominent COS activists remained deeply concerned about the glaring financial inequalities between assets in the Society's various districts. These inequalities mocked the Society's claim that all responses to deserving applicants were methodically designed and distributed in carefully measured amounts, untainted by human inconsistency. The financial records of COS District Committees reveal the reality: disturbing differences in the quality of the response and that the fact that the variations tended to be closely related to locality (see Table 3.1). What made it more distressing was that because of their shortage of funds and contrary to logical expectation, COS Committees in poorer districts were unable to match the COS relief provided in wealthier parts of the metropolis.

None were more concerned about these disparities than the Earl of Lichfield. He believed that the 'question of central collection, distribution and control' of funds lay at the 'very roots of the prosperity and well-being of the Society'. Although driven by the persistent discord within his beloved Society to the point of resigning from the Chairmanship of the London COS Council, Lichfield tenaciously pursued the need to fund COS District Committees more equitably. He argued that the money raised by the four 'richest' Committees equalled the whole income (including grants from the Council) of the 12 Committees in other parts of London – namely, St Pancras North, St Pancras South, Holborn, Shoreditch, Bethnal Green, Whitechapel, St George's-in-the-East, Stepney, Mile End Old Town, Poplar, St Saviour's and St Olave's. What made matters worse was that while the population of the area dealt with by the 'twelve poorer Committees was double that dealt with by the four richer', the 'average expenditure of the latter group had been six times as much as the former'. As Lichfield remarked, these disquietening inconsistencies were in spite of the four richer Committees having dealt with fewer cases than the 12 poorer Committees. The answer was that regardless of commonsense, the amount of COS relief given in the richer districts *per capita* was 'eleven times as much as that distributed by the poorer Committees'.[4]

The COS District Committees in the poorer areas of London found that 'employers and the tradesmen class generally' shunned their approaches to participate and were unwilling to subscribe funds. COS appeals for donations continued to have 'no effect whatever'.[5] In the

Table 3.1 Grants, establishment and 'other' costs for the 'richest' and 'poorest' COS Districts during the financial year 1876–7 together with the number of persons assisted in calendar year 1877

District	Grants from COS Council £s	COS Establishment costs £	'Other costs' (Note A) £	Number COS assisted 1877	Area in acres	Population in 1871	Rateable value 1876–7 £ 000's
4 'Richest'							
Kensington	–	429	484	402	2190	120299	1211
Paddington	–	710	314	454	1251	96813	1079
St George's (Hanover Sq)	−350	683	1429	426	1943	155936	2022
St Marylebone	−50	489	604	308	1506	159254	1305
12 'Poorest'							
N. St Pancras	+40	198	138	65	{2672*	{221465*	{1305*
S. St Pancras	+100	295	504	74			
Holborn	+140	157	110	64	784	162819	805
Shoreditch	+90	140	208	124	648	127164	515
Bethnal Green	+165	166	182	149	755	120104	320
Whitechapel	+114	160	106	72	378	75552	317
St George's\ East	+131	137	312	142	243	48052	189
Stepney	+203	254	138	35	462	57690	272
Mile End	+167	197	111	55	679	93152	297
Poplar	+192	215	260	133	2335	116376	485
Poplar	+192	215	260	133	2335	116376	485
St Saviour's	+167	270	203	127	1119	175049	838
St Olave's	1154	276	346	140	1503	122398	741

Sources: COS Council and District reports 1876–7 and 7th Annual Report LGB, PP XXVI.1, (1877–8), Appendix D, p. 388.

Note A: 'Other costs' include (1) sums received from charitable persons and agencies for relief of cases including convalescent cases; (2) sums granted from COS general fund in relief of cases, including purchase of mangles, bread to vagrants, etc; (3) loans; and (4) sums arranged by Francis Peek. This latter item refers to his gift of £1000/ year for School Board cases after COS investigation; for further details see 7th Annual Report of COS Council (1876), pp. 11–12.

*N. St Pancras and S. St Pancras data are combined for Area, Population and Rateable value.

mid 1880s, the Fulham and Hammersmith Committee were still having to admit that although their total expenditure was £398 17s 7d, they had managed to collect only £46 19s locally.[6] The COS Council's explanation was that 'until the principles of the Society are more heartily and fully recognised, many parts of London must depend for some of their leaders and workers on those districts in which there are more men of leisure'.[7] The trouble was that the Society had failed to induce a sense of it being a worthwhile attraction among the leisured classes for spending even a limited amount of time in disagreeable slums. In 1890 a COS report remained deeply concerned about how the 'finance and organisation' of the Society would be maintained. Again, the only solution offered was that District Committees should become more effective fund-raisers in order to reduce the 'increasing drain upon the Centre'.[8]

Succeeding annual reports of the COS Council included details of their 'objects and methods', their 'constitution' and a description of what workers could 'do in charity organisation'. The report for 1889–90 also informed the public that the main objective of the 'Society for Organizing Charitable Relief and Repressing Mendicity', as they continued to be called formally, was to 'Improve the Condition of the Poor'. They intended to achieve this by:

- propagating sound principles and views in regard to the administration of charity;
- promoting the co-operation of charitable institutions;
- initiating the establishment of new institutions which accorded with their principles;
- discussing associated practical questions and methods of promoting thrift and self-dependence;
- convening Special Committees to inquire into and report on 'comparatively technical questions' concerning deprived social groups;
- investigating and suppressing, by prosecution or otherwise, improper claims on the charity of the benevolent by begging-letter writers and others; and
- supplementing the resources of the District Committees by the personal assistance of Council paid officers and by providing grants and other 'adequate help' in the cases of difficulty.

On their part the COS District Committees were expected to:

(a) carefully inquire into the truth of the statements of all applicants;
(b) apply in each deserving case 'susceptible of permanent benefit' the assistance of charity as likely to make the applicant self-dependent;

(c) obtain the various kinds of help required from those interested in the applicants, from their relatives, from charitable institutions and from private persons;

(d) make loans without interest and grants where the necessary help cannot be obtained elsewhere;

(e) procure pensions from charities and from private persons for chronic cases with evidence of good character, of thrift and of reasonable efforts to provide for the future;

(f) send reports ('gratuitously') to 'legitimate inquirers';

(g) bring into co-operation with each other and with the Poor Law authorities; the various charitable agencies in the district;

(h) make the District Committee representative of local charities and the centre of reference; and

(i) repress local mendicity.[9]

The content of the propaganda above had remained essentially unchanged for 20 years. It was published in the vain hope that the public would become convinced that they were actually 'organizing' the charities of London. The reality was that 'from the very start' the District Committees had failed abysmally to attain many of their basic targets. Most importantly, they had not achieved their 'first purpose of co-ordinating the work of all the local charities and the Poor Law and of registering and directing all applicants for aid'.[10] The COS displayed a long-term reluctance to admit that most other bodies had rejected the Society's seminal concept of harnessing under their own organizational rules the relief work of London clergy, ministers and charities. This unwillingness to accept reality provided an indication of their own facility at self-delusion and confirmed how hopelessly they were adrift of contemporary attitudes and social aspirations. In their report for 1889–90 the London COS Council were still attempting to convince the public that 'charities could be organised tomorrow if their managers were charitable enough'. By this the COS meant that other charities should accept their principles. Allegedly, such a step would educate those of goodwill to 'abjure second-rate work', lead them to try above all things to be thorough, ... and 'for the sake of their own work become organisers'.[11]

By the late 1870s a number of Council members were challenging whether it was appropriate for the COS to continue in quite this lame manner – i.e. unable to offer adequate support to the aged poor who, after searching investigation, had been found to be both highly respectable and thoroughly deserving. A circular dated November 1878 was sent to COS District Committees asking to what extent they had been willing or able to support 'Deserving Chronic Cases'. Furthermore, assuming they had sufficient means at their disposal, what should be the Society's future policy? Of the 37 COS districts replying, 9 had never entertained the granting of pensions and a further 9 said they had been unable to provide a pension because of tight funds. Other districts reported variously that: the number of 'old and deserving applicants' was very small; most were 'ineligible' under COS rules; they had no special pension fund and they could see 'no prospect' of creating one. Only St Georges'-in-the-East, Stepney and Whitechapel Districts reported positively. This was because they had each been able to refer really 'deserving chronic cases' to the recently established Tower Hamlets Pension Committee which included COS supporters.[12] In this way they had been able to provide pensions selectively to the 'provident poor' in parts of the East End of London. During the calendar year 1878, there were in total 43 Tower Hamlets pensioners at a gross cost of £284 19s 0d. This suggested an average weekly pension of 2s 6½d. During the year there had been a total of 44 deserving chronic cases referred to the Tower Hamlets Committee by the three COS District Committees named above. Of these new cases, some of which were couples, 20 had been refused a COS pension as they were mainly judged to have shown insufficient providence in the past. This weakness had made them 'workhouse cases'.[13]

The lofty approach adopted by the COS to potential pensioners in the East End typified their attitude to social matters generally. They assumed that the general public was not only inferior but were also gullible. An example was the COS's dogged persistence year after year to create the illusion that their London District Committees abounded with proficient organizers who were consistently earning the respect of other charitable and relief bodies. One of the few localities where some semblance of the COS ideal situation did develop for a while was St Marylebone. There, as mentioned in the previous chapter, the activities of Sir Lyndoch Gardiner, the Rev. W. Fremantle, Octavia Hill and others, succeeded for a few years in moulding a meaningful rapport with local Guardians and voluntary groups.[14] Even at St Marylebone, from the second half of the 1870s there was little indication of continued COS involvement with other relief agencies. The COS Council were eventually driven to soften the wording of the objectives for their District Committees. By the turn of the century COS members were advised to learn 'how to befriend persons in distress in the best way' and, where possible, to spread this knowledge by bringing other agencies into co-operation with one another. Although their underlying purpose of organization remained deeply rooted, they erased such provocative references as the COS's earlier commitment to prevent 'the misapplication of relief and the evils of "overlapping"'.

The Society published advice on what 'workers' and 'money' could do in the cause of charity organization. 'Workers' were advised that their main focus should be on 'training, visiting and helping'. COS recruits were asked 'to assist *regularly* in the general work of a District Committee, even if it be only for a few hours on a day or two in a week'. COS visiting of the poor in their homes as a means of strengthening their character was viewed as vital. The Society explained that 'these persons (not unlike many of their betters) are often without the commonest ideas of thrift in food, dress, etc, often incur ruinous expenditure, especially at funerals; and are often ignorant of the most ordinary rules of sanitation and cleanliness'.[15] The Society published a request that money from well-wishers could either be sent to them for 'any special purpose' or for use in the COS General Funds. Potential donors were told that if sent to the COS for general administrative purposes their contribution would help:

> to make association in personal work possible to many who spend time and thought in assisting the poor in poor districts. It provides them with the means of carrying on their work; for learning the cause of distress in applications for assistance; for searching out the best kind of help; for detecting imposture; in a word, for 'discriminating'. It aids in introducing better methods of relief; in introducing reforms in charitable administration; in testing and propagating principles and methods of relief, and having them discussed.[16]

In spite of such claims couched in considerate terms, they failed to convince most people that they had genuinely softened their approach. The public continued to associate the COS mainly with rigorous investigation which all too often resulted in a heartless meanness in relief matters. The Society were being 'so frequently criticised on the ground that its administrative costs were unduly high when compared with its "expenditure in the relief of distress"', the *Charity Organisation Review* around the turn of the century continued attempts to display the COS in a more favourable public light. An article entitled *The Charity Organization Society: Its Objects and Finance*, almost certainly written by Charles Loch, requested that the Society should not be judged merely by the magnitude of its expenditure as against working expenses. They were asked to build their assessment on the 'ability and devotion with which its members carry out its recognised object and by the prudence with which they administer the funds entrusted to it'.[17] It was claimed that COS District Committees raised monies for relief 'in a manner quite unlike that of an ordinary relief society'. Allegedly, the COS alone possessed the fund-raising methodology and the moral mission to extract every possible penny from the applicant's friends and relatives prior to consideration being given about possible approaches to wealthier sources. The informal support traditionally provided by family and friends was in the form of food, fuel or clothing and was rarely taken into account by the Poor Law or most charities. These authorities tended to ask merely about alternative income in the form of wages when assessing what may be the extent of their relief. The difference claimed by the COS was that their rigorous methods of investigation were unique in enquiring more realistically into how deeply relatives and friends should dilute their own resources before the Society could even consider extracting relief from wealthy strangers.

Between 1876 and the end of the century the presentation of COS data relating to their applicants for relief was modified on a number of occasions, see Table 3.2. Each change was allegedly designed to provide the public with more details about the scope of COS activities. In reality, each presentational change succeeded in a further shrouding of the unit value of provision meted out by the Society to deserving applicants. Prior to 1882 the COS data had divided their responses to applicants under three main headings, namely: 'dismissed/not assisted', 'referred' and 'assisted'. The first category was further subdivided between data for those 'not requiring relief', the 'undeserving', 'cases for the Poor Law' and those 'otherwise ineligible'. Similarly, referred cases included separate data about the number of applicants referred to 'the Guardians', 'local agencies' and to 'private persons'. As regards those who were assisted directly, the COS divided their information in order to show whether applicants had been provided with a grant, a loan, 'employment' or a 'letter for hospital'.

From 1882, a partial curtain was drawn across COS data. Whereas they continued to publish a detailed breakdown of those who were 'not assisted', they combined the number of those they had referred elsewhere with those directly assisted. Both of the latter categories were now grouped under a 'total number'. The implication being that each of them had been 'assisted' by COS intervention either directly or indirectly. Further lack of clarity arose from the presentational changes in

Table 3.2   Total number of applications, those not assisted, referred and assisted by London COS Districts 1876–99

Year	Applicants not assisted and applicants withdrawn		Applicants referred		Applications assisted		Total applicants
	Number	% / total	Number	% / total	Number	% / total	
1876	7 195	38	6 794	35	5 184	27	19 173
1877	7 328	40	5 831	31	5 346	29	18 505
1878	6 105	40	4 225	28	4 781	32	15 111
1879	9 236	42	4 892	22	7 817	36	21 945
1880	9 369	45	4 673	23	6 728	32	20 770
1881	11 175	43	5 496	21	9 381	36	26 052
			*Referred and Assisted**				
			Number	% / total			
1882	10 975	55	8 953	45			19 928
1883	11 234	56	8 659	44			19 893
1883–4	9 980	48	10 772	52			20 752
1884–5	10 356	48	11 086	52			21 442
1885–6	11 565	44	14 566	56			26 131
1886–7	11 532	45	14 000	55			25 532
1887–8	11 322	46	13 431	54			24 753
1888–9	10 015	48	11 054	52			21 069
1889–90	11 579	54	9 823	46			21 402
1890–1	11 983	51	11 493	49			23 476
1891–2	12 469	56	10 385	44			22 854
1892–3	13 926	57	10 501	43			24 427
1893–4	13 059	58	8 586	42			22 645
1894–5	12 947	55	10 656	45			23 603
1895–6	11 324	56	8 817	44			20 141
1896–7	10 290	58	7 524	42			17 814
1897–8	9 793	59	6 686	41			16 479
1898–9	8 727	59	6 066	41			14 793

Sources: COS District Committee annual returns and the summarized data of applications assisted, withdrawn and not assisted when available in subsequent Council reports. Occasionally the two data sets differ slightly in which case the latter have been given precedence.

Notes: (a) * from 1882 the data assisted and referred were not provided separately. Refer also to the 27th Annual Report of the COS Council (1896), p. 29 which comments contrarily to their own tabular data published with the same report; (b) prior to 1884 data referred to calendar years because this coincided the financial year of the Council. From 1883–4 the Council changed their financial year to coincide with that of the District Committees, namely, 1st October to 30th September the following year.

the previous sub-divisional data related to the 'sources from' and the 'modes in which' the COS had assisted applicants. This change provided fertile ground for COS double counting.

From 1883–84 there was a further break in the continuity of COS data when the Council changed their financial year which hitherto had coincided with the calendar. Now it matched that used by the District Committees which ran from 1 October to 30 September of the following year. In an attempt to deflect outside criticism about excessive overhead costs, District Committees were asked to separate those donations intended to offset administrative costs from explicit relief contributions. This enabled the Society to claim that every penny sponsored to assist a specific 'special case' would be so directed.

Table 3.3 provides a breakdown of how deserving COS applicants were assisted. It illustrates how grants remained easily the most common type of COS assistance, at least until around 1890, in spite of regularly being ridiculed by the Society as morally the least appropriate form of assistance. Grants were seen as being neither reformative nor of permanent benefit. During the 1890s the COS circumvented this seemingly paradoxical situation by clamping down on formal publication of grant data by camouflaging them as 'other relief forms'. The steady fall in the number COS loans across London is discussed in more detail later.

The COS Council's 1894–95 report expressed concern that their publications were not providing an adequate picture of their efforts across London. They concluded that their published data had therefore tended to be 'in a manner delusive' so as to minimize 'the actual work' of the Society. They claimed that the 'assisted' column of data supplied by them and their District Committees meant 'actual material relief' and that, in addition, 'much was done by way of reference', which they reckoned remained 'uncredited to the Society'. COS data are not easily reconciled with this claim. Indeed, awareness of the COS's insatiable thirst for favourable publicity makes it unlikely that the alert C.S. Loch or his cohorts would have persistently laid aside such excellent propagandist opportunities for quietening the antagonist tongues mounting against them. In their drive towards a more favourable image, the Council were also keen to push their claim that an 'unassisted' case often entailed as 'much labour and thought as one which was eventually marked off as being "assisted"'.[18]

Figure 3.1 provides background to the Council's later inclination to avoid public focus on the increasing proportion of applicants who were 'not assisted' by the COS either because of rejection or withdrawal

Table 3.3 'Modes of assistance' provided to those investigated by the COS in London Districts. Tabulated are the number of applicants. Data at five year intervals between 1874–5 and 1899–1900

Year	Grants	Loans	Employment	Letter to hospital	Emigration	Surgical apparatus	Convalescent aid*	Pensions	Admitted to Homes	Other relief forms
1874	2712	1049	401	593	–	–	–	–	–	–
1879	4354	1045	651	1267	–	–	–	–	–	–
1884–85	7348	948	537	3382*	–	–	–	214	821	–
1889–90	4920	686	817	1118	92	1033	2278	203	213	–
1894–95	–	556	728	982	51	1051	2054	247	339	4174
1899–1900	–	277	520	616	23	716	1265	192	181	4897

Sources: Data are from the COS Council's annual reports. Data for 1874 and 1879 are for calendar years. Later data are for financial years 1 October to 30 September.

*is the total number receiving letters to hospital, medical assistance and convalescent aid.

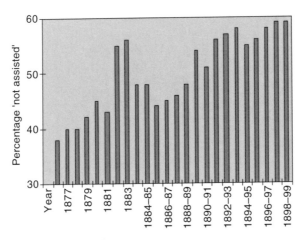

Figure 3.1   Applicants to COS District Committees in London who were 'not assisted', 1876–99.

of their application. In 1876 there had been 38 per cent of applicants 'not assisted' which itself was an increase from the 34 per cent turned away by London COS in 1871. As the 1890s were drawing to a close the proportion had grown so that almost three out of every five COS applicants received no assistance whatsoever other than a homily on thrift. Whereas the COS could attempt to use this huge rejection rate as positive evidence of their investigative skill in exposing fraudulent claimants, there was the overriding countervailing factor of it providing ready ammunition for the many who were ready to label COS members as cold-hearted ideologues. A further point to be borne in mind is that many poor people, aware of the Society's harsh reputation and worried that they too would be labelled by the COS as 'undeserving', saw little point in subjecting their family to the humiliation of protracted probing that could all too easily be fruitless. In the mid 1880s the COS had 'strongly urged' other charities involved with relieving the poor to recognize that 'a refusal to give (coupled often with advice, and always with sympathy) is often the truest kind of help'.[19]

Very much in accord with what the Earl of Lichfield had been arguing since the early 1870s, when applicant data at district level are compared across London for the later years of the century, the response characteristics depart sharply from the desired image of COS scientific conformity. For example, there continued to be large variations between districts as to the proportion of applicants they refused to help. Whereas in 1898–99, on average across London the COS were 'not assisting'

59 per cent of applicants, some districts regularly turned more away. Chelsea COS District Committee refused to assist 73 per cent of those applying for assistance while St Marylebone turned away 67 per cent. In bizarre contrast, the COS in Greenwich rejected only 26 per cent of their applicants and nearby Lewisham 34 per cent. The geography of the foregoing examples could encourage the simple conclusion that variations in COS rejection rates were further indication of the response chasm between wealthier districts and the poorer districts such as those in the East End. This division by wealth was a cogent factor, but not the only one. The overbearing attitudes of assertive COS District Committee members were another powerful input and could, on occasions, be the overriding factor. Whereas in 1898–99, wealthy St George's Hanover Square – where Committee members were set on assisting those with a relatively genteel past who had fallen on hard times – chose to turn away only 44 per cent of their applicants, the Committee in poverty-stricken Bethnal Green rejected 72 per cent of those who approached them. Overall, the large and often illogical differences in responses which persisted between COS districts did nothing to confirm the scientific impartiality claimed for COS investigative methodology. Some of the reasons why the COS in London chose to dismiss cases as being 'ineligible' for assistance can be gleaned from the following case-studies:[20]

> We believe that the man bore a good character but why he was out of work was not so clear. If, however, charitably intentioned people had stepped in and provided fully for the necessities of the family, would it not have been only natural for his neighbours to have said 'Why should we work, when we can get what we want without working for it?'. The *Police News* is not particularly nice reading and Lady Visitors would not therefore be likely to observe how a man, apparently out of work, was making money by lending his room for the purposes and immorality and crime.[21]

> A man of twenty-two, with a wife of the same age and one child, who, being unable to obtain employment in consequence of his being subject to epileptic fits, asked to be sent to Canada; the Committee saw no reason for saddling the colony with so helpless a family of persons who had so small an idea of thrift and providence.[22]

> A young man, aged 18, was sent to the office from the casual ward. ... Inquiry was made of the foreman of the works where applicant was employed. From him we learned that the man was

originally met by him begging in a public house; he offered him work ... after seven weeks' work the young man gave it up saying he was going back to his grandfather in Birmingham. The foreman soon discovered that he was keeping very bad company, was living with a profligate woman, and had become thoroughly depraved and worthless.[23]

M.G., a widow, applied for assistance to enable her to get a mangle. From enquiries it was found that she would not be able to get a living with a mangle, as there were already too many in the neighbourhood. She afterwards obtained one through another source; but, after less than two months, had to dispose of it at a loss through not being able to get work.[24]

A summary of COS Council and District Committee expenditure during a number of the years between 1884–85 and 1900–1 discloses various financial trends occurring within the Society, see Table 3.4. The Council's own expenditure between 1884–85 and 1900–1 had increased from £4413 to £5461. The general administrative expenses of the District Committees had remained more or less constant over the same period except that the total cost of Secretaries' salaries had more than doubled. This is further indication of the growing COS difficulty of attracting suitable gentlemen who were able or willing to spend their time unpaid in support of the cause. COS District Committees continued to open their offices daily except for Sunday. Most were open from 10.00 am to noon with a substantial minority also opening for one additional predetermined hour in the late afternoon each weekday. The General and the Decision Committees of each district deliberated at least weekly. The Decision Committee in wealthier districts tended to convene more frequently. At both St George's (Hanover Square) and at Paddington, COS stalwarts got together most days for 'decision-making'.[25] In the mid-1880s, London COS overheads cost on average 'about 7 shillings for every case dealt with'.[26] Or, as expressed more dramatically by the Holborn COS Committee about their own efforts, 'the average expense per head' incurred in confirming the credentials of each deserving applicant was £1 9s 1d.[27]

Payment to special cases, usually in the form of pensions, something which had been frowned upon by the COS founders, now occupied the paramount place in COS relief methodology. In total, they cost the London COS £30 434 in 1900–1. The COS continued to be coy about the monetary value of individual pensions. It suited the COS that the public should make assumptions about the generosity of COS pensions

Table 3.4 Summary of the expenditure of the Charity Organization Society Council and London District Committees during financial years 1884–1900

	Expenditure on 'organization' in £s					Cost of relief in £s				
	1884–85	1888–89	1892–93	1896–97	1900–01	1884–85	1888–89	1892–93	1896–97	1900–01
Expenditure of Council:										
Gross General cost at Central Office	4 213	4 989	5 183	5 661	5 461					
Medical Secretary	200									
Miscellaneous interim relief						6				
Special cases						233	243	105	153	374
Convalescent cases						1 858	627***			
Surgical appliances						107	118***			
Emigration cases						270	355	94	107	
	4 413	4 989	5 183	5 661	5 461	2 204	1 258	460	247	481
Expenditure of District Committees:										
General Expenses	8 846	9 371	8 944	8 971	9 004					
District Secretaries & Auditor	1 285	1 416	2 490	2 557	2 933					

					Grants*				
					3527	3846	3016	1692	873
Loans and 'returnable grants'					1535	1068	262	81	35
Special cases, incl pensions**					13659	16344	23335	28196	30434
Grants to local institutions					47	–	–	–	–
Gross for Council and District Committees	10131	10787	11434	11528	11937 18768	21258	26613	29969	31342
	14543	15776	16617	17189	17398 20972	22516	27073	30216	31823

Source: Annual Reports of COS Council, four-yearly intervals from 1884–85 to 1900–01.

*The Council claimed that besides the sums entered for relief, other sums had passed direct from the donor to the recipient after consultation with the District Committee. In spite of their District Committees being used to authorize any such donation, the COS seemingly made no attempt to estimate their value.

**'Special cases' are cases in which money has been procured from a society or individual. They included 'convalescent', 'surgical' and 'other cases' as well as pensions. See Table 3.7 for assessment of typical unit value of COS pensions.

***During the year 1888–89 the arrangements for conducting the Convalescent and Surgical business between the Council and Committees were altered.

based on the premise that since the Society so persistently derided the paucity of statutory doles, the value of their own assistance must, by implication, be distinctly more substantial. In addition, the public were not dissuaded from assuming that the COS were referring to their own relief patterns when they airily advised others that 'by multiplying the dole by twenty, the worthy man was raised up with his family out of the ranks of penury, and placed upon a platform where he could achieve a future career'.[28] COS propaganda implied that each deserving case was assisted substantially, it being far better 'to spend the money that would have been frittered away' in paltry sums by '*adequately* relieving (sometimes with comparatively large sums), those to whom a temporary assistance during illness or misfortune may be of long term benefit'.[29] A primary COS maxim was that charitable assistance should be granted only to industrious persons in temporary distress from causes other than their own misconduct or improvidence, '*where such relief was likely to be of permanent benefit*, but not otherwise'.[30] The public were told that any assistance short of making each applicant 'independent of charity and of Poor Law relief in the future ... is not really adequate'.[31]

In view of the extravagant claims over a protracted period about the appropriateness of their own relief provision and how favourably it compared with the value inadequacy of Poor Law doles, it is useful to compare the relief from both sources. From most Poor Law unions, a deserving outdoor adult pauper could expect about three shillings weekly on their own account, although some London guardians, such as at St Pancras, provided up to four shillings. A parent's dole was usually augmented for dependent family members if recommended by the Poor Law relieving officer. The relief process used by the statutory body was described in evidence given to the Royal Commission on the Aged Poor (1895) by J.H. Allen. As a guardian, he was quite satisfied that 'the position of those poor who apply for outdoor relief is (was) sufficiently inquired into' by his relieving officers without assistance by 'any voluntary agency'. According to Allen, decisions on doles were made only after relieving officers had first ascertained 'the outside help, whether from relatives, or from charity, or from work, which the applicant can rely upon' before it was then supplemented by a sum 'sufficient to keep the individual who is applying'.[32] The habit of local guardians of using doles to supplement other income had, of course, long been frowned upon and harangued by successive governments, with echoing support by the COS since 1869. They all agreed that wage subsidization was a system 'attended with many evil consequences which could not fail to have a very demoralising effect' on the poor.[33] It is clear that, in practice, the COS Agent when assessing what might be an appropriate relief level followed paths identical to those trodden by the relieving officer. The differences between the two establishments lay in the depth of the personal probing and the interpretations applied with the information derived. The gross annual cost of COS pensions across London increased significantly during the 1890s to become easily their most dominant form of relief. Even then, an impression of the relatively small scale of COS activities at the macro level can be gauged by comparing their gross relief expenditure in 1900–1 of £31 823 with the cost of Poor Law outdoor doles alone of £227 537. This latter figure was net of all establishment salaries and other administrative expenses. The total expenditure on relief by the Poor Law authorities in London was £1 258 896.[34]

A flavour of the type of applicant approved by the COS, and an impression of the quality of help the society then provided when in the form of grants, can be gauged from the case-studies published by various COS Districts to exemplify their work. When divulging details of specific 'cherry-picked' cases, the COS were less constrained about publishing information than they were about providing micro data concerning their general relief patterns. Published case-studies of assisted cases usually quoted values that were substantially higher than the average COS grant shown in Table 3.5. Typical of those which show the signs of being cherry-picked case-studies published by the COS were:

The Bethnal Green Committee asked for £3 for a very respectable widow aged 76. Her husband worked for an employer for 25 years and was a member of two clubs.[35]

G.L., a widow, four children, three dependent, applied for assistance to enable her to get a mangle. The case was found to be deserving. A mangle was obtained for her at a cost of £5. £1.10s. was given by the Committee (Shoreditch), and the remainder was obtained for them, from other sources.[36]

A New Start – A family of three had to spend six weeks in the infirmary through the illness of both the parents. The father was a watchmaker, of good character, and a first-class hand, but on recovery found his place filled up. Supported them for a fortnight, giving him the means to seek for work. He soon found a regular situation in Staffordshire, where we paid his fare, redeemed his tools, and sent him off with a sum in his hand for the first week. The cost was £4.10s, of which the Rector contributed £1.10s.[37]

A young man desirous of emigrating to New South Wales was granted £1.10s, the remainder of the money being found by his father and a lady who had known the family for some years.[38]

This was the case of relief secured by providing a mangle with the accompanying custom. This Committee headed a subscription-list with 30s. and the woman's friends who were interested in her raised the balance.[39]

Turning to COS loans, as we know from Chapter 2, in the COS's formative years, loans were the most highly recommended form of relief. So much so that the COS were 'determined to institute a system of loans throughout the metropolis'.[40] Loans were said to have special attractions both for the recipient and for the giver. Apart from their theoretical advantage of being a perpetually recoverable and rotating financial asset, the COS saw loan repayments as providing great therapeutic value. They elevated 'the tone of the poorer classes by inspiring feelings of self-reliance and independence'.[41] This intrinsic curative quality of lending, as distinct from giving, had been illuminated to the COS by the

Table 3.5   Value of grants, loans, and 'special case' pensions, provided by COS metropolitan districts, together with COS establishment expenses for financial years ending 1883–4 and 1891–2

Expenditure	1883–84 (£ s d)	1891–92 (£ s d)
Establishment costs:		
COS District Committees	9,024	11,380
COS Council (a)	4,516	4,845
Total	13,540	16,225
Grants:		
Number	6,314	5,424
Total annual value	4,360	2,865
Average unit value	13s 10d	10s 6¾ d
Loans:		
Number	852	570
Total annual value	1,480	288
Average unit value	1 14 7d	10s 1¼ d
Special cases including pensions (b)		
Total annual value	10,836	21,409

Sources: Annual reports of COS Council.

Notes: (a) Council costs are taken to be the expenditure shown in their financial accounts for the particular year on 'General Account'; (b) The categories 'pensions' and 'special cases' were often combined in COS financial reports and this practice is continued here.

'joy and sense of duty honestly discharged when the poor creatures returned the money'.[42] In the 1870s the COS told all those who would listen that whenever feasible, assistance should 'take the form of loans with proper security for their repayment by weekly instalments' as this promoted 'frugality and self-respect' amongst the poor.[43] At that stage, the COS had convinced themselves that loans were that part of their activities which few other charities, let alone individuals, could match.[44] Ostensibly, this was because COS investigative techniques had been instrumental in making the provision of loans to the poor economically viable to the poor. A searching investigation allegedly exposed the miscreant as well as spotlighting the deserving.

As implied in Chapter 2, with the passage of time, these early bullish COS attitudes lost their vigour as the veracity of the Council's rhetoric was seen to fade. The popularity of loans tailed off sharply after the widespread incidence of defaulting in the 1880s. For example, St Olave's COS reported having advanced loans totalling £64 with repayments of only £24 4s 6d.[45] In 1890 the gross value of loans over the whole of London was only £560 compared with £1929 in 1876. By the end of the century a mere £35 was on offer with many COS District Committees sufficiently disenchanted as not to offer loans at any price.

Why did COS loan defaults become so prevalent? One explanation may be that, contrary to COS claims about the high quality of their investigative techniques, they failed in practice to determine either the worthiness of loan recipients or their guarantors. Occasionally, the COS themselves admitted that, 'at times, after the fullest investigation and the most careful thinking', they still found cases did 'not turn out so well as they had hoped'. They even went so far as to concede that 'on several occasions' it was decided their 'inquiries had probably not been extensive enough' and had caused them to make a 'judgement' on 'insufficient data'.[46]

Another possible explanation for loan defaults was that whereas COS investigative procedures may have been reasonably effective, the stark socioeconomic vagaries faced by the metropolitan poor frequently made it impossible for even the best-intentioned candidates to repay their debts. Comments from COS Committees in poorer districts lend weight to this explanation. The Stepney Committee described how in the financial year 1883–84 'the condition of people was getting worse and worse'. St Saviour's Southwark, told of a 'great outcry on the condition of the poor and the state of their houses', while St George's-in-the-East reported the 'precarious' existence of 'dock labourers and needle-women', with wages 'very low'.[47] In addition, the COS in Stepney believed fewer people were applying to them for assistance because work was so 'chronically slack'. Earnings were so low that 'a larger proportion have sunk below the state in which timely help might have enabled them to raise themselves to independence'.[48] When things were especially bad even the COS Council had to agree that a fundamental problem existed in the East End. Like 'some other parts of London', there was seen to be a 'low level of existence – life often without energy or resources which might enable it to rally, dependent on unskilled labour, irregular employment, and wages insufficient for sustenance'.[49]

The opposing trends of declining COS loans while 'special case' pensions were increasing reflected succinctly the change in attitude forced on the Society during its early decades, as indicated in Table 3.5, above. Initially, the COS had insisted that its role was essentially a provider of last resort. It repeatedly emphasized its determination not to become yet another charity among the many already attempting to relieve the needy. The Society's purpose was seen to be that of harmonizing what they described as the irresponsible haphazard activities of existing charities and the combining of them effectively with the economic processes of the Poor Law.[50] Bullish COS expectations of achieving this prime objective disintegrated when they found that local guardians and charitable bodies shunned their schemes. To attain any meaningful involvement in the charitable arena, it had to subjugate the ideal of promoting themselves as being the organizer of other funds. Circumstances demanded that they became providers of poor relief themselves. In its endeavour to plaster over this forced change, the COS claimed that the character of their assistance was unique. It was allegedly structured so as to be always 'individual, personal, temporary and reformatory'.[51]

We must now question why then, contrary to much of what the COS had argued earlier, pensions became such a dominant part of COS operations? When the COS had so resolutely supported George Goschen's Minute in 1869 and the LGB's crusade against outdoor relief, the COS had projected their opinion that long-term assistance outside of the workhouse was abhorrent, whether provided by charity or by the state.[52] Helping the impotent poor by regular charitable gifts or pensions was seen to undermine their spirit of independence and to erode personal providence. Pensionable provision opened the door to idleness, debauchery and drunkenness. Charitable offerings to the poor, previously considered as innocent Christian gestures of compassion were now highly suspect. Allegedly, socio-scientific knowledge possessed by the COS had exposed much charity as being sinful, irresponsible and economically disadvantageous.[53] In 1876 the COS expressed horror at 'the folly of sapping the independence of the poor by a system of doles, for which they learn to be for ever looking, instead of their own providence and exertion'.[54] Even then, early indications were that COS action on the ground did not always follow the recommended pattern. In a report to the Local Government Board, Col Lynedoch Gardiner described how in COS activities in St Marylebone 'small pensions were given to the most deserving chronic cases'.[55]

As the 1880s approached, references to 'special cases' appeared more frequently in COS publications. District Committees expressed their regrets about 'deserving' old people being brought suddenly to destitution while the COS lacked the financial wherewithal to assist them financially. The Paddington COS Committee admitted that on occasions 'hundreds of men and women are thrown out of work and are therefore in distress for no fault of their own'. Nevertheless, they considered that the kind of 'special case' most deserving of COS attention was the 'broken-down semi-genteel' person who, because of his socially superior background, invariably needed 'particular delicacy of handling'.[56] Apparently, when such people had collapsed into penury they deserved a particularly sympathetic COS response. It seemed unreasonable to the Society that those who had known better days should be expected to suffer the same humiliating stigmatization of the workhouse as had the permanently poor.

The official COS stance on pensions gradually moved from abhorrence to admiration. Eventually, their District Committees were instructed to 'procure such pensions from relations, friends, former employers, charities and charitable persons', in that order.[57] Even then, the COS considered it necessary to tell the public plainly that their pensions were 'not raised without much trouble' to themselves. They grumbled about the effort involved in their collecting the various small pension elements from sponsors and the resultant chore of them having to be 'put together' regularly involving 'a good deal of labour'.[58] Such COS complaints were at variance with their admission that quite often their Committee 'merely' collected and distributed the allowance from 'relatives, former employers, clergy, etc'. The COS in Whitechapel reported that a 'fair average of the help given by relations' was between 2 shillings and 3 shillings weekly. COS theorists found it extremely difficult to sell the concept universally that the prime essential when considering the creation of one of their pensions was always to extract what they could from relatives and friends. Outsiders saw clearly that, all too often, the latter were themselves merely scraping by. Even 'fellow workers' in the COS hesitated about pressing 'upon the old woman' that it was her primary duty to support their efforts to gather every conceivable support from her family before even contemplating topping up to meet her prescribed needs from relatively wealthy members of the public.[59]

Awareness that not all their volunteers were willing to exert sufficient strictures on the needy poor forced the COS to turn increasingly to professional help. As the COS explained, the trouble was that 'people of means and leisure have other concerns, and more immediate interests, than to make friends of, and systematically to try and know the poor'.[60] When the COS did eventually get round to appealing publicly for the funding of one of their 'special case' pensions, they requested that the donor commit themselves specifically to the needs of the distressed individual. This nurtured the hope of creating a sense of long-term responsibility with donors; a personalizing fund-raising technique still widely practised throughout the voluntary sector. The COS did not find it easy to obtain money from the 'well-to-do'. The relatively rich in Paddington COS Committee complained about their own already stretched finances. The result had been that as a Committee they found themselves 'literally living from hand to mouth' on all fronts. Evidently, lack of charity was still dire. Even when attempting to provide for men 'of good character', who had done their best to make a provision for sickness and old age, they still encountered 'continual difficulty'. Similarly, the wealthy Kensington District Committee reported that there were 'so few who are willing to bind themselves to the payment of even a small sum'.

The COS Council proudly described their tactics for extracting funds from relatives and loved ones when publicizing the 'successful activities' of the Battersea District Committee, see Table 3.6. They pointed with satisfaction to 'the amount of money that has been contributed by the relatives and friends of those in distress'.[61] This was said to contrast with the conventional haphazardly distributed charity which allegedly ignored the 'moral obligations of relatives'.[62] As the Stepney Committee put it, 'if there are relatives able to assist, we make our help conditional on theirs'. The COS remained puzzled as to why the public continued to accuse the Society of 'treating the poor in a hard, unsympathetic way'.[63]

Long after the COS had got themselves irrevocably immersed in pensions, Charles Loch remained distinctly uneasy. He warned against the danger of them becoming nothing but 'an ill-regulated system of allowances, not unlike outdoor relief'. He recognized the 'great temptation' of giving pensions to 'respectable old people' but urged that they should never be given in such a manner as to 'weaken providence and family ties'.[64] Loch also spelt out the difficulty experienced

Table 3.6 Sources of funds used by Battersea COS District Committee when compiling pensions, 1898–9

	£	s	d
(1) Contributions from the applicants and their relatives	165	11	2
(2) Contributions from employers	24	17	0
(3) Contributions from applicants' personal friends	424	16	9
(4) Contributions from local clergy, not including relief given direct on Committee's advice	113	4	1
(5) Contributions from charities, general and local	150	6	9
(6) Contributions from local Committee and their friends	308	18	2
(7) Refunds from Convalescent Homes, etc	29	2	10
(8) Payments from other COS Committees	44	8	2
(9) Result of Appeals through Golden Book	107	4	0
Total for the financial year	1 368	8	11

by the Society in 'procuring' the necessary assistance to provide personal supervision of adequate quality to make certain that pensions were channelled into the right direction. He consoled himself in the belief that this difficulty itself would check the granting of COS pensions because the enforced 'need of scrutiny' was 'beneficial' to all concerned.[65]

Table 3.7 shows the average weekly value of COS pensions in certain metropolitan districts for various years between 1884 and 1887, highlighting the variation in weekly value ranging from 1s 11d to 5s 4d. Further, the annual report of the South St Pancras COS Committee suggests a huge variation between the unit values provided to their 18 pensioners. Their most generous pension was worth £32 1s annually, equivalent to about 12s 4d weekly. At the lower end of the St Pancras scale were pensions with an annual value of only; £7 16s, £8 5s, £4 8s, £5 8s, and £1 respectively.[66] Similarly, the St James, Soho and West Strand COS District Committee pensions can be shown to have an average weekly value of 3s 11d although the range was considerable. Some of the weekly pensions were shown to be:[67]

1. Widow living with widowed son and family	3s 0d
2. Old man able to work a little to meet 2s	1s 0d
3. Old woman, nearly blind, living with married daughter	2s 0d
4. Old woman able to work a little, to meet help from daughters	1s 0d
5. Old woman in Home, to meet 3s from niece and friends	1s 0d
6. Old man, to meet 3s from sons	3s 0d
7. Old couple, to meet pension from Bookbinders' Society	3s 0d

Table 3.7   Assessment of the unit weekly value of a typical pension as provided by COS London District Committees in the 1880s

Pension provider	Number of pensions	Total annual value of pensions	Equivalent unit average weekly value
Stepney COS	46 (a)	£462 (a)	3s 10d
St Pancras (South) COS	18 (b)	£249 (b)	5s 4d
39 COS District Committees	390 (c)	£1,950 (d)	1s 11d
St James and Soho COS	18 (e)	–	3s 11d
Poplar and South Bromley COS	15 (f)	£200 (f)	5s 2d
Tower Hamletts Pension Committee	100 (g)	£700 (g)	2s 8d

Sources (a) to (g):
(a) Sixteenth Annual Report of COS Council, (1883–4), p. 128.
(b) As above, p. 221.
(c) Seventeenth Annual Report of COS Council (1884–5), p. 23.
(d) As above, p. 116.
(e) Annual Report of St James, Soho and West Strand COS (1887), p. 13.
(f) Annual Report, Poplar and South Bromley COS (1887), p. 4.
(g) *Charity Organisation Review* (November 1886), p. 401. The Tower Hamlett Pension Committee was established by prominent COS members, notably Messrs A.G. Crowder and Arthur Wedgewood, as a means of creating pensions for those 'to whom the idea of entering the workhouse is the least tolerable' and were principally intended for residents of Whitechapel, St George-in-the-East and Stepney. See *Charity Organisation Review*, November 1886, p. 401; *Charity Organisation Review*, August 1885, p. 341.

An assessment of COS pensions a few years later provides further data on the number of pensioners and their cost. In the early 1890s, COS pensions at Whitechapel varied between 1s and 8s per week. Kensington had raised weekly sums of varying amounts for 56 pensioners at a total cost during the year 1891–92 of £605; the 54 pensioners at St George's (Hanover Square) received an annual total of £650; while the 78 St Marylebone COS pensioners received 'nearly £700' during the same year 1891–92.[68] Collating the data from these three 'wealthy' districts, an annual average pension can be calculated to be £10 8s or four shillings per week.[69] During the financial year 1894–95 the 1089 COS pensioners in London received a total of £12 222 indicating an average weekly payment of around 4s 31/2d.[70] It was becoming conventional for most COS pensioners in the 1890s to be women since women usually outnumbered men by about four to one.

Another source for COS case studies on pensions were the 'Notices and Advertisement' columns of the *Charity Organisation Review*. These confirmed that many COS pensions had a weekly value of 3 shillings or less; some examples follow:

- Pension 12 301: 'The Mile End Committee wish to continue a pension of 2 shillings a week for an old woman of 74 years ... '.[71]
- Pension 12 339: 'The Poplar Committee wish to raise a small pension, 3 shillings per week, for a respectable widow. Relations are helping'.[72]
- Pension 12 379: 'The Mile End Committee wish to raise a pension of 2s. 6d. a week for a single woman, aged 62; she for several years supported not only herself but her mistress with her needle. The mistress is dead, and she can now earn only 2s. or 2s. 6d. a week. The church allow her 2s. a week and with a pension of 2s. 6d. she could keep away from the Poor Law'.[73]
- Pension 12 406: 'The sum of £6. 10s. is wanted by the Stepney Committee, to provide an allowance of 2s. weekly (including arrears), to supplement a pension granted by the Tower Hamlets Pension Committee to a most deserving woman, aged 71'.[74]
- Pension 12 417: 'The Bethnal Green Committee wish to raise a sum of £2.12s. as a pension of 2s. a week for six months, for an old tailoress of 65, who, owing to her fingers being crippled by rheumatism, can earn little more than 3s. a week'.[75]

The realization that COS pensions were frequently worth no more than the typical Poor Law dole strikes at the very heart of COS propaganda which repeatedly ridiculed the latter for their inadequacy. There is also convincing evidence that COS pensions were specifically designed to augment other incomes, a practice savagely attacked when carried out by the Poor Law authorities. COS propaganda often proclaimed that charitable agencies had no need to restrict expenditure because of their power to appeal to the wealthy and the benevolent. They implied that as a consequence, the voluntary sector could naturally be expected to treat the deserving poor more generously than did the Poor Law. Such impressions could hardly have sat easily on London COS consciences when their District Committees were repeatedly being faced with intense difficulties in extracting funds from their rich acquaintances, even when their benevolence would have been directed towards helping the most deserving cases.

There was an essential difference between COS pensions and Poor Law doles which the former constantly emphasized. COS pensioners were never allowed to assume that assistance was theirs of right and they must always remain deferential as well as deserving.[76] Pensioners were constantly reminded how beholden they were to the Society for bringing together such kindly sponsors but that they must never expect a COS guarantee of permanence. The COS reckoned that 'hard-won experience' had spotlighted how laxity by their own members when providing benefits, eroded what limited public support they might enjoy.[77] The LGB Inspector, Henry Longley, a prominent ban-ner-bearer in their crusade against outdoor relief, supported a measured provision of scientific charity 'when absolutely necessary'. Equally, he shared COS 'anxiety that for the good of recipients charitable help should remain precarious' and 'intermittent'.[78]

Let us now consider the type of person likely to be chosen by the COS to be the recipient of one of their pensions. These were usually either middle class who had seen better times or were 'worthwhile' respectable working class approved by COS investigators for their 'thrift and upright-ness, family duty and the like'.[79] The Society were 'glad to note among their applicants an increasing number of persons of a better stamp' who were 'a real pleasure to help through their difficulties'.[80] Such people were seen to possess 'exceptional worth and respectability'. For example, there was the 'widow of a military officer' for whom it was considered 'the prospect of becoming dependent on parish relief is extremely painful and repulsive'.[81] Other COS case-studies, in which they described this 'better-class' of person whom they most wished to help, include:

- 'Case 11 151 ... 5 shillings a week ... for a widow of 68, somewhat above the ordinary class'.[82]
- 'Case 12 124 ... a pension of 10 shillings per week for a single woman, aged 78 ... She belongs to a better class, feels her position much, and dreads being compelled to go into the workhouse'.[83]
- 'Case 13 016 ... an allowance of 8s.6d. weekly to a very respectable couple ... the man has also been a *Freemason*'.[84]
- 'Case 12 851 ... a pension of 8 shillings ... for a thoroughly respectable woman'.[85]
- 'Case 13 958 ... complete a pension of 10 shillings-a week ... for a very respectable old butler, aged 74'.[86]

Occasionally, Committees in poorer districts challenged the COS Council's advice about investigators adopting a softer approach towards people who had known better times. For example, the St Olave's Committee rejected their Council's view that it was 'unnecessary in dealing with more respectable applicants' to subject them to the 'ordeal of investigation'. Experience learned at St Olave's had shown that the 'petty meanness and want of straightforwardness of some of the better class of applicants often caused far more trouble … '.[87]

It is useful to discuss the contribution Charles Loch and Bernard Bosanquet made to the public awareness of COS activities. Both were managing editors of a stream of authoritatively written pamphlets, books and newspaper articles as well as being dominant contributors to the *Charity Organisation Review*.[88] Each projected an impression of omniscience designed to project the COS as natural leaders in all matters relating to the condition of the poor. Unfortunately for the COS, not only did they fail to reach a popular readership but were also unable to convince many of their wealthy adherents to dig sufficiently deeply into their treasure chests. As a consequence, many COS activities constantly teetered on the brink of insolvency. Nevertheless, sufficient of the Society's well-placed members who had social connections remained loyal – emotionally, if not financially – to ensure that COS views continued to be heeded by decision-makers in Whitehall. As a consequence, the COS, which had in the meantime become the Establishment's referee on social matters, remained influential throughout the last three decades of the nineteenth century. No Royal Commission bearing on the condition of the lower social classes was envisaged without COS involvement.

The impressive contribution Loch made in pushing the Society and himself to the forefront of social matters is illustrated by the special reports published by the COS while he was the Society's Secretary and in practical terms, its chief executive. The reports were not primarily aimed at the public, who remained largely disinterested in COS procedures, but at persuading decision-makers in Whitehall and elsewhere about the sanctity of COS doctrine. The semi-official façade of COS reports was not accidental as their printing was commissioned to Spottiswoode and Co., responsible for printing many of the government's publications.[89] Furthermore, Loch ensured that the COS presentational style mimicked officialdom. Minutes of evidence in COS reports were often recorded in a day-by-day pattern, with each question put to the witness numbered sequentially and his answers recorded *verbatim* as was typical of Parliamentary Committee enquiries.

A COS special Committee was appointed in 1887 to study soup kitchens and the cheap food supply together with the provision of meals for poor children. Its report, *Charity and Food*, followed in the wake of earlier COS publications on the same subjects.[90] It argued that to supply food free or below cost without personal inquiry was a false and dangerous charity for schoolchildren as well as for adults. The 'evil effects' of this type of support were clear to the COS. They alleged that such provision weakened the needs and duty of the family and encouraged mothers in lazy habits. It was also said to lead to the misuse of the rates levied for educational purposes.[91] A follow-up report some years later, *The Better Way of Assisting School Children* (1893), recommended that, after appropriate COS investigation, help should go to deserving families with needy children. On the other hand, those exposed as being 'negligent, improvident or worthless' should be prosecuted and forced upon the Poor Law.[92]

Special COS committees were established, some under the chairmanship of the eminent surgeon Timothy Holmes, to 'consider and report upon the public and charitable provisions made for the care and training of feeble minded, epileptic, deformed and crippled persons'.[93] Two books emerged in 1893, both with a significant input by Charles Loch. The first, *The Feeble-minded Child and Adult*, described the causes and characteristics of feeble-mindedness. It proposed that School Boards should provide special schools and appropriate funding. Feeble-minded adults should be provided for in special homes supported where possible by voluntary contribution. Where contributions were needed from guardians they should be free from stigmatization. The second volume, *The Epileptic and Crippled Child and Adult*, was similar in 'scope and spirit'.[94] It presaged continued government activity and culminated in the *Royal Commission on the Care and Control of the Feeble-Minded* (1904–8) of which Charles Loch was a member.

Another useful COS initiative, again with Loch as its motivator, has also gained long-term plaudits from social administrators. It involved the introduction of trained almoners into hospital outpatients' departments. The capable Miss M. Stewart was transferred from the COS Secretariat during winter 1894 for trial work at the Royal Free Hospital. Next year her appointment was confirmed as permanent, with the Society guaranteeing half of her salary.[95] The usefulness of Miss Stewart's efforts gradually led to other hospitals employing trained almoners with the Royal Free becoming a kind of training ground.[96] Young and Ashton have described how the almoner was 'in an excellent position' to know whether patients were able 'to contribute to the cost of their treatment in hospital'.[97]

What the COS described as being the confused administration of medical charities led to the Society making them targets for reform. The

COS campaigned to 'organize' an improved response from provident dispensaries, in particular, to GPs' 'hasty diagnosis and a bottle' without investigative reference to a patient's home surroundings. According to the COS, this slackness had led to 'hundreds of poor women' being misleadingly tempted to 'live upon drugs, tonics and cordials'.[98] The COS maintained that the remuneration of general practitioners was being eroded by persons who were well able to pay fees taking unfair advantage of free medical care. In 1888 the COS had appointed a special committee to examine what they saw as confusion in the provision of medical aid. They successfully petitioned the House of Lords for the appointment of a Select Committee to inquire into the 'overlapping services' of voluntary hospitals, Poor Law infirmaries, provident dispensaries and out-patient departments. Although the House of Lords Committee appeared to support COS ideas on medical organization and in spite of the subject being doggedly pursued by the Society throughout the 1890s, no legislation emerged.[99]

An attempt in the 1870s to 'organize' medical charities had led to the appointment of a special committee in 1879 to examine the placing of persons in Convalescent Homes. The COS Convalescent Homes Committee proposed a system whereby Homes should send notices of their vacancies to the COS who would act as a clearing-house. Thirty-six Homes had soon been attracted to the scheme prompting the COS to claim that the success had accrued from their investigative procedures which were rooting out cunning 'undeserving' people and preventing them from hoodwinking misguided medical practitioners. The COS explained that convalescent aid had originally been established 'to deal with the after-time of illness in which change and good food promoted a speedier cure'. But once Homes had been created, doctors had become carelessly inclined to provide a certificate for convalescence to any patient who, 'living in a crowded town, showed signs of debility, even if he suffered from no definite illness or disease'. This lack of discretion on the part of GPs was detected by the COS as creating a 'convalescent class' of person who would go 'from one convalescent home to another or use a convalescent home as holiday resort'.[100] The COS perceived their role as that of interceding by means of case investigation so as to erase the social irresponsibility they claimed to be prevalent among some sections of the medical profession. After the initial burst of co-operative interest, the rigidity of applied COS practices blunted enthusiasm. As a result, the number of convalescent cases 'dealt with' by the COS declined sharply. Compared with the 2000 and more convalescent cases mentioned annually in London COS reports during the 1880s, 1768 cases had passed through COS hands in 1896–97 and only 1265 were 'dealt with' in 1899–1900.[101]

There were long-term sorties by the COS into rationalizing the activities of voluntary medical dispensaries with Poor Law hospital out-patient departments. These, coupled with the COS campaign to 'organize' Convalescent Homes led to the appointment of Lieut Col Montefiore as the special COS Secretary to the Medical and Convalescent sub-committee, a post he held from the mid-1880s to his retirement in 1909. Montefiore's brief also included the Society's drive to undermine what it alleged to be the habit of many Surgical Aid Societies of supplying surgical apparatus without appropriate prior investigation. Here again, after early interest in COS ideas, experience of how they were being applied in practice led to a decline in the number of surgical aid cases they were invited to investigate. There were only 716 cases in the last year of the nineteenth century compared with nearly 1000 looked into by the COS two years earlier.

The common thread running through the various COS attempts to involve themselves in social matters was their determination to apply the basic concept of rigorous investigation coupled with co-ordinated organized effort from charitable bodies. As discussed above, by judicious selection of particular aspects of charitable work, the Society did contrive to contribute more effectively than they did by their overbearing but fruitless efforts at intimidating all other relief bodies into submitting themselves wholesale to an investigative and 'organizing' schema. By applying their methodology to specific social problems such as homelessness, the mentally defective, Convalescent Homes and free meals, the COS were more successful in persuading others, at least for a while, that they had something worthwhile to offer.

An example of COS failure when venturing into a broader organization of charities is instanced by the Combined Collection of Charitable Contributions scheme, attempted along the lines of that used by the Liverpool Central Relief Society.[102] The London COS replica launched in 1883 had gained the co-operation of 11 societies by 1884–85, involving total collections during the year of only £3203. The snag was that these were but a small fraction of the London charities concerned with the condition of the poor. The vast majority had not deigned to become involved. After further brief mention by the COS in 1888 to the effect that the Combined Collection system was being 'slowly developed', it vanished without trace from mainstream COS literature.[103]

Another area where the COS failed to get their way was in Loch's idea of reorganizing old endowed charities, preferably in association with the voluntary societies. After campaigning for years, Loch was eventually disappointed when the reorganization of London's endowed charities took place in 1890 with no provision for COS involvement. Emigration was another facet of London life in which the COS attempted to become the dominant player only to see early signs of success fade away. In 1886, they formed a sub-committee to assist in the emigration of families after their personal circumstances had been investigated and judged 'deserving' by a COS District Committee. From 1890, the Society co-operated with the East End Emigration Fund. By 1893, the number of cases increased so that during that year 337 case families were assisted in emigrating, mainly to Canada, South Africa, Australia and the USA. By the end of the century, case family emigrations involving the COS had dropped to 18 although emigration generally had continued to rise.[104]

During the 1890s when the various innovative initiatives were being attempted by the COS, they continued to struggle to attract volunteers. By 1900 the total number of volunteers claimed by London COS to be operating in their District Committees was 1240. Some of these volunteers were 'able only to attend Committee meetings' on odd occasions but, it was claimed, that 'at least 650 persons' were actively taking part in the Society's work. Even then the COS complained that, 'much of the time of the more experienced members of the Committee' was spent in the training new workers.[105] No matter how the COS Council blustered about their efficiency as an organizing Society, it is clear that in practical terms they had failed to rationalize relief to London's poor. By 1900, there was no possibility of COS District Committees achieving their original target of 'combining the machinery of legal and charitable relief under one roof' with 'the guardians, the clergy, and the visiting ladies sitting round a table' dealing with 'each case according to its merits'.[106] Widespread rejection by other relief agencies meant that the original meaning of the word 'organized', as featured in the Society's title, was strangely at odds with reality.

The total income of the London COS Council for the financial year ending 30 September 1900 was £15 027 15s 7d, as detailed in Table 3.8. The Council's general account expenditure for the same year was £4 259 12s 7d. This included C.S. Loch's salary of £800 and those of the two Assistant Secretaries, receiving £350 and £250 respectively. Included in the administration cost was £273 15s for an Accountant, £195 and £194 19s respectively for the two shorthand writers, £123 5s 2d. for the general clerk, £100 for the copying clerk, £69 5s 1d for the junior clerk, £130 for an 'inquiry officer' and £102 5s for other 'inquiry officers',

Table 3.8   Total London COS Council receipts for the financial year ending 30 September 1900

Subscriptions and donations to COS Council*	£9 886 0s 1d
Funds received: for 'special cases'	£1 793 14s 1d
for 'relief generally'	£ 77 13s 8d
for 'convalescent cases'	£1 606 4s 1d
for 'surgical appliances'	£ 298 9s 0d
for 'emigration fund'	£ 149 12s 0d
for 'District Committee Aid fund'	£ 20 10s 0d
from sales of books and papers	£ 253 9s 7d
From sundries, interest and b/f from previous year	£ 942 3s 1d
Total receipts for year	£15 027 15s 7d

*The Council subscription list included around 1500 names, some of whom had donated no more than a few shillings: Thirty-second Annual report of the COS Council.

presumably employed part-time. The Council's annual publication account showed a total expenditure of £553 14s 10d, indicating a net deficit on publications slightly in excess of £300. More than two-thirds of publication loss was attributed to the production and distribution costs of the *Charity Organisation Review*. This signalled the continued COS inability to attract sufficient interest in its main propaganda outlet to make it viable.

During the 12 months ending 30 September 1900, the sum of £4 814 17s 8d is shown in the accounts to have been distributed by the Council to the District Committees. This included £2 572 1s for District Secretary's salaries and £1 854 11s 5d for the central relief account, almost half of which had gone on payments for 'special cases'. A further £1 940 7s 7d had been spent by the Council on the sub-committee account covering payments for convalescence, surgical appliances, emigration, 'medical working' and expenses on conferences and exhibiting in Paris. After accounting for a small sundry item of 9s 3d, the Council reported a favourable balance at Bank (Coutts & Co.) of £604 2s 3d.[107]

At the turn of the century, the COS Council had a nominal strength of 150. These included the President (the Archbishop of Canterbury), 37 Vice-Presidents headed by HRH the Princess Louise, the Chairman (the Rt Hon. Lord Avebury), 2 Vice-Chairmen, 3 Treasurers, 10 representatives of metropolitan charities, 19 'additional' members and District Committee representatives. A few names still remained intact from the 1872 Council list, see Table 2.1, above. These included the Duke of Norfolk, the Marquis of Lansdowne, Lord Leigh, Lord George

Hamilton, Lord Ashcombe (formerly George Cubitt, MP), The Viscount Goschen (the Rt Hon. G.J. Goschen, MP), Miss Octavia Hill and the Rev. Canon Barnett. By 1900, females featured much more prominently among the council's various sub-committees. A significant number of females were now being nominated as District Committee representatives on the Council.[108] Auditors continued, as in 1872, to be members of the Exchequer and Audit Office, Somerset House, thus retaining another quasi-official veneer to COS affairs.

What then had been achieved by the COS in their first 30 years from 1869 to the end of the century? Extreme Smilesian concepts applied to the poor no longer suited the mellowing mood of the middle classes in general. More of the middle class were now prepared to accept that, particularly in the urban context, working people could find themselves little better than flotsam in an unpredictable economic maelstrom. The poor themselves fought shy of becoming involved with the COS. This forced the Council to admit that 'large sections of the working class' added to the Society's 'popular unpopularity'.[109] From 1875 the COS presence in London was one of attempted consolidation rather than of robust expansion. The number of COS District Committees had reached 40 in the mid-1870s and since then had made little meaningful progress in terms of either membership or local income. Over the same period the COS Council income had more than doubled: from £5830 in 1875 the central annual revenue had grown to over £15 000 by 1900.[110] The fundamental COS problem, something that showed few signs of being resolved, was that the funds acquired locally by their District Committees had remained 'practically stationary' for 25 years.[111] Throughout that quarter-century the amount distributed in relief by the richer districts remained greater than that of the poorer districts and so persistently discredited COS claims that their 'scientific' investigative methodology was always impartial.

The number of applicants to the COS had been 19 173 in 1876. They had then increased in some years, particularly when trade was slack. A peak in excess of 26 000 was reached in 1885–86 and stayed above 20 000 for ten years or so before dropping below 15 000 by the end of the century, see Figure 3.2. The increased proportion of applicants turned away empty-handed from COS offices without help meant that the fall in numbers of persons actually assisted and referred elsewhere by the COS became even more marked in the 1890s.

The possibility that individual poverty may be related to faultlines in the nation's socioeconomic structures was never entertained by the

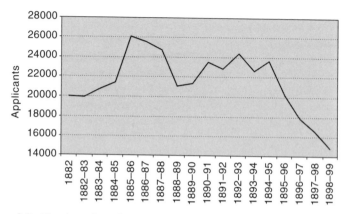

Figure 3.2   Number of applicants either referred or assisted by London COS between 1882 and 1898–99.

COS. Even towards the end of the century, the Society still rejected mounting evidence of widespread metropolitan squalor and domestic misery. Charles Booth's descriptions of how London's poor existed from hand to mouth, were dismissed as being 'characteristic of the chaotic condition into which the so-called science of economics has fallen'.[112] According to the COS, weakness of character remained a much more cogent explanation of personal failure than that of being unemployed. When Helen Bosanquet was asked how families were expected to exist in insuperable domestic circumstances, she brushed the question aside as a 'vain and idle hypothesis' because always 'social conditions *will* permit them'.[113]

It was apparent by the end of the century that although they had retained friends in high places, the COS had been unable to prevent fundamental change in social attitudes towards the poor. The London Society and their acolytes had to face the reality that the socio-political responses to charity organization were becoming increasingly negative with the passing of years. The COS blamed the 'general advocacy of socialism' for altering the standpoint of many people 'in regard to their social obligation'. The state and the local municipalities were both condemned by the COS for being undesirable instruments set on mischievously attempting to equalize economic conditions by adjustments to the interests of the different social classes. The COS lamely explained their own lack of social impact by claiming that their failings were 'entirely consistent' with the regrettable contraction of interest in personal and voluntary work. Relief, not charity, was said by the COS to now dominate people's thoughts.[114] How the COS rearguard action against the impending forces of New Liberalism was fought with some limited success in the early years of the twentieth century, only to later wane and wither, will be discussed in the following chapter.

4

1900 Onwards – a Half-Century of Change and General COS Decline

The closing years of the nineteenth century cast doubt on the impregnability of Britain's economic, political and industrial supremacy. However, there were still sufficient favourable factors to satisfy British optimists that their nation justifiably carried the prefix 'Great'. 'Empire red' continued to dominate the classroom globes. As the Capital of these far-flung lands, London's buildings and thoroughfares reflected pride and grandeur. The City remained the unchallenged hub of world commerce, trade, banking and finance. Sterling seemed impregnable and 'as good as gold'. The Home Counties middle class were pleased that much of industry's stench had been kept away, located in the Midlands and the distant North. They retained the satisfaction of knowing that their River Thames remained a crucial conduit of world trade.

The economic growth of Britain, expressed as GDP per head, had continued for decades at one per cent per year up to the outbreak of war in 1914. It seemed irrelevant to many that the other industrializing nations such as the USA, Germany, Japan and France were improving their GDP at a significantly faster rate. It was comforting for Britons to delude themselves into believing that this could be entirely explained by the belief that these countries had much catching up to do. When British growth rates slowed after hostilities ceased, it was a dangerously misleading cocoon for these people to know that most other global competitors had also been severely hit. Indeed, as far as the nation's decision-makers in south-east England were concerned, the British economy was as robust as could reasonably be expected after the justifiable exertions and economic repercussions of war. Admittedly, the distant staple industries of textiles, coal, steel and shipbuilding were sickly. Fortunately, they seemed to be largely the problems of other people and weighed little on the lifestyle of those in the more forward-looking Home Counties.

Those faults that were diagnosed as existing in British industry could seemingly be traced, by those not involved, to worker laziness. The COS adopted this line. Their solution for the economic difficulties of the 1920s was that industrial workers should face reality and 'take their coats off to make the best of a difficult job'.[1] The London COS saw the positive nurturing of personal qualities and individual character as essential for the well-being of the country. They explained that this was important because each individual was a function of that 'organism' described as 'society' and that their 'virtues and capacities', however diverse, were complimentary to each other.[2] For the COS, no state welfare programme would ever replace 'the neighbourly service of the settlements' or the personalized service provided by caring individuals whose energies had been 'correctly' directed towards child-care, nursing or education. In attempting to explain why 'socialist' concepts were overtaking individualism, the Society argued that the long-term structured thoughts and processes associated with manufacturing led naturally to a more collective type of social administration. For them, it was 'noteworthy' that the 1860s had witnessed not only the important scientific discoveries of the biologists Darwin and Huxley but had also produced the COS. This 'coincidence' was taken to prove that British society should tune their individual imaginations to be more in touch with the life sciences and biology, just as these were allegedly 'marching hand in hand' in the USA. It was claimed by the COS that when such re-tuning occurred on this side of the Atlantic, their ideas would soon 'regain their ascendancy'.[3] The COS remained convinced that it was introducing science into charity with its belief that there was a subjective aspect of dependency. Members argued that the cause and certainly the cure for dependency lay crucially in the character of the recipient, proving that his needs were 'immaterial' as well as being 'material'. The Society alleged that this 'scientific' approach differentiated the COS from the many charities emphasizing that religious conversion could itself satisfy the weakness in the subjective aspect of dependency.[4]

But as the 1920s wore on even the most diehard COS supporters could not fail to recognize that in the existing political climate any idea of themselves gaining the ascendancy among British charities was little better than a pipedream. The COS were frustrated when succeeding British governments persisted in spurning individualistic advice while compounding the 'disastrous folly' of pouring 'more and more on rates and taxes'. The COS saw it as symptomatic of a mad world that there seemed to be little awareness of the associated danger that such unwise government policies would lead to institutions such as themselves becoming submerged. Equally, they were anxious to reassure their public that although as an institution their 'death by drowning had come near at times', they remained afloat. They told the public that each person who approached the COS for assistance would be reassured that they would always be welcomed with that special brand of COS sympathy and patience making them feel they were the only one in the world with a problem.[5]

The big political disappointment for those still proselytizing crude Smilesian principles was the disturbing tendency, particularly among Liberals, towards pampering the poor. Worrying cracks had begun to appear in the COS's own intellectual edifice in Victoria's time. They had been furious when Joseph Chamberlain, who himself had been the first Birmingham COS President, launched a disturbing political trend when, as President of the Board of Trade in 1886, he initiated non-stigmatic, non-skilful and non-competitive public works programmes.[6] Another major jolt to COS thinking came early in the twentieth century when Campbell-Bannerman's government allowed Local Authorities to provide free school meals without what the COS regarded as appropriate attention to parental circumstances. More frustrating still was the 1908 Old Age Pensions (OAP) Act followed three years later by the National Insurance Act. Such policies had for many years been savaged by the COS as being irresponsible and likely to create 'new evils' by aggravating the social problems they were intended to solve.[7] Allegedly, the state proposals neither placed sufficient emphasis on rewarding the thrifty nor accorded worthwhile attention to weeding out the undeserving. The COS Council's report for 1907–8 criticized the heavily increased financial burden placed on citizens by state involvement. Self-reliance was said to be weakened and faults of individual character strengthened. The COS also warned that the continued failure of voluntary helpers to 'come forward in large numbers to fulfil the obligations which the state imposes' would inevitably lead to these departments being managed by salaried officials. They forecast that as a result, they would lose 'most of the characteristics that will make them useful to society'.[8]

In practice, the COS found it hard to select suitable cases for those volunteers they did manage to recruit. The Society described their difficulties in finding cases which matched the particular volunteer's own temperament, held their interest, gave them responsibility and yet did not suffer from the inevitable 'occasional nature' of voluntary service.[9] Although the COS were understandably keen to project the 'voluntary' image, the backbone of their District Committees, prior to the First World War, had already become mainly salaried. In 1913, within the London COS, there were: 19 Secretaries, 13 District Secretaries, 4 Organizing Secretaries and a General Organizing Secretary, H.L. Woollcombe. Secretaries were paid £150 (men) and £100–130 (women); District Secretaries £170–200; Organizing Secretaries £250 (men) and £200 (women).[10]

In spite of their many disappointments, the COS maintained a stout verbal rearguard action against interventionist legislation. Committed as they were to the organization of charitable provision, it was embarrassing for the COS to recognize that signs of a haphazard voluntary sector remained everywhere. They had to admit that, in spite of all their efforts, charities of all kinds 'multiplied with bewildering rapidity'.[11] This admission was coupled with the unconvincing argument that because charitable and Poor Law expenditure had grown while poverty remained, there was proven need for all interested parties to recognize the value of COS methodology. As late as the 1930s, the Society continued to issue warnings about the 'dangerous' emergence of new voluntary organizations. At the same time, it extolled how its own Enquiry Department continued to expose the duplicity of newcomers. Many had allegedly been exposed as tricksters suitable for inclusion on the COS's Cautionary Card.[12] Of particular COS concern was the fact that massive unemployment had led to a growth in the number of Societies offering assistance to the homeless. Many of these emergent societies were said to depend upon house-to-house collections for their funding. According to the COS, they often displayed shocking profligacy in paying their collectors a commission of 33 per cent and occasionally as much as 50 per cent. The COS claimed that the old-established homeless societies were 'well equipped and capable of dealing with homeless men on constructive lines'. They saw 'no possible justification for additional "Homeless Societies"'. The night shelters created by these emergent Societies were designated by the COS as 'little short of a social menace'.[13]

Although the COS's confrontational stance on state provision provided an obstacle, their image among Whitehall's decision-making establishment had not been tarnished irreparably by the early twentieth century. Retention of a partial gloss had been helped by their exalted Council members and assiduous senior salaried staff who had continued to pressurize politicians and Whitehall mandarins alike. The

COS continued to be invited to join Government Committees and Royal Commissions. During the 1890s, Charles Loch and Albert Pell, MP had forcibly represented the COS on the Royal Commission on the Aged Poor. In 1904 Loch became a dominant member of the Royal Commission on the Care of the Feeble-minded and drafted the greater part of its final 1908 report. At much the same time, as leader of the six-strong contingent on the renowned Royal Commission on the Poor Law and the Relief of Distress (1905–9), he kept the COS in the public eye.[14] Any involvement by Loch could never have been passive in any case. The strain of participating so wholeheartedly in public service while actively continuing with his COS Secretarial duties contributed to his deteriorating health and eventual retirement.[15] It did not lighten his task for him to be subject to the growing perception that his relentless efforts to propagate COS principles as a Royal Commissioner had fallen largely upon deaf ears among Liberal politicians and the public generally. In his more private reflections, Loch must by now have suspected that he had nailed his lifetime talents to what had become a tattered banner. By the outbreak of the First World War, the COS was finalizing the transition from being an eminent group of right-wing elites superbly confident that, with the quality of their breeding and position, they were naturally able to depend on the support of contemporary governments, to a situation where their opinions were often being ignored and even derided.

The COS insisted tenaciously that paramount in promoting individual independence was 'social utility of thrifty ways of life and saving'. This was too uncompromising a concept for Edwardian Britain, an age seeking enlightened social reform. Eventually, even the seemingly impervious London COS Council had to admit that their growing unpopularity was 'hard to bear'. This led to the formation of yet another COS 'Special' Committee to examine how hurtful and injurious criticism could best be alleviated by the COS.[16] The Committee recommended deletion of reference to the 'repression of mendicity' from the COS's full title. In 1910 it became 'The Society for the Organization of Charitable Effort and the Improvement of the Condition of the Poor', apparently aimed at providing 'a more accurate impression' of COS objectives. Such changes were like shuffling the proverbial deckchairs. Change of title was far too little far too late, especially as it was rarely, if ever, subsequently used, even in London COS Council annual reports. The 'Special' Committee also observed that even within the Society, there were disturbing conflicts of opinion. One internal group ominously advocated the adoption of a more conciliatory attitude towards dissenters. The Council snuffed out such weakness by deciding that while Society members must be prepared to cope with internal differences of opinion they should always remain aware that, after thorough debate, there must be no dilution of COS principles. A fundamental COS flaw was therefore perpetuated by the Society consistently seeing itself as being a cut above other charities and never afraid to say so. In this vein, the Society extracted encouragement from Sir Geoffrey Butler's comment that while social workers in general were 'admirable people', when compared with COS volunteers they were merely like a 'well meaning Militia compared with the Guards on parade'.[17]

Loch's health broke irretrievably in the summer of 1913 when he was laid low with a serious stroke. He failed to recover fully although he lingered on the sidelines for another ten years. The Rev. J.C. Pringle succeeded him as General Secretary in 1914. Towards the end of the First World War, Pringle obtained leave of absence from the Society to serve as an Army Chaplain. After overseas service he returned to the COS in 1919. Within a short time he resigned as their Secretary after being appointed Rector of St George's-in-the-East where he stayed for six years. Upon Pringle's departure, H.L. Woollcombe was promoted to Secretary and then, after his death in 1923, Fox-Strangeways succeeded him temporarily. Within two years Pringle had decided to return as COS Secretary where he remained until shortly before his death in 1938.[18] Throughout his time with the Society, Pringle was stimulated by what he remembered as Loch's moulding of a 'Parochial Service' and of the nearest to 'perfect human relationships that the world had ever seen'. At the same time he recognized that Loch had blundered most 'heroically' in failing to convince the 'average beer-swilling Englishman' that the Parochial Service concept was the only correct interpretation of the objectives and the teachings of T.H. Green.[19] Loch's failure to convert the public had, in Pringle's opinion, resulted in a 'progressive and now long since absolutely complete exclusion from Whitehall and Parliament' of the COS viewpoint.[20]

Loch's departure from the helm left the entrenched COS conviction that haphazard charity was mischievously wrong unchanged. Although public opinion was steadily moving away from Victorian Individualism so as to leave them even more intellectually isolated, the COS remained adamant post-war that the many ill-directed charitable appeals 'tended to deaden our natural sympathies and blunt the edge of our discrimination'.[21] Every head of a family throughout the nation was held by the COS as being responsible for providing against the 'ordinary' contingencies of life. Allegedly, social advance could come only through increased thrift and self-reliance. At the same time, state involvement must be 'restricted within the narrowest limits'. According to the COS, the post-war spread of official and voluntary assistance towards the unemployed, the ex-serviceman, public health and education was fundamentally flawed by its indiscrimination. The Society warned persistently about what it alleged to be the social dangers of compulsory state insurance against sickness, accident or unemployment.[22] Men 'suffering from a disability' which did not 'prevent them from working' should not benefit from state allowances for their wives and children. Able-bodied war widows were said to have been 'needlessly' granted pensions and child allowances.[23]

Austin Hopkinson, MP, with more than 20 years of close association with the COS, likened them to English monasteries prior to the Reformation. They too had 'organised charitable impulses' when required but after dissolution there had been a foolish attempt to make the state act 'in a way in which only individuals can function'. Hopkinson considered it unfortunate that people had been encouraged post-war to believe that the 'charitable state' would create a 'new heaven and a new earth' and a 'land fit for heroes' for which no-one need pay. The Charity Organization Society was, according to Hopkinson, in its essence, 'a protest against that point of view'.[24] COS realization that their star was no longer in the political ascendancy prompted them to reminisce about on how different things might have been had late-Victorian governments followed their advice more closely. The Society wistfully prefaced their 1926–27 report with Alfred Marshall's evidence to the Royal Commission on the Aged Poor in 1895:

> I may say that a suggestion has been made, I think by Professor Sidgwick, that in certain cases the Charity Organisation Society might distribute public money. That is one method of attaining very much the same result as that which I rather prefer to get by another method. I wish that no relief should be given at all, except interim relief, until the case has been examined by the Charity Organisation Society. The Guardians, acting with the advice of the Charity Organisation Society, to have much greater freedom of classification in workhouses and outside workhouses according to thrift and past conduct than they have at present.[25]

The COS greatly regretted that Marshall's guidance had been ignored. They accepted that the 'socialist' climate of inter-war Britain made it even less likely that, as a Society, they would be courted by a contemporary government. Even then they refused to be deflected from what had become hopelessly outdated ideas. As if to confirm their inflexibility, they quoted proudly from 'an illustrious and kindly critic of vast overseas experience but long out of touch with the details of things at home'. He had observed in the mid-1920s that the COS had changed 'a great deal since the time of Loch and his friends'. But he in turn had been contradicted in a 'twinkling' by another unnamed good friend and critic of the Society who believed; 'not one jot or tittle, the COS changeth not'.[26] The Council drew comfort from this 'confirmation' that their principles remained as inviolable in 1928 as they had been in 1869. They deplored the current erosion of individual character caused by state benefits, such as when Hackney COS District Committee had quoted the case of a man 'to whom dependence on outdoor relief and unemployment benefit was utterly intolerable'.[27]

Selective COS case-studies continued to be published. Some illustrated 'deserving' cases that the COS had helped and others the undeserving that the Society had refused to help. They even afforded themselves the occasional humorous anecdote about their social contacts, as in the last of the three cases that follow:

'A man of 75' who the COS were helping over 'three operations for cataract lived on his savings (so there *are* people who save) and then, as soon as he was fit, went to work again as a matter of course'.[28]

The Lewisham Committee refused to help an ex-convict who asked for a cornet in order to join a band and who said no one would help him to make a fresh start although he did so want to go straight. It was not that he was an ex-convict but the discovery that the cornet given to him the previous week by another society had already gone into the pawnshop, which finally discouraged the Lewisham Committee.[29]

From Fulham comes the story of a request for a large-sized perambulator for twins whose father had recently returned from a sanatorium and whose mother would be otherwise unlikely to be able to give them an airing. Knowing the family, Fulham gave the perambulator with some reluctance and shortly afterwards learnt that not the perambulator but one of the twins had been 'given away'.[30]

As early as 1894, the COS's Mrs Dunn Gardner had stressed the necessity for more systematic training and shortly afterwards 'a scheme of training through lectures and practical work was instituted'. This developed into the School of Sociology with E.J. Urwick as lecturer and tutor to the 16 students enrolled. In 1912, mainly through lack of financial support while under the COS wing, it amalgamated with the London School of Economics to become the Department of Social Science and Administration.[31] Although still respected in the emerging 'social worker' profession for their contribution to the methodology of social administration, the COS perspective, as regards the actual provision of relief and other benefits, became progressively irrelevant. Clement Attlee went so far as to claim that the 'dominant voices of the voluntary sector during the inter-war period were all from outside the COS'. In social service the COS held only a 'minor place', offering little that was 'constructive to the post-war world of social provision'.[32] No matter how the COS from time to time attempted to court popularity by cloaking its propaganda in honeyed words about its devotion to improving the condition of the poor, few were fooled into believing it was other than the inflexible purveyor of elitist values.

As the Society's influence in high places dwindled, the COS attempted to maintain the public illusion that it remained a close advisor to government. COS annual reports recorded any indication that it might have the listening ear of Whitehall. It found it especially comforting when it could imply publicly that its advice had actually been heeded. An example is the COS Council's 1935–36 report. It claimed that the Society's 'experience and opinions' had been sought by four government committees. These had covered: (1) lump sum compensation; (2) probation of offenders and matrimonial conciliation; (3) adoption of children; and (4) the rehabilitation of persons injured by accidents.[33] In each instance, COS evidence unsurprisingly emphasized the crucial importance of casework study being applied before any decision was made on development of a personal plan to strengthen an individual's character. The COS were baffled as to why, as an institution committed to improving the condition of the poor, they had come to be so publicly rejected in principle and abhorred in practice. They found it 'small wonder if the COS worker, tenderly estimating the chance that a family, not very robust and not very wise, will make good in a chaotic, wintry, difficult world, is astonished to discover that he had become an object of vehement misunderstanding and attack'.[34]

The number of applications to London COS District Committees in the early years of the century had been relatively low. Then, after rising to a higher plateau by the middle of the first decade of the new century, they dropped again around 1912 when the economy

Table 4.1 Total number of applicants, applicants 'decided', 'assisted', 'not assisted' or 'withdrawn' by London COS District Committees between 1900–1 and 1913–14

Year	Applications 'not assisted' or 'withdrawn'		Applications 'assisted'	Applications 'decided'*	Total applications
	Number	Percentage of total applications			
1900–1				14 059	
1901–2				14 555	
1902–3				17 996	
1903–4				19 115	
1904–5				19 631	
1905–6				20 590	
1906–7				20 335	
1907–8				18 900	
1908–9	13 123	60	8 079	20 656	21 783
1909–10	13 289	60	8 463	20 002	22 320
1910–11	11 670	61	7 351	18 028	19 279
1911–12	11 637	61	7 849	18 336	18 949
1912–13	10 110	59	7 116	16 399	17 251
1913–14	10 113	59	7 508	16 564	19 074

Source: Data are extracted directly from the appropriate Annual Report of the COS Council; 'assisted' applications include those helped from Institutions, Guardians, Individuals, applicants' relatives and 'other sources'; *'decided' applicants were those considered by the District Committee as 'dealt with' and 'closed'. It will be noted that between 1908–9 and 1913–4 the sum of the number of applicants tabled as 'not assisted' or 'withdrawn' and the number shown as 'assisted' in any one year does not precisely equal either the number of applications 'decided' or the 'total' applications.

strengthened preceding the 1914–18 war, see Table 4.1. Unfortunately, the annual COS 'returns' data for numbers 'assisted' and for those 'not assisted' or 'withdrawn' are not to hand for the twentieth century prior to 1908–9. From that time the percentage of total applications either 'not assisted' or 'withdrawn' in the average year prior to the outbreak of hostilities hovered around 60 per cent, much as they had been during the 1890s.

The COS remained particularly proud of their ability to mobilize the co-operation of an applicant's relatives and friends towards satisfying the needs of that applicant. The following two case-studies exemplify the COS processes:

A young widow with three children, whose husband had died of cancer. During his last illness much help was given to him and after his death attempts were made to enable the widow to support her family. It was found she had relatives, living in the country near to a steam laundry, who were willing to let her part of their house and to look after her children while she went out ironing. The family were moved to this place, where the woman is now earning good wages and supporting herself and children.[35]

C.D., a widow of 79, was referred to us by the Guardians to whom she had reluctantly applied because her two sons failed to help her. She was in receipt of an annuity of 4s. a week secured to her by her late husband and lived with a daughter, herself a widow, who was already helping but could not give all that was needed. The Guardians considered that the sons could provide the small weekly sum still required but suggested that we should try and obtain it by persuasion if possible and so avoid enforcing payment through the Poor Law. A clergyman on our Committee, who was interested in the family, visited the sons with the result that they now help their mother regularly.[36]

The COS Council also published the occasional case-study illustrating how they had obtained more parental responsibility, for example:

K.L., the daughter of a carman, exempt from school owing to threatened consumption. The home was a miserable one, and the mother had for a long time traded on the child's ill-health, sending her with notes to beg for money or clothing. On the hospital doctor's advice we sent her to the country for three months with excellent results, the father contributing 1s. 6d. a week towards the expenses. It was arranged for her to go to a Sea-side Training Home belonging to the Metropolitan Association for Befriending Young Servants. The parents, however, insisted on having her back, although it was explained to them that she would lose her best chance of recovery. Naturally she soon lost all good she had gained, and is now under hospital treatment. Before blaming the parents too much for her selfishness, one is inclined to wonder whether the greater responsibility does not rest with the lady who so readily responded to the pencilled notes brought by the ill-clad child, even when it was pointed out to her that such giving could not but do more harm than good.[37]

The desperation of workers finding themselves without income during industrial disputes forced many to approach the COS against their normal inclination. They were not guaranteed much sympathy. According to the COS Council, 'strikes and threats of strikes had squandered the very means of bringing a true social amelioration' to the doors of the people.[38] Even before the 1914–18 war, L.V. Shairp, a COS 'Travelling Secretary', was horror-stricken that relief from the voluntary sector was being widely supplied to strikers. He argued that whereas 'starvation may be said to be the weapon of capital', it was equally correct to recognize that the 'Relief Fund may become the corresponding weapon of labour' and could materially affect the issue of the dispute. According to Shairp, at times of exceptional distress, as in a recent London Dock strike, the public had been led to regard a whole district of the metropolis as if it were a parched desert. He saw 'a hundred watering-pots' of mischievous charitable relief sprinkling indiscriminately across the smitten area in the form of soup kitchens, appeal funds and newspaper subscription lists. It seemed to Shairp as being 'in the last degree unreasonable that method and experience should not be allowed to guide our emotions'. He saw great danger that when we are called upon 'to pity the mass, we often lose our heads and do infinitely more harm than good'.[39]

As regards unemployment generally, the COS repeated its determination not to help the lazy. Finding work for applicants 'who have not energy or perseverance' was exceedingly difficult. Two contrasting cases from Battersea illustrate the Society's meaning:

> Case A – In January last, in conjunction with the Soldier's Help Society, we obtained a berth as carman for a man who threw it up after one day's trial, saying the hours were too long. In this case we were defeated by the applicant himself.

> Case B – A man was invalided out of the Army after eleven years' service with a 'very good' character. His own efforts to find work were unavailing. We got him some odd work – a few days a week. Shortly afterwards he called to tell us of another firm who were taking on hands. A letter of recommendation was given him from the office and he obtained regular work. Here the man himself co-operated with the Committee and the result was success.[40]

'Public relief on a large scale' was predicted by the COS as being likely to diminish the chance of people returning to the 'ranks of independence'. The following case-study from Whitechapel was used to illustrate its perspective:

> A.H., under 30 years of age, a wooden tea-chest maker, with a wife and one small child, applied for work in January 1904. He bore a

good character with his employers. He was referred to the Unemployment Committee under Mr Long's scheme and obtained work in the country until the spring. He was then offered emigration but preferred temporary work. He was again in difficulties the next Autumn and was given work by the same agency until the spring of 1905 on a definite promise by him that he would emigrate. In the spring, however, he changed his mind, as 'he would wait until the new Bill was passed'. He is still in casual work and has every prospect of being unemployed this winter.

During the First World War the number of applicants annually contacting the COS dropped but remained consistently above the 10000 mark, see Table 4.2. Unemployment, underemployment and industrial dispute were now no longer the main underlying causes of distress. Problems were more likely to be war-related, matrimonial or otherwise domestically inclined. During and subsequent to the war, the London COS usually found it possible to assist more than half those knocking on its door, regardless of numbers. This was a distinct improvement on the level of favourable COS response compared with previous periods. After the hostilities had ceased there was a jump in the number of applicants, coinciding with military demobilization and economic slump. By 1920–21, numbers had approached 15000 and rarely dropped below this level during the next 20 years. In fact, the economic shocks of the early 1930s pushed the number of applicants above 17000 before a gradual decline as the improving economy and preparation for another war made searching for work a little more satisfying.

Inter-war, the growing number of men forced through lack of work to depend on Poor Law relief and Unemployment Benefit made it 'extremely difficult' for the COS to restore men to independence. The Society saw this as perhaps 'the most striking and melancholy feature' of its activities in a world 'inhabited by people who for the most part avail themselves of everything that can be got'.[41] They were outraged when in 1934, despite their protestations, the Unemployment Assistance Board took over the relief of able-bodied poverty and freed it from Poor Law stigma. The COS objected to: the lack of ultimate sanctions; the decision to ignore malingering; the lack of organized casework; the neglect of restorative methods; and the absence of Work Centres. People who accepted such benefits were allegedly being degraded to 'an almost sub-human way of life'. While by now the COS reluctantly had to accept that unemployment could be a contributory factor to social problems, they believed these were being unnecessarily

Table 4.2 Total number of applicants, applicants 'decided', 'assisted', 'not assisted' or 'withdrawn' by London COS District Committees between 1915–16 and 1944–5

Year	Applicants 'not assisted' or 'withdrawn'		Applicants 'assisted'		Applicants 'decided' number	Total applications number
	Number	Percentage of total and of 'decided' ( )	Number	Percentage of total and of 'decided' ( )		
1915–6	5 673	46 (50)	6 767	54 (60)	11 342	12 357
1915–6	5 673	46 (50)	6 767	54 (60)	11 342	12 357
1916–7	4 434	44 (50)	5 229	52 (59)	8 920	10 169
1917–8	4 108	39 (43)	5 786	55 (60)	9 620	10 459
1918–9	4 284	39 (44)	5 946	55 (62)	9 734	10 851
1919–20	5 794	44 (46)	7 169	54 (57)	12 560	13 240
1920–1	7 461	51 (53)	7 253	49 (52)	14 001	14 714
1921–2	6 544	47 (48)	7 113	51 (52)	13 657	13 982
1922–3	6 303	44 (46)	7 359	51 (54)	13 662	14 315
1923–4	6 607	44 (46)	7 814	52 (54)	14 421	15 026
1924–5	6 346	44 (45)	7 840	54 (55)	14 186	14 574
1925–6	6 613	44 (45)	8 019	53 (55)	14 632	15 090
1926–7	7 168	46 (46)	8 296	53 (54)	15 464	15 713
1927–8	7 192	43 (46)	8 567	51 (54)	15 759	16 836
1928–9	7 028	46 (46)	8 186	53 (54)	15 214	15 355
1929–30	6 725	45 (46)	8 010	54 (54)	14 735	14 876
1930–1	7 694	49 (50)	7 565	48 (50)	15 259	15 646
1931–2	8 788	51 (52)	8 016	47 (48)	16 804	17 191
1932–3	8 489	49 (52)	8 099	47 (49)	16 588	17 187
1933–4	8 327	47 (48)	9 169	52 (52)	17 496	17 722
1934–5	7 321	46 (47)	8 114	51 (53)	15 435	15 856
1935–6	7 129	46 (48)	7 841	50 (52)	14 970	15 560
1936–7	6 836	48 (48)	7 958	56 (56)	14 244	14 299
1937–8	6 825	44 (45)	8 286	53 (55)	15 111	15 524
1938–9	7 201	44 (46)	8 492	52 (54)	15 711	16 488
1939–40	6 329	39 (39)	10 101	62 (62)	16 330	16 358 (X)
1940–1	6 000	32 (32)	12 823	68 (68)	18 806	18 801 (X)
1941–2	5 298	33 (35)	9 860	62 (65)	15 158	15 895 (X)
1942–3	5 340	33 (35)	9 783	60 (65)	15 123	16 238 (X)
1943–4	5 382	31 (32)	11 424	66 (68)	16 806	17 335 (X)
1944–5	4 277	28 (30)	9 988	66 (70)	14 265	15 163 (X)
1945–6	4 321	28 (29)	10 664	70 (71)	15 025	15 261 (X)

Source: Data are extracted directly from the appropriate Annual Report of the COS Council; 'assisted' includes those financially and 'otherwise' helped; •'decided' meant applicants considered by the District Committee, 'dealt with' and 'closed'. It will be noted that the sum of the percentage of applicants tabled as 'not assisted' or 'withdrawn' and the percentage shown as 'assisted' in any one year often does not total exactly 100 per cent. During the 1920s and 1930s the percentages related to the 'decided' number of applicants, shown (), more frequently present an accurate total. Number of applicants suffixed (X), from 1939–40 to 1944–45 continue to depict those approaching COS District Committees requesting assistance. They do not include those asking for advice from associated Citizens Advice Bureaux and Legal Advice Centres. During the immediate post-war years the total number of callers to the London CABx averaged around 100 000 annually.

complicated by a 'relaxed system of allowances and doles, doles without end and without conditions'.[42] The COS saw it as an urgent national task to stop the rot and accept the need for 'moral re-armament'. Their case histories illustrated what they saw as a serious human problem:

> James is thirty years old and has not done a day's work for ten years, during which time he has married and brought six children into the world. He now draws 42s. a week from the Unemployment Assistance Board which is more than he ever earned. His dole would be several shillings larger but for the fact that his wife clings to a foul tenement where the rent is only 6s. 3d. a week. The NSPCC has been after the family. James himself is well dressed and has a bicycle. His reputation is that he has not lifted a finger to find work and his only remark, on interview, was to demand his extra winter allowance from the UAB.

> ——— is a London man of twenty-one, single, who calls himself a shop assistant. He lives with his mother, who has a widow's pension of 10s. He himself draws 19s. in summer and 21s. in winter from the UAB. He had one week's employment in 1934 and one day in 1936. All offers of training have been refused as he says he would like a job near home. The Exchange said that his attitude made it difficult to submit him for vacancies as a bona-fide worker and that he has not been known to seek any work on his own account.

> Julius is twenty-nine and lives in London. He draws 45s. 6d. from the UAB and has done no work since 1936. He has a wife and five children, on behalf of whom the NCPCC has had to intervene more than once. Julius has refused low-paid work in hotel kitchens or selling ice-creams. Truly he does better on the dole. Several times he has turned down the offers of training at a Ministry of Labour centre.[43]

During the Second World War, COS applicant numbers grew. Callers were now more likely to bring family disturbance problems associated with the war such as: evacuation, enemy bombing, housing and furniture shortages, armed forces recruitment and psychological disequilibrium. Around two out of three COS applicants received some form of help during the conflict, see Table 4.2, above. The threat of war had meant that in Whitehall, long-term memories acknowledged the favourable potential, when emergency circumstances demanded, of COS procedures on administrative structures. Under the direction of the National Council of Social Service, the COS took on the running of Citizens' Advice Bureaux (CAB) in London.[44] Eighty CAB offices were available for action in London when the war began. More than one million citizens approached the Bureaux for advice and guidance during the hostilities. Other wartime activities for the COS included: free Legal Advice Centres; receiving and transmitting messages for the International Red Cross; the British War Refugees Fund and the Polish Relief Fund.[45] The Society also organized schemes that included the provision of free false teeth and spectacles for the needy. A disturbing growth in the number of 'irregular' adoptions of children was spotlighted by the COS and its efforts were an important contribution leading to the Adoption of Children Act (1940). Titmuss records how the COS and other organizations such as the Society of Friends and Settlement Workers 'helped to "hold the line" during this period while the official machine was beginning to take effective action'. He believed that the sight of 'Red Cross labels and the emotional stimulus of bombing broke down traditional dignities and liberated a spirit of helpfulness'.[46] The various services in which the COS became involved during wartime were funded externally. Annual grants for running the CAB came from the Ministry of Health and an early grant of £6 200 came from the British Red Cross after air-raids began in 1940. Other monetary contributions came from the British War Relief Society of the USA and the COS War Distress Fund.

During the hostilities London COS District Committee work settled down to providing a service much as normal but with added disquieting ingredients associated with the war. There were also lighter moments as when one elderly lady found romance and became happily married following a COS placing. Another old lady set them an unusual problem:

> She wished to go to a billet with two orphan great-grandsons and a parrot, said to be a "most refined bird". No one south of the Tweed would undertake this oddly assorted party, but a stout-hearted Scot agreed to have them and gave them a royal welcome in Edinburgh.[47]

On 16 June 1944, the London COS workload changed overnight with the start of flying-bomb attacks. The Society was 'besieged by badly-shocked people begging to be sent to the country'. COS volunteers were claimed to have successfully 'pestered their friends all over the country' to find shelter for distressed families.

Towards the end of the Second World War there were new problems for the COS befitting its post-war title of The Family Welfare Association. The housing shortage caused by bombing together with London house building restrictions had led to overcrowding and

domestic strain. Furniture scarcities were aggravated by returning evac-
uee children. Psychological troubles and the necessary social adjustments of ex-service men and women loomed into prominence.
Post-war, young couples, already tight for space by the necessity of living with parents or in-laws, brought intolerable overcrowding with the
coming of a baby.[48] A flavour of some of the family problems confronted by the COS is illustrated by the three following case-studies:

A husband had been sent home on compassionate leave to cope
with the advent of an unwanted coloured baby. In co-operation
with the Moral Welfare worker and a woman doctor, all the help
possible, both material and spiritual, had been given to this sad
little family, and the soldier, on leaving the office, was heard to
remark: 'Every time I come to this place I leave with a lighter heart'.

Another Committee cites the case of a woman who applied for extra
furniture in view of her children's return from evacuation. This led
to a long and intimate relationship between Mrs X and the office, in
the course of which, after many hindrances and delays, Mrs X was
sent away for overdue convalescence. Her husband, who had been
so difficult that Mrs X had had to claim police protection, was sent
for later to share her holiday; a piece of wisdom which resulted in a
greatly improved atmosphere at home.

Robert, a 17 year old boy, whose case illustrates the personal aspect of
the Association's (FWA) work, has been able to train as a Merchant
Navy radio officer because the Committee in the district where he
lives advanced the necessary funds, which he and his father under-
took to repay. Unfortunately he failed by one point in his examination and at first flatly refused to try again. However, after a fortnight's
holiday, spent chiefly on the skating rink, he agreed to return to
school, passed easily, and is now half-way round the world.[49]

It is interesting to compare and contrast details of London COS cases
for the year 1900–1 with those for 1938–39, Tables 4.3 and 4.4 respectively. When the twentieth century dawned, there were 40 COS District
Committees located across the capital. Cases for the year 1900–1,
detailing the number of applications decided, the sources of assistance
and 'some forms of relief', show that by far the largest form of relief or
assistance numerically was the nebulous 'other' category, see Table 4.3,
below. This was usually little more than a euphemism for a small
financial or material grant that did not fit comfortably into COS

recommended assistance patterns. Also numerically prominent and demanding substantial financial outgoings, was medically orientated assistance. This took the form of either hospital treatment, supply of surgical apparatus, convalescent aid or help in gaining admittance to a Home. COS pensions were flourishing, with 257 newly recorded across London during the first year of the century. However, the 258 loans that year were small in number compared with a decade earlier.

Returns for 1938–39 show that prior to the Second World War the number of London COS District Committees had drifted from 40 to 31, see Table 4.4. 'Other' forms of assistance, mysteriously, still dominated numerically as a category even though mention of grants had crept back into the tabular frame as being provided specifically for the acquisition of stock, equipment or 'removal'. Medical assistance under various headings remained prominent. For some years the Society had proudly recorded its efforts towards improved health as being the 'strongest impulse at work'. In the 1930s the increased proportion of COS expenditure allotted to 'special cases' was interpreted as confirming the COS's 'close and happy alliance' with hospital almoners, the Invalid Children's Aid Association, the Tuberculosis Care committees and Scholl Care Committees.[50] 'Loans' had been obliterated from COS annual returns as long ago as 1908–9 although some may have occurred within that element of COS District Committees' revenues attributed to 'applicants'.

COS pension provision through the early years of the twentieth century is noteworthy. As discussed in Chapter 3, pensions had become a dominant part of COS relief after an inauspicious start in the 1870s. By the calendar year 1900 there were 1259 COS pensioners. 1040 of these being over the age of 65 years. On average, each COS pensioner received a weekly allowance of just under five shillings. Of these, 1006 were female and just over 50 per cent were widows. About one-third of the women were spinsters. The total number of pensioners remained fairly constant up to the First World War. They did not fall below the 1220 recorded in 1909, nor did they exceed the 1426 recorded in 1906.

The effect of the 1908 Old Age Pensions (OAP) Act was to reduce the unit value of COS pensions more than it did their actual number, see Table 4.5a. The Society claimed that prior to the legislation it had been common practice for it to provide a weekly pension of 5 shillings above rent for one 'thoroughly deserving' person and 8s for two such people. Further assistance was occasionally provided when COS investigation indicated the need for clothing or medical help.[51] The OAP legislation brought most people over the age of 70 years a non-contributory means-

Table 4.3 Tabular statement of cases for year ending 30 September 1901 returned by District Committees

Committee	Referred to other District Committees	Inquiries to other District Committees	Number of applications decided	Sources of assistance					Some forms of relief								
				Institutions of local agencies	Guardians	Individuals	Other sources of assistance	Reports sent out	Employment	Emigration	Hospital treatment	Surgical apparatus	Convalescent aid	Pensions	Admitted to Homes	Loans	Other forms of relief
Kensington	21	0	696	85	6	27	202	603	11	1	3	15	33	10	8	12	227
Fulham (4 months)	35	198	294	56	5	53	10	234	8	0	19	15	24	6	2	6	33
Hammersmith	43	188	224	42	0	12	36	150	8	0	11	8	15	3	3	7	36
Paddington	68	385	674	150	4	129	227	424	36	1	23	23	41	14	10	27	265
Chelsea	23	196	333	20	2	66	1	192	18	1	9	3	32	8	0	7	39
St George's	66	673	871	663	23	533	0	836	153	1	23	36	44	7	3	2	247
St James's	91	674	381	66	4	53	30	299	12	0	5	14	17	4	3	9	63
St Marylebone	42	444	677	242	6	46	0	440	35	1	31	29	42	9	8	19	136
Hampstead	69	143	228	56	1	48	52	59	23	1	8	26	34	6	6	4	34
North St Pancras	55	243	302	80	2	71	26	336	26	0	24	24	60	6	17	9	32
South St Pancras	56	361	469	116	1	76	38	139	10	1	9	20	43	6	2	1	82
Islington	47	364	426	131	4	65	94	312	16	4	8	31	51	6	22	11	85
Holloway	63	180	314	64	22	94	24	265	15	4	11	19	44	6	10	8	86
Hackney		193	240	83	7	71	14	78	9	0	18	24	20	10	5	2	24

Dalston	18	166	147	32	8	29	19	70	17	0	5	7	17	4	1	7	31
Holborn and City	79	1446	473	160	0	63	62	437	28	0	14	28	19	15	3	1	121
Shoreditch	38	343	281	82	1	71	10	57	1	1	2	19	22	5	1	1	47
Bethnal Green	28	216	307	80	1	33	14	239	4	1	11	12	32	11	2	1	46
Whitechapel	58	226	202	35	4	37	12	88	1	1	4	7	13	12	0	0	24
St George's East	30	178	194	87	1	21	26	224	0	0	6	3	14	3	0	0	168
Stepney	69	188	226	80	1	18	15	50	3	1	40	9	6	10	6	3	31
Mile End	9	29	202	43	0	15	68	74	0	0	9	12	17	7	0	1	63
Bow	16	135	119	20	0	6	23	29	0	0	7	10	10	2	0	3	16
Poplar	13	173	236	38	2	16	50	71	1	0	5	14	30	2	2	1	34
West Ham	2	93	132	19	0	13	4	74	3	0	2	3	9	3	1	8	8
St Saviour's	35	387	362	126	3	53	55	143	13	0	6	22	50	14	2	8	93
Newington	64	326	639	131	1	90	118	99	6	0	21	53	88	7	4	9	127
St Olave's	23	251	498	163	3	83	18	286	11	2	31	51	73	14	4	31	78
Vauxhall	46	425	411	81	3	42	25	310	6	0	14	14	29	7	1	20	12
North Lambeth	56	259	421	61	5	11	14	228	19	1	12	15	40	8	7	4	67
Brixton	52	234	174	30	4	20	15	82	2	0	6	6	15	3	3	3	26
Wandsworth	33	123	269	54	4	46	15	130	5	0	4	19	28	5	7	0	37
Battersea	75	296	599	106	6	100	3	486	16	0	27	16	50	5	16	0	54
Clapham	72	254	320	72	6	68	0	285	13	1	13	22	30	6	9	1	37
Camberwell	127	339	506	162	4	145	7	381	5	0	18	34	63	8	5	0	68
Dulwich	1	107	122	11	1	17	41	33	0	1	1	10	19	2	0	0	24
Greenwich	4	99	141	166	0	18	84	425	7	1	67	26	133	1	1	24	105
Deptford	10	196	208	43	0	38	21	50	0	1	4	20	24	1	0	1	23
Woolwich	14	74	348	104	2	34	47	263	17	0	20	18	23	1	6	7	71
Lewisham	3	47	120	26	3	18	33	58	2	0	1	11	17	3	1		15
Total	1654	10852	14059	3866	150	2449	1553	9039	560	24	552	748	1371	257	181	258	2815

Source: Thirty-fourth Annual Report of the COS Council, (1901–2), pp. 56–7.

Table 4.4 Tabular statement of cases for year ending 30 September 1939 returned by District Committees

Committee	Referred to other District	Friendly visits	Enquiries for other Committees	Number of applications made	Number of applications decided	Number of applications withdrawn	Number of applications financially assisted	Number of applications otherwise assisted	Number of applications not assisted	Recommended to and assisted by Voluntary Institutions	Recommended to and assisted by Statutory Bodies	Cooperative with Public Assistance Committees	Assisted by individuals	Applicants and their relatives	Other sources of assistance	Work found	Grants for stock or equipment	Grants for removal	Psychological treatment	Medical help	Surgical appliances	Dentures	Convalescent treatment	Temporary allowances	Pensions	Provision for children	Other forms of assistance	Reports given
										Sources of help						*Some forms of assistance*												
Battersea	31	58	108	437	439	114	102	131	92	195	7	1	29	114	71	4	6	2	0	1	21	18	97	23	1	8	72	431
Bermondsey	8	26	109	790	701	75	285	187	154	478	52	39	72	84	0	7	16	9	0	8	24	49	51	71	0	71	158	436
Bethnal Green	0	5	45	273	294	81	95	35	83	125	0	0	8	30	2	2	0	1	1	8	15	18	23	5	1	1	52	298
Camberwell	67	65	195	1025	1008	243	380	201	184	502	88	18	126	155	39	4	42	21	5	20	48	74	58	112	2	41	196	999
Chelsea	6	17	113	267	233	63	83	42	45	79	15	3	6	20	17	4	9	5	3	1	9	16	16	20	2	7	58	300
Clapham	33	53	144	319	287	83	123	43	38	209	6	5	25	39	30	2	6	6	1	5	11	19	20	60	0	5	34	413
Deptford	4	53	127	325	331	46	95	136	54	186	23	5	37	42	52	9	6	10	0	13	23	28	18	17	1	14	129	337
Fulham	5	85	136	708	642	108	184	169	181	310	40	11	51	46	56	8	15	13	3	0	21	31	37	35	7	6	185	463
Greenwich	22	61	87	315	305	64	109	77	55	135	5	7	16	44	11	6	10	3	3	0	17	21	18	10	5	10	93	460
Hackney	46	48	233	420	375	105	74	60	136	141	3	2	14	27	22	6	16	1	0	0	13	14	13	16	4	7	47	280
Hammersmith	6	41	140	961	918	290	269	206	153	355	38	4	199	85	6	10	16	62	7	27	28	47	38	66	7	18	170	834
Hendon	13	47	71	284	281	60	85	62	74	94	14	17	14	50	24	2	9	5	3	0	7	24	19	20	0	27	47	301

Holborn	31	140	849	432	435	92	142	72	129	149	20	2	13	39	42	1	10	5	0	3	15	37	28	26	2	12	93	571
Islington	36	193	238	1388	1203	261	466	209	267	902	111	33	64	200	134	11	34	40	4	6	44	112	56	64	6	43	282	1536
Kensington	48	55	293	819	785	149	280	110	246	304	11	1	41	55	137	11	14	2	0	3	34	52	35	49	1	9	172	743
Lambeth, North	13	208	149	321	266	32	133	61	40	134	12	9	24	40	38	2	9	9	0	3	8	19	30	17	3	10	76	316
Lambeth, South	7	91	265	671	702	114	247	184	157	618	2	11	65	40	0	5	18	22	0	4	60	41	134	66	6	8	118	1035
Lewisham, East	6	46	76	717	621	72	294	102	153	313	30	3	15	141	35	5	32	6	0	9	36	33	73	80	1	31	94	357
Lewisham, West	8	54	69	322	316	87	92	54	83	136	19	8	23	48	25	14	2	4	3	3	11	11	18	13	3	26	32	479
Norwood	42	99	105	322	351	53	97	115	86	225	22	19	39	56	15	3	10	7	1	7	18	12	20	25	4	19	95	562
Paddington	9	69	223	874	811	219	233	103	256	256	18	2	166	41	17	0	5	22	0	2	9	28	22	34	3	16	241	868
Poplar	18	36	40	120	136	34	58	18	26	101	4	5	18	33	10	3	3	0	1	0	6	24	5	5	1	0	38	159
St Marylebone	6	26	324	329	320	72	73	77	98	111	7	3	32	31	20	0	8	6	1	2	11	15	15	13	1	11	73	341
St Pancras, North	5	97	113	686	648	113	131	223	181	342	58	2	37	48	100	6	50	11	0	6	15	22	40	72	1	13	166	779
St Pancras, South	4	46	288	521	535	156	165	72	142	293	3	0	25	47	63	3	13	7	1	1	19	36	29	41	6	14	100	273
Shoreditch	8	121	163	468	431	54	100	138	139	138	30	25	17	40	61	4	11	35	2	3	21	4	16	45	0	19	109	235
Southwark	4	74	272	686	684	226	255	137	66	557	32	12	92	145	120	11	17	27	7	3	36	84	43	32	0	19	154	1247
Stepney	55	128	60	385	354	134	103	44	63	197	21	16	49	66	20	6	6	10	1	6	10	64	28	13	0	7	57	456
Wandsworth	18	41	95	426	456	112	121	92	131	154	17	4	77	46	61	5	2	6	4	2	14	15	20	28	9	17	94	381
Westminster	25	75	574	489	445	89	130	62	164	188	11	4	40	38	28	7	29	24	3	1	23	11	23	27	2	9	52	659
Whitechapel	7	16	135	388	398	52	215	41	90	204	5	16	64	66	0	1	5	1	0	0	7	15	11	35	1	0	193	136
Total	591	2174	5839	16488	15711	13453	5219	3263	3766	8121	724	287	1498	1956	1256	167	460	341	45	139	617	994	1054	1136	74	494	3480	16685

Source: Seventy first Annual Report of London COS Council (1938–39), pp. 16–17.

Table 4.5a   COS pensions: numerical returns of pensioners assisted during the year ending 31 December of years from 1900–14, total pension expenditure during the financial 12 months ending 30 September and the approximate weekly allowance received by the average COS pensioner

Year	Data for 12 months ending 31 December					Data from 12 months ending 30 September		
	Total pensioners	Male	Female	Widows	Number over 65 years	Total value	Weekly value	
						£	s	d
1900	1259	253	1006	532	1040	16257	5	0
1901	1334	281	1053	577	1122	17719	5	1¼
1902	1276	275	1001	530	1081	18622	5	7¼
1903	1331	279	1052	549	1110	18227	5	3
1904	1274	258	1016	526	1067	19647	5	11¼
1905	1343	299	1044	546	1142	19357	5	6½
1906	1426	303	1123	589	1222	–		
1907	1374	273	1101	575	1094	20510	5	9
1908	1371	312	1059	568	1178	20688	5	9½
1909	1220	269	961	458	1001	16099	5	1
1910	1253	265	988	489	995	14842	4	6½
1911	1234	269	965	475	985	14964	4	8
1912	1286	276	1010	512	988	15228	4	6½
1913	1303	288	1015	528	1044	14868	4	4½
1914	1369	284	1085	548	1092	15323	4	4

Sources: Annual Reports of COS Council.

tested weekly state pension of 5 shillings. There was broad agreement that this was inadequate without a supplement from either savings, relatives, friends or charities. It did however provide a welcome cushion from anxiety for many old people, helping to make them 'independent for life'.[52] The OAP legislation was anathema to the COS in providing assistance regardless of a person's history. Allegedly, it wilfully discouraged thrift, did not relieve the sufferings of the poor and gave the idea that the state would eventually provide for all necessities.[53]

In spite of its resistance to the state OAP provision, the Society pragmatically advised each of its pensioners aged over 70 years to apply for the state benefit. The COS then took this into account when re-assessing how much it should pay the applicants so that they were no worse off. After 1908, the Society continued to be willing to consider new 'thoroughly deserving' cases and commended needy people who believed that they fitted this description to apply for COS support. The COS was also keen to consider short-term help to appropriate people if it avoided their having to approach the Poor Law. It claimed that similar cases of this type, where help was needed for a few months, were being referred to it by guardians and others. Provided the applicants reached 'the requisite standard of character and thrift' the Society considered that it should do its utmost to maintain them during the anxious interval between the breakdown of their own resources and the attaining of pensionable age.[54]

Table 4.5b shows the number of COS pensioners assisted during the years between 1925 to 1939 inclusive and their average weekly pension. In the years before 1925, the number of COS pensions had almost halved to 751 when compared with the 1369 who had benefited in 1914. By 1939, there had been a further decline to 569 of which

Table 4.5b COS pensions: numerical returns of pensioners assisted during the year ending 31 December of years from 1925–39, total pension expenditure during the financial 12 months ending 30 September and the approximate weekly allowance received by the average COS pensioner

Year	Data for 12 months ending 31 December					Data from 12 months ending 30 September		
	Total pensioners	Male	Female	Widows	Number over 65 years	Total value	Weekly value	
						£	s	d
1925	751	104	647	315	631	12 160	6	3
1926	777	118	659	310	624	13 664	6	9
1927	716	90	626	282	575	13 882	7	$5\frac{1}{2}$
1928	679	88	591	268	540	13 565	7	8
1929	737	100	637	285	582	13 736	7	2
1930	706	92	614	270	565	14 046	7	$7\frac{3}{4}$
1931	695	101	594	250	569	13 625	7	$6\frac{1}{2}$
1932	643	79	564	248	548	13 018	7	$9\frac{1}{2}$
1933	591	76	515	221	500	12 340	8	$0\frac{1}{4}$
1934	604	80	524	214	495	12 454	7	$11\frac{1}{4}$
1935	612	76	536	221	519	13 017	8	$2\frac{1}{4}$
1936	633	65	568	227	533	13 118	7	$11\frac{3}{4}$
1937	605	71	534	220	514	13 704	8	$8\frac{1}{2}$
1938	578	67	511	205	491	13 937	9	$3\frac{1}{4}$
1939	569	69	500	194	494	13 990	9	$5\frac{1}{2}$

Sources: Annual Reports of COS Council.

69 were male. Of the total, 287 were single women and 194 were widows. This reversed the single women:widow ratio relative to the pre-war period when widows had predominated.[55] Of the pensioners, 494 exceeded 65 years of age. While the average COS pensioner received 6s 3d in 1925 and was rather worse off in purchasing power than his pre-war predecessor, by 1939 the average pension had crept up to a more generous 9s 5½d.[56] An article in the *Charity Organisation Quarterly*, reporting on investigations of some London Boards of Guardians during 1927, showed that Poor Law relief often exceeded the typical COS pension being offered to thoroughly deserving people in the same locality. This was interpreted by the COS as indication of reckless extravagance of the Poor Law officials. But the greatest offence had been that committed by the West Ham Guardians who were not so much 'pouring two million pounds down the gutter, but mishandling the cases that came before them'.[57]

Turning now to COS finances during the twentieth century, it is interesting to first examine the comparative financial performances of the District Committees early in the century, see Table 4.6. Their revenues for the year 1901–2 indicate that the inequalities between rich and poor districts remained much the same as those deplored by the Earl of Lichfield three decades earlier, see Table 3.1, above. The richer districts of Kensington, Paddington, St George's (Hanover Square) and St Marylebone continued to attract gross revenues sufficient to meet both their administrative costs and the amounts they distributed in COS pensions, special cases, grants and returnable grants. This contrasts with poorer parishes where there was generally the need for substantial COS Council contributions to balance administrative costs which themselves were usually substantially less than those in the better-off districts. As an example, West Ham, one of the poorer districts, could only muster £26 locally towards its 1901–2 office expenses and required a top-up of £68 from a COS Council grant to meet its running bills. Similarly, St George's in the East struggled to attract £90 to offset its office costs and needed the Council's help of £112 to balance its books. In the same East End district, income for pensions was £289 and revenue for all other relief, including special cases, only totalled another £96. It is revealing to compare the relatively modest sums available where poverty was most widespread with those enjoyed by the COS in St George's Hanover Square, a much wealthier parish (and, furthermore, one which also carried the name of England's national Saint), see Table 4.6. This West End district was able to raise over £816 unaided to satisfy its high administrative costs. Donations

Table 4.6 Summary of receipts of London COS District Committees, 1901–2

	General receipts			Grants from Council			Receipts for grants and returnable grants			Pensions			Other special cases		
	£	s	d	£	s	d	£	s	d	£	s	d	£	s	d
Kensington	513	0	0		–		34	10	0	762	3	3	712	8	1
Fulham	59	4	6	60	0	0	11	9	10	349	8	10	288	2	3
Hammersmith	114	12	7	95	10	0	8	16	6	446	19	4	138	4	0
Paddington	414	13	6		–		57	8	0	1036	19	1	410	3	8
Chelsea	322	5	3		–		21	13	5	592	3	4	291	3	0
St George's (Hanover Sq.)	816	7	10		–		433	8	9	482	14	6		–	
St James's	232	14	6		–		18	6	6	427	17	4	388	10	2
St Marylebone	436	2	6		–		39	18	4	1083	7	11	576	19	5
Hampstead	286	4	6		–			–		661	2	4	546	5	9
North St Pancras	136	5	11	60	0	0	64	12	11	591	15	2	302	4	9
South St Pancras	297	8	0		–		459	13	8	916	9	5		–	
Islington	191	6	6		–		4	19	9	560	18	10	573	13	10
Holloway	61	14	6	108	17	0	8	19	0	512	18	8	319	19	0
Hackney	92	17	6	75	0	0		–		394	15	5	183	18	1
Dalston	51	7	0	132	15	0	8	7	6	113	14	0	220	19	5
City and Holborn	575	17	6		–		22	12	0	510	13	5	324	5	9
Shoreditch	94	1	3	103	0	0	3	1	0	464	5	7	265	10	9
Bethnal Green	159	13	6	19	4	6	5	0	0	273	11	9	174	1	2
Whitechapel	171	8	8		–			–		868	10	0	134	13	10
St George's East	89	19	6	111	15	0		–		286	16	6	96	0	4
Stepney	95	10	1	114	11	8	4	13	9	562	14	10	109	8	11
Mile End	99	18	0	134	17	6	131	12	6	427	9	2	156	7	10
Bow	23	10	6	182	0	0	0	9	0	388	11	6	108	17	1
Poplar	79	7	6	84	0	0	12	13	6	297	7	0	373	7	7
West Ham	26	2	0	68	0	0	31	17	10	79	6	10	56	1	9
St Saviour's	129	14	6	179	0	0	9	18	3	497	9	2	366	10	10
Newington	102	17	6	174	0	9		–		474	18	5	619	8	0
St Olave's	193	5	0		–		4	2	0	977	14	4	536	2	1
Vauxhall	124	10	1	136	0	0	14	17	8	362	12	5	255	17	4
Lambeth	129	19	0	87	10	0	3	7	0	336	7	3	345	16	8
Brixton	56	19	0	126	7	4		–		316	4	1	318	3	0
Wandsworth	159	2	0	85	0	0	11	16	0	200	4	8	412	5	0
Battersea	192	7	3		–		152	8	4	566	13	2	590	11	8
Clapham	105	1	6	30	0	0		–		352	17	6	478	5	11
Camberwell	172	13	6	55	0	0		–		448	15	4	455	7	11
Dulwich	53	0	0		–			–		220	2	10	100	13	10
Greenwich	143	3	0		–			–		90	13	6	104	9	5
Deptford	105	10	6		–		6	5	0	126	17	6	79	14	7
Woolwich	167	19	0		–		0	8	6	243	11	8	347	5	4
Lewisham	111	9	4	21	17	0	14	19	6	213	2	2	203	13	3
	7389	4	3	2224	5	9	1602	6	0	18522	18	0	11965	11	3

Source: Thirty-fourth Annual Report of the COS Council (1901–2), p. 81. For matching expenditure data by the District Committees, see ibid., p. 82.

and subscriptions topped £900 to meet the cost of the various forms of relief it distributed during the year. Income at Hanover Square was sufficient to allow it to also magnanimously contribute £75 to the Council for redistribution to poorer COS District Committees.[58]

Table 4.7 gives a summary of London COS District Committee expenditure on administration and on relief, prior to the First World War, at four-yearly intervals, namely: 1901–2, 1905–6, 1909–10 and 1913–14. It shows that between 1901–2 and 1913–14, spending on administration, euphemistically described by the COS as 'organization', grew from £17 605 to £25 634, almost a 50 per cent increase. Relief provision did not increase nearly so rapidly. The £33 204 spent on relief during 1901–2 had reached £38 604 by 1913–14, a rise of just 16 per cent, marginally exceeding the cost-of-living increase over the same period.[59] At the outbreak of war, special cases including pensions continued to account for by far the largest part of COS relief expenditure. It was much the same at Central Office although, in addition, a number of families were still being assisted to emigrate. There was an exceptional surge in COS emigration support around 1906–7, costing £13 520. Towards the end of that financial year the COS grew uneasy about the current economic downturn in the USA and how it might reflect adversely on job opportunities in Canada, destination of most COS-sponsored emigrants at that time.[60] Its concern was justified when a bad harvest led the Canadian Government to enforce stringent conditions for assisted emigration, mainly confining admission to agricultural workers. Consequently, during the following year, 1907–8, only 96 family cases were approved for emigration assistance by the COS compared with the 825 of the previous year.[61] About one-third of the emigrants in the COS bumper year of 1906–7 had been investigated and approved by the Special Investigation Committee dealing with candidates from Canning Town, Poplar and West Ham. Almost one-half of the emigrant households had a father who described himself as a 'labourer'. Among other 'Heads of Household' were bricklayers, carpenters, painters, carmen and coachmen with miscellaneous other trades making up the total.[62]

As regards the deep-seated financial problems of the COS itself, little had eased in the years prior to the Second World War. Most District Committees suffered a failure to attract local financial support. Across London, the total income attracted locally by the districts in their efforts to offset administration expenditure during the financial year 1937–38 was only £7 290.[63] Following the long-established pattern, COS districts collectively required Council grants of a further £3 467.[64]

Table 4.7 Summary of the Expenditure of the Charity Organization Society Council and London District Committees during financial years 1901–2, 1905–6, 1909–10 and 1913–14

	Expenditure on 'organization' (£s)				Cost of relief (£s)			
	1901–2	1905–6	1909–10	1913–14	1901–2	1905–6	1909–10	1913–14
Expenditure of Council Central Office:								
Special cases, etc.					512	1286	1610	1347
Pensions	5291	6869	7565	8297	238	9573	1315	497
Emigration					750	10859	2925	1844
Council total	5291	6869	7565	8297				
Expenditure of District Committees:								
General expenses	9404	10279	11445	11830				
Committee audit	210	205	221	50				
District Secretaries & agents in training	2700	3312	5273	5456				
Special work		846						
Grants					1112	467	–	–
Special cases, etc, incl. pensions					31342	37948	37744	36760
District committee Total	12314	14642	16939	17336	32454	38415	37744	36760
Gross total	17605	21511	24504	25634	33204	49274	40669	38604

Sources: Thirty-fifth, thirty-ninth, forty-third and forty-sixth Annual reports of the COS Council. *Much Central Office expenditure resulted from 'general administration' but other costs accrued from the administration of publications, medical working, almoners, emigration working, thrift and saving and district committee accounts. In Table 4.7, rounding of expenditure and relief to the nearest £ occasionally results in a slight discrepancy in totalling.

The inability of some District Committees to meet their establishment expenses had worsened. A look at the COS Council's summarized Council's Income and Expenditure General Account makes this clear, see Table 4.8. It illustrates how Central Office were having to offset the salaries and training costs of District Secretaries together with other district costs such as audit fees, National Insurance and superannuation contributions. When added to the Council grants already referred to, the accumulated district cost borne by Central Office was £10 770. This outweighed the Districts' own fund-raising efforts. The COS Council themselves would not have been capable of meeting the Districts' running costs had it not been for the 'extraordinary income'

Table 4.8 Income and Expenditure General Account for COS Council for the year ending 30 September 1938

Expenditure	(£)	Income	(£)
GENERAL EXPENSES including Central Office salaries of £2,956.	5 841	VOLUNTARY CONTRIBUTIONS	8 744
INQUIRY DEPARTMENT	752	INVESTED PROPERTY: interest and dividends	3 084
DISTRICT COMMITTEES		RECEIPTS ON ACCOUNT OF SERVICES	580
Grants £3467			
Salaries and training £7169			
Audit fees and travelling £13			
National insurance and superannuation costs £121	10 770		
LOSS ON PUBLICATIONS incl. COQuarterly, Charities Register, etc.	233	SUB-COMMITTEE ACCOUNTS	64
SUB-COMMITTEE ACCOUNTS incl. registration, medical, provincial	591	MISCELLANEOUS	492
		Balance: excess of ordinary expenditure over ordinary income	5 224
Total ordinary expenditure	18 187	Total	18 187
Balance brought down	5 224		
Balance, being excess of total income over expenditure	3 679 8 903	EXTRAORDINARY INCOME including legacies in cash and shares and gifts	8 903

Source: Seventieth Annual Report of the COS Council (1937–38), pp. 36–39.

Note: £ rounding in constituent elements of accounts occasionally results in small totalling discrepancies.

of £8903 made up mainly of legacies and the additional income of £3084 from investment interest, dividends and rent.

The inability of all but the wealthiest COS districts to attract a viable level of local support had by now continued unabated for more than half a century. The three principal sources of COS District Committee income had remained virtually unchanged over this period. They were: (a) private appeals; (b) charitable sources; and (c) payments from applicants.[65] The proportion each of these income sources contributed to the total relief of the Society in London over the ten years 1925 to 1934 for 27 of their district offices is shown in Table 4.9. Total COS income across London rose from £40 837 in 1925 to £42 514 in 1929 only to fall again by 1934 to £35 582. During this period some COS District Committees that had featured prominently in the Society's history, reached the situation where they no longer believed it worthwhile to continue to open their doors. Unlike the personal obituaries for 'old friends and supporters' which regularly featured in inter-war COS annual reports, the closure of a District Office rarely received a word of explanation. Such was the fate of a COS flagship, St George's (Hanover Square) where the early Committee had been so strident and disruptive during Council debates of the 1870s, particularly concerning the financial structure of the Society.

Of the three income sources shown in Table 4.9 for various District Committees, private appeals on average accounted for almost 30 per cent of the revenue. This included the income from generous individuals who had been touched emotionally by the unusually appealing circumstances of some specific case. The relative success of private appeals differed enormously from one COS District to another. A poor locality such as Bethnal Green might attract a mere 10 per cent of their revenue in this way. Other districts, often the wealthier ones like Chelsea and Kensington, collected around half of their relief funds from private donations.

The second avenue of COS income were charitable sources which accounted on average across the 27 districts for around half of their relief revenue. In COS terminology, charitable sources included all endowments and funds collected annually. Some of these were substantial amounts still being made available for the assistance of ex-service men and their dependants. However, there was significant variation in the contribution from this sector. Clapham and East Battersea raised more than 75 per cent of their proceeds from charitable sources whereas Norwood gained only 33 per cent.

The third main source of COS income was from the applicants themselves, their relatives and friends. Norwood managed to obtain only

Table 4.9   Monetary total and percentages of sources of relief income over a total of 10 years, 1925–34, London COS District Committees

District Committees	Monetary total (£)	Percentage of total		
		Private appeal (%)	Charitable sources (%)	Applicants' payments (%)
Battersea	13 336	29	53	18
Bermondsey	9 458	17	51	32
Bethnal Green	10 026	10	62	28
Camberwell and Dulwich	25 813	33	44	23
Chelsea	12 630	47	38	15
Clapham and East Battersea	11 155	11	76	13
Deptford	6 117	22	60	18
Fulham	15 356	32	46	22
Greenwich	6 191	28	48	24
Hackney and Stoke Newington	17 330	18	67	15
Hammersmith	11 520	34	41	25
Holborn, City and Finsbury	23 085	24	38	38
Islington and Holloway	25 089	16	66	18
Kensington	30 556	43	37	20
North Lambeth	11 755	20	62	18
South Lambeth	16 744	23	66	11
Lewishham, 1928–1934	8 537	26	49	25
Norwood and South Dulwich	11 808	57	33	10
Paddington	16 179	39	42	19
St Marylebone	9 735	33	44	23
North and South St Pancras	34 076	25	59	16
Shoreditch	13 555	27	56	17
Southwark	14 994	25	48	27
Stepney and Mile End	11 025	37	49	14
Wandsworth and Putney	9 423	41	36	23
Westminster	13 198	36	52	12
Whitechapel	6 180	35	53	12

Sources: Sixty-seventh Annual Report of COS Council (1934–35), p. 21.

10 per cent of its relief revenue by this route whereas Holborn, the City and Finsbury collected more than one-third from this route. The percentage of cases in which 'relatives and friends' had contributed increased markedly during the 1920s. Before the 1914–18 war, such cases had averaged 16 per cent of total applications but by the mid 1920s this had grown to around 40 per cent.[66]

Even the COS, blinkered members were, was as forced to recognize how relatively miniscule was its financial impact when compared with state expenditure on social benefits. The COS complained that 'it would be laughable, were it not so exasperating, to turn from the hundreds of millions spent by the state' to the relatively trivial 'exiguous sums' requested so ineffectually from the public by the COS to fund a 'competent service' from its District Offices.[67] In the 1930s, the COS was puzzled that the public were no longer prepared to believe its version of nineteenth-century society in which most poor people had contrived, while gaining great moral improvement, to overcome material shortcomings without welfare sickness benefits or a state pension. These anecdotal painful personal struggles drawn from the Victorian era were believed by the COS to have brought valuable therapeutic gains for the individual sufferers and taught them crucial lessons about the importance of independence and thrift.

At grass-roots level, not every COS worker had rosy memories about how COS attitudes had improved the condition of the Victorian poor. Gilbert Elliot, writing as a 'humble' member of a COS District Committee, said that although in the past he had seen 'much devotion and effort applied', he had also, 'from time to time' found his colleagues making decisions with which he could not approve. These were apparently made entirely 'on what are called COS principles'. Elliot criticized the Society's 'lust for indiscriminate investigation' and likened their *thoroughness* to Dickens' Mrs Squeers with a 'wooden spoon and the bowl of brimstone and treacle'.[68] T.E. Lloyd, expressing 'some observations as a COS worker', believed that originally the Society's principles were only guides to action. He alleged that they had been changed into rules that were totally binding. He instanced occasions when the COS 'never paid back rent, never helped deserted wives, never supplemented wages, and so on'. Lloyd maintained that as a consequence of these attitudes, COS committees had become 'chiefly concerned in the task of finding out how not to help their applicants'.[69]

The on-going COS difficulty which paralleled its scarcity of funds was the chronic shortage of new volunteers. This had not been alleviated by the COS's own self-imposed recruitment hurdle by which it continued to look for 'new blood', mainly at Oxford and Cambridge, long after the New Idealism of T.H. Green and Henry Sidgwick had provided cogent reasons why COS teaching must be viewed as obsolete if the sociopolitical *status quo* was to be maintained.[70] Ingrained suspicion and public dislike of its methods meant that few among the working class or lower-middle class responded to the wider-ranging COS recruitment drives that were occasionally launched. Consequently, a core weakness remaining with the Society was that 'volunteers were drawn almost entirely from the upper-middle class'.[71] The persistent shortfall in volunteer numbers was exacerbated for the COS by the difficulties associated with growing complexities in social class structures and administrative frameworks. There was an intensified need for existing COS volunteers to spend premium time in training newcomers into the evolving intricacies. The situation was then worsened by this tutorial effort being aborted when, after having become useful contributors to the COS services, the newly-trained volunteers left the Society for more amenable institutional work or for domestic reasons.

The COS was sanguine that it had struck a rich recruitment vein when Sir Charles Mallet wrote to *The Times* on 24 October 1928 proposing that men retiring from 'various services and avocations beyond the seas' might find satisfactory scope for their activities in the COS. Any limited success from Sir Charles' letter was short lived. Soon the COS was again grumbling that it was 'definitely not receiving adequate support' to relieve the 'very undue strain' volunteers were enduring in their remaining Offices. Nor were sufficient recruits forthcoming to even contemplate opening other COS Centres said to be 'urgently required' in the 'Outer Ring of London now containing $4\frac{1}{2}$ million inhabitants'. The COS admitted that, so far as people coming forward in the 1930s to support them, there was 'literally, no one available'.[72] In the 1870s, the London COS Council and District Offices had been overwhelmingly male. By the 1930s the picture had changed. Most of the District Committee Secretaries and Council representatives were female. At each of the districts of Greenwich, Hammersmith, St Pancras (North) and Westminster, even the position of District Chairman was occupied by a 'lady'.[73]

The COS Council report for 1930–31 was prefaced by an excerpt from a recent radio broadcast by the Prince of Wales which the Society had found most encouraging. Trailed by the COS under the heading *The Crisis* it warned that state-sponsored social services could be threatened by current economic exigencies. The Prince had told the country, much to the delight of the COS, that every person must realize the amenities of life, like its essentials, are best secured by personal effort and individual contributions of every member of the community. He had explained how there was not a sort of heaven-sent manna to be garnered and enjoyed without effort, service or obligation.[74] The support of the Royal Family for the COS had been unwavering. In the face of public rejection of the Society, Queen Victoria had remained their patron until her death after which Queen Mary had graced the role for many years.[75] Victoria's son, Prince Arthur of Connaught, had presided over the COS Council's annual meeting on 25 May 1914. Her daughter,

Princess Louise, Duchess of Argyll, continued as a COS Vice-President for over 50 years until her death in the late 1930s.

However, among those actually involved in 'Public Health and the Family' such as Nora Milnes, there were outspoken criticisms that a Society which 'adopts a case-front for its family case-work' and had not changed it for 20 years is proving that 'in many ways it is stagnating'. By the early 1930s, she believed the COS was 'just out of touch with the times' and interpreted their miniscule support from the younger generation as confirmation of her view. Milnes argued that 'no Society can live and flourish if it is to rely entirely upon the middle-aged and even point to the middle-aged as being the children among it'.[76]

In 1937, J.C. Pringle attempted to re-launch the basic COS concept that 'voluntary' caseworkers imparted a superior quality to social work and should be used when possible 'even if it is only to maintain STANDARDS of service'. Trained volunteers, he argued, would provide a criterion for the evaluation of the Public Social Services which by now covered 'such a large portion of the field'. Pringle was concerned about social theorists who proposed that all needs, troubles and perplexities of distressed people could be resolved by the Public Services. He doubted whether in this social climate, freshly ordained clergy and newly trained social workers could be expected to tackle individual problems in the COS manner with the *highest skill and with the most perfect understanding given to man*. Pringle thought it more likely they would follow the temptation to 'improvise some deplorably inadequate treatment, basely material in all probability and let them go at that'.[77]

COS wartime involvements with, for instance, the CAB and Legal Advice Centres, saw the Society putting patriotism before principle. It provided the Society with a much-needed boost in morale and in public awareness. The COS was now accepting, if temporarily, the reality that most services needed by the citizen were directed by central or local government. What is more, the Society was actually devising and implementing ways of advising enquirers, whether deserving or non-deserving, how to make effective use of wide-ranging public services. It became clear that the even more complex range of social services planned for the post-war period, would present the COS with the dilemma of modifying its principles permanently or of facing oblivion. The Society was not without advisors, including the uninvited though well-meaning. Writing an open letter to the COS in 1943, Cherry Morris predicted that after the war social workers and social work agencies would have a large part to play in building a 'brave new world'. She believed that COS workers themselves recognized that 'drastic, even revolutionary' changes were necessary if the Society were to rise 'pheonix-like out of the ashes, revivified and certainly renamed' to seize the opportunity to help those in distress and to train students both for state and voluntary service. Morris complained that far too much time was being spent in COS offices on detailed, 'indeed ponderous investigation', for the performance of small services under a name 'so obnoxious to modern ears and the principle of deterrence'. She pleaded for an urgent COS re-think so as to achieve more 'flexibility' and a better 'sense of proportion' because such a 'chance will never come again'.[78]

Benjamin E. Astbury had succeeded the Rev. Pringle as London COS Secretary on his death in 1938 after having held a number of posts within the organization since 1930. He had a very different background from his predecessors. One of eleven children, he lacked public school or a full-time university education. After being invalided out of the Army, he gained practical experience about the condition of the poor, principally as Secretary to the Council of Social Welfare in Chester.[79] Astbury replied to Cherry Morris's call for the Society to re-think its social role with the claim that 'all and, indeed, more than the points raised by Miss Morris' had already occupied the 'close attention and consideration' of the Society. 'The vexed question of a change of name' had evidently taken priority but older COS members remained 'strongly of the opinion that much of the "goodwill" of the Society would be lost in any change of title'. On the other hand it was said to be clear that present-day clients disliked the word 'charity' and that there had eventually been agreement that 'the Society shall change its name at an appropriate time'.[80] With refreshing realism, Astbury recommended that voluntary societies should face the fact that the state would in future undertake fuller responsibilities for the needs of its citizens. He believed that voluntary societies should therefore:

(a) be prepared to take their share in initiating reforms in the social services;
(b) press for employment of trained social workers in those services;
(c) endeavour to eliminate overlapping among themselves; and
(d) engage in pioneering work as far as possible.

Astbury also accepted the need for improving committee procedure, training of students and reviewing office management. However, his awareness of the COS's parlous financial circumstances led him to remind members that filing cabinets, typewriters and duplicators cost a 'considerable amount of money'. He warned that because the COS had to count every penny, each item would need to be carefully considered.[81]

Whether Astbury's reply to Morris's call for radical COS changes was as convincing as she would have wished is doubtful. There was nevertheless a clear acceptance from Astbury that he, at least, now recognized the undeniable need for all post-war voluntary societies to find an accommodation with what would inevitably be an even more interventionist state.

Throughout the Second World War there had been no hiding the fact that 'the ordinary expenditure' of the COS Council was regularly exceeding its 'ordinary income'. Although during 1941–42, the Council had been 'greatly encouraged' by the 'gracious and generous action of His Majesty the King in doubling the amount of his subscription', the Council's satisfaction merely clouded the underlying reality that year after year the financial accounts of London COS were in deficit, see Table 4.10.[82] In 1943–44, the Society lamented that their ordinary income was 'no greater than it was 30 years ago while its obligations and commitments are more extensive'.[83] Two years later, and by now functioning as The Family Welfare Association, the deficit of ordinary income compared with ordinary expenditure of £15 489 was seen to be 'critical', although partially offset by extraordinary income. This included revenue from the première of a film (*The Bells of St Mary's*) as well as the more conventional legacies, special donations and other extraordinary items.[84] The deficit seemed to drop to £9803 during 1947–48, doubtless helped by the presentation of the published accounts being 're-arranged'.[85] By 1948–49, any effects of creative

Table 4.10 London Charity Organization Society: Ordinary Expenditure compared with Ordinary Income during and post the Second World War

Financial year *1 October to 30 September*	*Excess: ordinary expenditure over* *ordinary income (£)*
1939–40	4 681
1940–1	4 487
1941–2	7 175
1942–3	10 115
1943–4	8 817
1944–5	9 765
1945–6	15 489
1946–7	21 304
1947–8	9 803
1948–9	27 070
1949–50	2 915

Source: Data extracted from Annual Reports of the London COS Council.

accounting had worn off and business consultants were appointed to advise on further economies. By the time their plan was approved in August 1949 it was already 'apparent even more drastic action was necessary'.[86] Rationalization pruned London activities down to 9 Areas and one District in Hendon. Even then the Society incurred a deficit for the year of £2915. The necessary offices and operational funding for the CABs and Advice Centres continued to be provided by the appropriate municipal and government departments.

There had been something of a psychological boost for the COS from William Beveridge when he addressed the London COS's Seventy-fifth Jubilee Meeting in 1944. He said that the 'main doctrine of their Society is based on humanity and reason' and that the only help which is worth giving is 'that which is adequate and restorative'. Beveridge told his audience that whatever the state did there would remain 'scope for personal help' and for a society like the COS that would make 'charity constructive and healing'. The Society was heartened that the 'author of the State schemes for "organised general provision to prevent distress"' could make such encouraging comments. Thus, especially at a time when it was itself reviewing its own function and structure to meet the demands of a new social order which, 'during its seventy-five years of pioneering work, it had done so much to bring into being'.[87]

Chapter 6 of this book takes up how, long before Beveridge's post-war pleasantries, COS social rigidities had attracted an irretrievable accumulation of public mistrust. The Society's good points, of which there were a number, had largely been forgotten in the cloud of suspicion surrounding most of their pronouncements. The favourable aspects of COS social organization and training had stood them in good stead at times of exceptional distress such as when managing the Lord Mayor of London's nineteenth-century Appeals. When the fabric of London society was again under serious threat in the late 1930s it was the same COS organizational skills that were called into play by the Establishment. The COS fulfilled the task asked of it with characteristic determination. Unfortunately for its own future, the COS was not sufficiently pragmatic to modify its ideas towards compatibility with the needs of an emerging modern nation.

5
Charity Organization outside London

The flame of charity organization spread rapidly. In the UK, by the turn of the nineteenth century, close to 100 towns and cities had formed a COS. Some provincial groups started from scratch; others, from existing societies, were keen to change their format to that advocated by the London COS. Overseas, the interest shown in COS methodology was phenomenal. In Germany, where some COS roots have been detected, rapid early growth took place in major cities. But it was in the USA that COS methodology took hold most strongly. During the early decades of the twentieth century, few American towns lacked their own COS. How this USA enthusiasm developed strongly and then declined in the 1930s is largely the subject of the second part of this chapter.

Britain's provincial centres soon took steps to follow the London COS. The message of charity organization that circulated from the late 1860s around London was taken up in the provinces and beyond. By March 1873 there were six 'country associations' affiliated to the metropolis. These COSs were located at Brighton, Chester, Eton, Kingston upon Thames, Oxford and Scarborough. During the quarter ending 29 March 1873 they had together 'dealt with' a total of 437 cases. Of these they had assisted 129 applicants, referred 134 elsewhere and 'dismissed' 174, mainly because the latter were judged to be 'undeserving' or 'ineligible'.[1] Existing charities were also being re-organized along COS lines at Birkenhead, Reigate and Winchester.[2] From 1872 onwards the London COS issued a number of 'County Papers'. They included, *Suggestions on the best Method of Organising Local Charity Associations with Offices as contemplated by the Society for the Organising of Charitable Relief and Repressing Mendicity*. Attached to this pamphlet were price-lists of 'appropriate' stationery which embryo COSs could obtain from London. They included drafts of printed invitations and handbills announcing a projected public meeting, preliminary circulars, envelopes from sub-scribers, sheets of tickets (numbered and unnumbered) and placards, all of which could be bought in lots of 500 or 1000. Each COS propaganda item had blank spaces to be completed with appropriate local names, venues and other particulars.[3]

Between 1875 and 1914, there was a steady build up in the number of provincial COSs and similar institutions supporting their principles, see Table 5.1. By the turn of the century 66 Charity Organization Societies operated within the UK. These, together with other institutions func-tioning with the blessing of London COS, made a grand total of 96 nationwide. Most big towns had their own organizing group by this time. Some were successors to prominent Societies – already involved in providence, relief or mendicity – who had decided to augment their existing operations with the concepts of investigation and charity organization. Among the most prominent of these were the Liverpool Central Relief Society and the Manchester and Salford District Provident Society. During the early twentieth century the number of COSs

Table 5.1　Provincial Societies organizing charity to the methodology approved by the COS Council in London and 'in correspondence' with them

| Year | *COS*[1] | *Title of Provincial Society* | | | | |
		Mendicity Society[2]	*Association for the poor*[3]	*Inquiry address*[4]	*'others'*[5]	*Grand total*
1875	12					12
1880	49	18	7	–	18	92
1885	51	11	7	–	16	85
1890	62	8	6	–	16	92
1895	64	7	6	–	18	95
1900	66	3	7	2	18	96
1905	71	3	5	10	19	119
1910	91	3	7	11	29	141
1914	88	3	6	12	36	145

Sources: Annual reports of London COS Council.

Notes:

[1]Includes all societies with 'charity organization' in their title, also Associations for Organizing Charitable Relief.

[2]Includes all societies with mendicity in their title other than those already covered by also possessing 'charity organization', see (1) above.

[3]Associations for Improving the Condition of the Poor (mainly located in Scotland).

[4]Addresses to which 'inquiries may be sent'.

[5]'Others' include Charitable Societies, District Visiting Societies, Central Aid Societies and Relief Associations.

expanded further. The rate of increase was particularly sharp between 1900 and 1910 with two counties showing strong COS growth, Lancashire and Yorkshire. These were also the counties where newly-formed Guilds of Help and similar groups were in fact blossoming even more strongly, something we will discuss shortly.[4]

Most early provincial Committees fought shy of becoming formally affiliated to their London COS Council. While they could not avoid being the recipients of London's powerful pronouncements on principles, provincials tended to shrink from being more intimately embroiled with the centre than was necessary and preferred to retain the less onerous 'in correspondence' status.[5] This reduced the possibility of the central COS Council pressurizing them into producing more statistics and reports on top of their already formidable paperwork burden. They also knew, particularly in the early decades, that provincial data were closely examined by COS pundits in 15 Buckingham Street, WC. They were then often used as targets for scathing comments from the metropolis about the alleged shortcomings of their country cousins in falling short of COS principles. By 1890, of the 62 provincial COSs then existing in the United Kingdom, only 25 were federated or affiliated to London. Eventually, the formal use of these divisive COS categories was dropped.[6] Not all provincial groups listed by the London COS Council as being kindred spirits on matters of charity organization chose to carry the acronym COS, see Table 5.1, above. Scottish organizing Societies often adopted the title 'Associations for Improving the Condition of the Poor'. In South East England they frequently described themselves as 'Central Aid Societies' while others were known as 'Mendicity Societies'.[7] The geographical distribution of the 96 Societies approved by London COS at the turn of the century was as follows:[8]

Cities and towns in England, Wales and the Channel Isles 77
Cities and towns in Scotland 10
Cities and towns in Ireland 3
County associations in Ayrshire, Dorset, Gloucestershire,
 Herefordshire, Wiltshire and Worcestershire 6

During the 1880s the occasional conference of provincial UK organizing Societies was assembled by the London COS. The conference at Oxford in October 1890 was judged to be such a great success as to become the forerunner of a more frequently held series of conferences. After the conference in London during May 1893, annual conferences then tended to be held at other venues, including Rochdale, Cheltenham, Leicester, Glasgow and Clifton (Avon). To retain control of activities 'in the country' and to ensure that conference discussion did not stray from the correct ideological furrow, the London COS Council had formed the Provincial Sub-Committee in March 1892. Its active Honorary Secretary, Nevil Masterman, generated a great deal of two-way correspondence between London and the provinces. He made numerous visits out of town during which he strongly encouraged provincial COS members to attend and learn from London office procedures.[9]

The recruitment of COS visitors was always a festering problem in the provinces in much the same way as that suffered in many London districts. In what had remained a male-dominated institution throughout the nineteenth century, there was usually not much encouragement for ladies to progress within the Society. Only a famous few, possessing exceptional personal qualities such as Octavia Hill, Henrietta Barnett and Helen Bosanquet (née Dendy), in London, defied the convention whereby the COS provided only subsidiary roles for the fair sex. Even then the cynic could point to how both Barnett and Bosanquet owed some measure of their success to the prominence of their husbands. Indeed, neither woman would have disputed the advantage gained from their domestic association.

The sexist tone of provincial COS operations generally can be gauged from the attitude of the Rev. R.P. Hooper, Vice-Chairman of Brighton COS. He had 'serious' doubts about using any ladies for the 'important' task of COS visiting. His own experience had convinced him that 'ladies working among the poor were apt to wish to help undeserving cases' and as a consequence were 'habitually deceived by the poor'. Hooper described how seemingly destitute cases had been materially assisted by the Society's lady visitors only for their male agent colleague to discover the recent beneficiary 'revelling in porter and beefsteak'.[10] In accord with this male chauvinism, neither Brighton COS nor Rochdale COS had female Committee members.[11] Leamington COS went a stage further by forming themselves into 'a purely male Society' in 1893.[12] It is hardly surprising that Nevil Masterman had to admit that having studied 'the annual reports of about ninety provincial societies' he had found that 'only five or six seemed to employ lady volunteers to any considerable extent', other than in the simplest of tasks.[13]

In the COS's formative years, social structures had allowed provincial gentlemen to take on the unsalaried role of Hon. Sec. At that time, the few provincial secretarial representatives who were women were isolated. They included Cambridge, where Lady Wilson shared the chore with the Rev. A.P. Wodehouse and Leicester COS where Mrs Edward Paget and Miss H. Ellis divided the office responsibilities three ways with G.H. Blunt Esq. By 1914 a totally different picture existed. The recruitment of lady visitors still held considerable difficulties but the problem of attracting gentlemen to fill the secretarial role without recompense was virtually insurmountable. As a consequence, the number of salaried female provincial COS secretaries, each requiring a lower salary than would a male counterpart, jumped sharply upwards in the twentieth century.[14] Even this state of affairs was not achieved easily. As persistent problems remained in filling vacancies at London COS district offices, there was little surprise in Council that there was also 'a dearth of trained candidates for provincial appointments'.[15] When vacancies were filled, the female appointees frequently did not view them as long-term opportunities, causing COS provincial administration to be often in a state of flux. During and after the First World War this situation worsened. By 1935 the centralized Associated Societies Committee, responsible for liaison between London COS Council and the provinces, had only three men among its 15 members.[16]

The increase in the number of provincial COSs during the early years of the twentieth century did nothing to inhibit the mushrooming of miscellaneous charities engaged in haphazardly assisting the poor. Nationally, the economic outlook was bleak. The 1903–4 winter found 31 soup kitchens operating in Manchester and Salford. Increased numbers of night shelters were opened in the same locality for homeless out-of-work men. They included the Wood Street Mission hostel which the long-established District Provident Society, in carrying the COS banner locally, viewed as 'notorious' for not applying any 'test of worthiness'. Other shelters for the homeless in the Manchester and Salford area were provided by charitable groups such as the Church Army and the Salvation Army both of whom were perceived by charity organizers as being thoroughly irresponsible.[17]

The widening poverty in a depressed economy, and the deplorable condition of the poor around the turn of the century, exercised the minds of decision-makers inside and outside Parliament. The Edwardian well-to-do could scarcely help being disturbed by factors such as: the meagre physical calibre of men recruited for the Boer War, the persistence of distressingly high levels of infant mortality, the moral degeneracy among the urban poor and the appalling environmental squalor revealed by such as Seebohm Rowntree and Charles Booth.[18] Long-term unemployment problems began to impinge on the lives of citizens hitherto widely recognized as being respectable and good-living. MPs became worried about spreading dissatisfaction leading to public order disturbances in major conurbations. Labour registers, launched by some provincial COSs, assembled, for the perusal of employers, details of unemployed workers they had investigated and found to be 'respectable'. The lengthening of the out-of-work lists confirmed the deepening trough of despair associated with unemployment. As regards relief, provincial COSs were only prepared to help 'want of work' cases who were married men with families, were of good character and were likely to obtain work in the immediate future.[19]

There was disquiet among some middle-class factions on the appointment of the 1905 Royal Commission on the Poor Laws by the outgoing Conservative administration. This was because the Liberal Party had already hinted that, should they come to power, they would build on the precedence of Chamberlain's 1886 Act and use unstigmatized state assistance to replace traditional voluntary initiatives for assisting disadvantaged groups. Progressive citizens argued that it was no longer appropriate to depend entirely on charitable whim to support the needy. Worrying words like 'socialism' and 'collectivism' were sufficiently in the public domain to disturb and alert better-off sections of the community about a potential threat from a dissatisfied workforce. In this social climate, it is hardly surprising that the early twentieth century saw various reactionary groups across the country stung into mounting last ditch attempts to convince national and local governments that, as volunteers, they could effectively monitor, rationalize and organize support for the poor in their own locality. In addition to the various Societies listed in Table 5.1, above, and accepted by the COS as working within their rigorous rules, other groups were emerging unilaterally which the COS were unwilling to authenticate as genuine participants in their own methodology. In spite of the differences perceived by the COS, to the cursory observer, the emergent Societies shared many of their ideas, especially those involving co-ordination of charitable activities. Prominent among these nascent groups, particularly in the industrial North and the West Midlands, were the Guilds of Help.[20] These mainly comprised middle-class provincials keen to improve the condition of the poor but unwilling to apply the more rigorous unpopular COS attitudes. The Guilds' spontaneous growth, sparked by the prevailing climate of change, may be regarded as a turning-point in the history of social service.[21] The enthusiastic public acceptance of the Guilds' more conciliatory responses emphasized the withdrawal from the old order. The implicit assumption that improvement in the condition of the deserving poor should be the exclusive preserve of a socially favoured class entirely responsible for formulating the rules of benefit was increasingly shunned.[22]

The first Guild of Help was launched during 1904 in Bradford where the local COS were said to have been 'quite inadequate' in solving the widespread poverty and atrocious housing.[23] The Guild soon flourished and imitative units followed rapidly in surrounding urban conurbations.[24] Within five years there were more than 60 Guilds of Help, mainly concentrated in towns away from the south east. They claimed great success in recruiting 'eager' volunteers.[25] Of the 83 Guilds functioning by 1917, the vast majority remained in a stand-off situation with the London COS and its acolytes.[26]

A conceptual similarity between the Guilds of Help and the COS was that both claimed theoretical roots in the Elberfeld system.[27] Bradford Guild of Help interpreted the Elberfeld administrative procedures for practical use in the UK by arranging themselves into four divisions, each with ten districts. With ten helpers to each district together with a district head and secretary, the Bradford Guild needed to recruit 450 helpers.[28] Other cities and towns planning to institute Guilds of Help were similarly dissected and organized according to population size. Larger cities like Manchester and Sheffield required more than four divisions so that each local Guild in centres of this size needed to muster a total of around 1000 volunteers. This was a tall order but there were claims that, for a while at least, recruitment levels were sufficiently encouraging to maintain the momentum of the projects. The same enthusiastic climate was claimed for smaller conurbations such as Halifax, Middlesbrough and Croydon, each theoretically requiring 200 to 300 helpers. Such arrays of personal helpers had been the unfilled aspirations of the COS movement for more than 30 years. An example of how far some of those still flying the COS banner had been driven by volunteer shortages to depart from the organizational ideal emanating from London, was indicated by the Manchester and Salford District Provident Society (DPS) which mainly conducted their charity 'organizational' relief work from one centre, in Deansgate.

W. Milledge, Secretary of the Bradford City Guild of Help, described the purpose of his organization as being 'a method of popularizing the best aims of the COS'.[29] These comments annoyed Leicester COS. They urged that 'no notice should be taken' of the misleading implications behind Milledge's remarks. The London COS attempted to remain disdainfully cool about those newcomers who, they believed, degraded the principle of charity organization. COS frustration at losing ground relative to the newcomers was shrouded in the delusory belief that for them to achieve popularity, they must first 'raise torpid public opinion up to its own lofty level'.[30]

Although there were distinct similarities between the social aims of the Guilds of Help and the COS, there were also fundamental differences between the emergent 'New Philanthropy' and the 'Old Philanthropy' associated with the COS.[31] One difference was that the New Philanthropists, as represented by the Guilds of Help, adopted positive attitudes towards working harmoniously with public bodies. Secondly, each Guild was genuinely free to tailor their affairs to match local requirements.[32] Thirdly, the Guild movement displayed more respect for the environmental plight of poor people, accepting that faults in societal structures could cause poverty.[33] A fourth difference was that the Guilds fostered 'local patriotism' in an endeavour to 'create an interest in all matters of local importance'.[34] This 'community' view of the Guilds aimed at attracting men and women, irrespective of class or creed or 'scientific' knowledge of social problems. Guilds invited all people of goodwill to combine in combating 'the misery and destitution of their fellow citizens'.[35] A fifth crucial difference, and what made them especially attractive to the public at large while guaranteeing their rejection by COS pundits, was that Guilds of Help put less emphasis on 'real inquiry'. Charles Loch icily blamed the Guilds' more conciliatory investigative attitude on their naiveté. He forecast that 'in time' they would come into line with the COS on the subject.[36] The Guilds' reply expounded the view that whereas the COS believed those who sought charity should prove under investigation that they were deserving of support, they themselves, as Guilds of Help, proactively sought potential cases for their friendship.[37]

Laybourn has claimed that by 1910, in northern towns, the Guild movement had already surpassed in size and equalled the influence of the COS.[38] Opposition to the Guilds by COS supporters was said by W.M. Boscoby to arise from the 'fundamental principle of jealousy'.[39] Charles Loch remained annoyed by the Guilds' failure to conform with COS principles. He pointed out that in some places Guilds were actually 'attempting to be the organizing society' while elsewhere they were competing head-on with COS stalwarts. Seeing the ominous writing on the wall arising from the strong surge of interest in the Guilds of Help and similarly motivated groups, the London COS sent them invitations calling for joint action. Naturally, there was the COS understanding that the newcomers would conform to the proven stricter principles of the established COS. Loch even offered the concession that, since there was common ground, the COS and the Guilds of Help should 'join hands or divide the work between them and so advance to make a more complete organisation'.[40] A few Guilds were attracted by Loch's overture but most were apprehensive about entering joint harness with the spurned COS. They surmised that such an association carried the danger of impeding their own public image, especially in localities where the COS brand of charity organization had been tried and had failed. The Guilds also suspected that were they to become associated with the COS, future friction was likely with a supposedly equal partner who on past experience, would have little compunction about depicting themselves as being superior.[41]

An impression of the discord that simmered between the COS and the Guild movement at local level can be gauged from events on Merseyside. Shortly after the Bradford experiment got underway, W. Grisewood, the experienced Secretary of the old-established Liverpool Central Relief Society (CRS), who were affiliates of the London COS, epitomized the attitude of charity organizers. He conceded that 'friendly visiting' by the Guilds of Help did provide the advantage of bridging the 'chasm between the poor and the well-to-do'. However, in Grisewood's opinion, they failed to meet the main point of controlling and regulating 'the actual administration of relief in its main channels of Poor Law relief and voluntary charity as to direct it to the advancement, material and moral, of its recipients'.[42] It was hardly surprising therefore that when the Liverpool Council of Voluntary Aid (CVA) was formed in May 1909, having close links with the Guilds of Help movement, they were not welcomed by the CRS. F.G. D'Aeth who had worked tirelessly for years in the poorest sections of the City, was the first CVA secretary. He soon experienced nothing but lukewarm recognition from the CRS. They perceived the Council of Voluntary Aid as transgressors into what they had viewed as being their own specialized social territory. CRS truculence was still dominant when, in 1918, Dorothy Keeling became Secretary of the CVA's Personal Service Committee. She quickly became aware of possible administrative differences with the CRS but hardly bargained for the intense obstructionism which did materialize. Two points of conflict rumbled on throughout the 1920s. First was the intense CRS criticism levelled personally at Keeling for assisting wives deserted by their husbands. Second was that the CRS remained adamant that applicants should always first be divided into the 'deserving' and the 'undeserving', regardless of the immediacy of their personal plight.

To the intense annoyance of the CRS, the Council of Voluntary Aid's more lenient policy proved much the more popular throughout the city. So much so that a decade later, after nearly 70 years of service to Merseyside, the CRS accepted that their influence had mortally waned.

They ceased independent operations at the close of 1931 to become subsumed into the Liverpool Personal Service Society (as it became known) with Keeling fully responsible for all enquiry, relief and almoner work.[43] Birmingham COS had found themselves in a not dissimilar position as early as 1908. An emergent Aid Society formed from a reorganization of various West Midland Societies committed to working along Guild of Help lines were soon attracting more workers than the COS.[44]

Although the Guilds' more flexible approach to social problems allowed them make impressive early progress, albeit regionally, their efforts were insufficient to convince state decision-makers that, after the First World War, the organized voluntary sector could sensibly be left to resolve alone the mounting number of social problems. Nevertheless, in retrospect, the Guilds can be recognized as a useful transitional mode between the COS's Victorian rigour and the less austere welfare approaches that were to follow. The Guilds of Help turned out to be bright but non-expansive stars. Laybourn describes them as a brief 'heroic attempt to make philanthropy far more effective, efficient and sympathetic'. At the cessation of the 1914–18 hostilities, Whitehall initiated a restructuring of social institutions leading to the 'effective demise' of Guilds of Help as an independent force.[45] The establishment in 1919 of the National Council of Social Service (NCSS), with its objective of formulating national policies for voluntary work in co-operation with the state, led to the Guild movement becoming a willing participant in a novel venture.[46] In the post-war period, when the National Association of Guilds of Help were approached by the NCSS about possible co-operation, they fell into line to the 'fullest extent'. Realistically, they accepted that they would fast become but a constituent part of the newly formed body although in localities where they were particularly strong it was agreed that, for the benefit of the public, Guilds could continue under their original banner.[47]

Before the end of the First World War the COS movement throughout the United Kingdom was creaking badly. The London COS Provincial Sub-Committee reported that it was 'very greatly to be regretted' that some COS outposts who had 'done most useful work in the past' were now finding it necessary either to 'suspend their work or to close down altogether'.[48] Other provincial COSs, including those at Reading, Wimbledon, Croydon and Kingston upon Thames, kept themselves afloat by fusing with diverse 'Civic Movements' to form Councils of Social Welfare. It was not surprising that these provincial COSs did decide to co-operate with the social service councils because during preparatory meetings leading to the formation of the NCSS, the COS had been actively represented by the Rev. J.C. Pringle, F. Morris Esq. and Miss Thompson. Indeed, Margaret Brasnett recalled the important COS contribution in helping to develop an appropriate NCSS constitution.[49] Then, in careless disregard of their own diminishing influence as a front-line social force, the London COS got cold feet when the moment of decision came to become permanently associated with the NCSS. The COS Council decided to retain their independence despite the awareness that they would be standing even further adrift from the mainstream voluntary sector. Here was yet further indication of how the COS's obduracy regarding the inviolability of their own principles acted against their long-term interests. Their increasingly isolated position had been deepened. Post-war, the COS again became a social leper, largely shunned by other charities and by government agencies. What is more, without the responsive ear of government that they had once enjoyed, they had no reasonable hope of again becoming a major contributor to future debate on social conditions. The stumbling block remained as before: the COS Council could not envisage being part of an organization where they themselves were not the final arbiter of decisions. Whereas the COS claimed a willingness to 'seek co-ordination with official agencies in all possible ways' they could never accept a scenario where they may be subordinate to them.[50] As discussed in Chapter 4, under the future emergency circumstances associated with the Second World War, the NCSS and the COS later worked effectively together on specific ventures. These included the establishment of the Citizens Advice Bureaux (CAB) where the NCSS found themselves involved in a relationship to which the COS's contribution was 'friendly but aloof'.[51] The COS's abhorrence of indiscriminate charity remained undiminished. They continued to promulgate their unfashionable message to a dwindling audience. The COS's abrasive attitude guaranteed the continued 'odium of all those who could see no reason why a man, finding himself in need through no fault of his own, should be refused help'.[52]

The outcome of inter-war institutional changes in the voluntary sector in the United Kingdom and Northern Ireland can be gathered from Figure 5.1. Other than relating to a later period, these data are from similar COS sources to those used in Table 5.1, above.[53] The later data expose that, with so many of their 'approved' provincial societies having disappeared, largely through lack of support, the COS had been forced to modify their public stance, at least superficially. To present a more favourable image of the condition of the charity organization

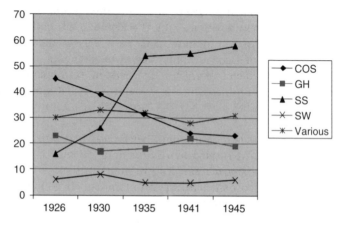

Figure 5.1   Charity Organization Societies, Councils of Social Service, Guilds of Help and other societies in the UK.

Sources: Data from the appropriate *Annual Charities Register and Digest.* Note that, in the Figure, due to lack of data, the years 1926 and 1941 have been substituted as representing years, for the years 1925 and 1940 respectively.

Key: COSs = Charity Organization Societies including the Liverpool CRS; the Manchester and Salford DPS and COS Enquiry Offices; GH = Guilds of Help; SS = National Council of Social Service; SW = Social Welfare Associations; 'Various' includes Central Aid Societies, Associations for Improving the Condition of the Poor, etc.

movement in Britain and to camouflage their own decline, the COS now included the group names of provincial organizers of charity groups which, as the COS knew all too well, had not the slightest intention of accepting their own rigorous format, see Figure 5.1, above. At the same time, the COS adopted a conciliatory façade stating that it was 'obvious the standard and method of casework cannot be every-where the same'.[54] Such a concession on the part of the COS would never have been contemplated prior to 1914. Even now it did not sig-nal a genuine change in the attitude of COS policy-makers but did imply recognition that their charisma had lost much of its gloss. By 1926 only 42 provincial COSs remained from more that twice that number pre-war. During the next 20 years COS numbers in the provinces gradually trickled away. At the end of the Second World War there were a mere 23 provincial COSs in Britain. As their supporters fell by the wayside, the London COS circulated their shrinking numbers with a rallying memo 'emphasising our common principles'.[55]

Not surprisingly, the social welfare institution that progressed most in Britain during the 1920s and 1930s was the NCSS. Starting afresh in a post-war period of goodwill and unhampered by outdated social theory, the NCSS established its own public image as the dominant co-ordinating body.[56] They gradually spread their influence through the major cities and towns in the United Kingdom. Other than the COS, most institutions committing themselves in any way to the organization of charity became associated with the NCSS. Where local groups continued to use their previous title, such as some Guilds of Health and Social Welfare Associations, they are shown separately in Figure 5.1, above. These groups, together with those included as 'Various', such as the Central Aid Society, the Associations for Improving the Condition of the Poor and the Mendicity Societies, broadly retained their representation across Britain during the inter-war years.

Finance was always a recurring problem for those attempting to keep the COS flag aloft in the provinces during the 1920s and the 1930s. The London COS Associated Societies Committee (successor to the COS Provincial Sub-Committee) was regularly confronted with 'very critical' financial situations. Struggling COSs throughout the country found 'it very difficult to carry on their work through lack of money'.[57] Provincial COSs earlier 'formed in high hopes' had 'not survived'. Those contriving to cling to existence were reported by London COS to be facing 'all the difficulties due to the shifting of the fulcrum' of Britain's social structure.[58] As the provincial network withered, in number and in quality, so the London COS Associated Societies Committee's reports endeavoured to comment enthusiastically on what positive items that could be dredged from the deepening gloom. One edifying piece of news was the appointment as Lord Mayor of Leicester of W.E. Hincks, Secretary of the local COS. London COS described him as 'the most effective municipal worker and leader in Leicester'. They even extolled him as being 'the wisest and most forceful personality' of the COS movement throughout the country.[59] This was indeed a rare accolade for the COS central caucus to confer upon someone outside of their own tight circle.

Worsening COS finances in London meant that pruning became essential in the central organizational structure that dealt with the provinces. When Miss Marsland, the COS's 'capable' travelling secretary, retired in 1929, financial stringency made 'it impossible' for her 'valuable function' to be perpetuated. London COS had no doubt that should a 'suitable person' be found as her replacement and the money made available 'for salary and expenses' the benefit would be large to 'all engaged in Charity Organisation'.[60] Ten years after Miss Marsland's retirement, the COS Council were still pleading fruitlessly to their well-heeled members that 'the desirability of having a visitor able to go round in the country is very urgent'.[61]

As late as 1937 the COS Council in London indulged themselves in the delusion that nationally they were setting up a 'rich network of cross-connections between the multitude of dispositions' in social service. They claimed to be committed towards weaving 'proliferating systems into a connected mass'.[62] Such misleading propaganda was circulated among the faithful when the COS were well aware about the reality of their declining social influence. They knew, for example, that while they were publishing extravagant claims about burgeoning provincial activities, the Charity Organization Societies of Skipton, Shrewsbury and York were being forced to close their doors through lack of financial support and a dearth of willing volunteers.

Charity organization overseas

The concept of charity organization, as formulated by the COS Council in London, proved to be enormously attractive overseas. Information about the names and addresses of 'colonial and foreign' societies practising charity organization were published regularly from 1882 as part of London COS's annual report. Organizing Societies were shown to be operating in Britain's major colonies, including: Australia, Canada, India, New Zealand and South Africa (Natal); across Europe in: 'Austro-Hungary', Belgium, Denmark, France, Germany, Greece, Holland, Italy, Russia, Spain, Sweden, Norway, Turkey (Istanbul) and in the USA. After the initial surge in the number of countries attracted by the organizing concept, further international expansion outside this range of countries virtually ground to a halt, see Figure 5.2. During the early 1880s, the countries outside Britain that had most COS offshoots were: Germany (29 branches), France (19 branches) and the USA (18 branches). During this period it was in the USA where London's influence was to become most marked and it is here that we will mainly concentrate. At the turn of the century there were over 130 urban groups across the United States which were associated with the charity organization movement. By the outbreak of the First World War, that number had doubled, see Figure 5.2. Delegates from organizing societies in the USA and elsewhere overseas were welcomed with open arms at COS jamborees in the UK.[63] Similarly, United States conferences were often instructed by COS 'experts' from Britain.[64]

The advance of charity organization in the USA was encouraged by the social environment where many Americans believed themselves to be part of a land dripping with honeyed opportunity. The majority who were doing well rarely had time to realize that national prosperity had not seeped through to all levels of society. Many of those among

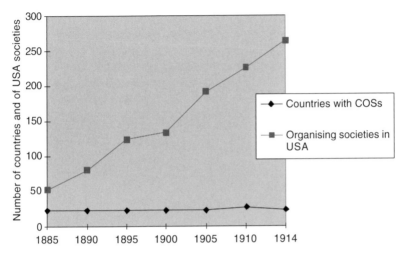

Figure 5.2 Number of countries outside Britain with organizing societies and the number of such societies in the United States

Sources: *Annual Reports of the London COS Council.*

the middle classes who did occasionally become concerned about the plight of the less fortunate decided that the poverty-stricken must be suffering privation as a direct result of their own indolence, improvidence or addiction to alcohol. Well-to-do Americans in the nineteenth century often encouraged the impression that degenerates should be shunned as either being victims of irrecoverable hereditary misfortune or because they were guilty of inexcusable laziness. These parallels with the traditional attitudes paramount in the old country are not surprising. Imported into the USA with earlier British settlers were ideas that had initiated many of the early American institutions concerned with the condition of the poor. The influence of the Old English Poor Law still showed itself across the USA in a jumbled concoction of local almshouses. Into these disparate institutions, lacking the conformity attempted with the 1834 Poor Law Amendment in England, were herded the 'old and the young, the sick and the well, the mentally normal and the mentally deranged, the epileptic, the blind, the alcoholic and the criminal'.[65] Only in the 'most general sense' was it possible to speak of a 'system of relief' at all as 'it applied to the States'.[66]

In spite of the haphazard nature of poor relief, the spirit behind the crusade against outdoor relief instigated by the Poor Law authorities in England during the 1870s was taken up wholeheartedly across the USA. Charitable Americans were persuaded, should persuasion be necessary, that once a poor person had sampled outdoor relief they would henceforth consider it to be their basic right. Allegedly, this made out-relief 'a great promoter of pauperism'. Not only did Americans latch on to the ideas behind the 1871 'crusade' against outdoor relief in England, they applied the concept more rigorously and with greater effect than did most English Poor Law unions. Whereas in Britain the number of people on outdoor relief continued to far outweigh those of workhouse inmates, in most USA cities inmates outnumbered external beneficiaries. New York had twice as many persons within their state institutions in 1873 than were receiving relief outside.[67] One explanation was that the low unit outdoor relief values were often accompanied by the additional humiliation of having personal details published in the local press, including the recipient's name and the miserable unit value of their relief.

Prior to 1863, Federal and State governments throughout the USA had avoided responsibility for local almshouses. Then, the Massachusetts State Board of Charities was established as a 'watchdog of the treasury and the law' with powers to 'inspect, report on and suggest improvements' of all such institutions within their boundaries. Other states quickly followed suit. When, in 1874, the first National Conference of Charities and Correction (NCCC) was convened it formulated a modest code of public social service which was to serve the USA for around 60 years. Annual conferences of the State Boards of Charities provided regular forums on how people could best supply subsistence relief while ensuring that provision was only when absolutely necessary and then of minimum cost. The alleged perils of outdoor relief, both for the individual recipient and for the nation, were repeatedly featured at the annual get-togethers of State Charities, much in the way the subject was aired regularly at Poor Law Conferences in Britain.[68]

Before the import of charity organization ideas from London during the 1870s, there had been earlier attempts in major USA cities to form groups claiming to share the motives of preventing pauperism and improving the condition of the poor. Noteworthy were the Societies formed in New York (1819) and in Boston (1828), both structured on lines similar to Thomas Chalmers' ideas of 'locality' as practised in the Scottish parish of St John's, Tron in Glasgow.[69] The early New York Society for the Suppression of Pauperism advocated dividing the city into 'Elberfeld like' districts. Administrators in each district were then to recruit visitors eager to: call on the indigent; establish savings banks, benefit societies, life insurances, etc.; procure the abolition of street begging; refuse support to paupers who have not gained a settlement; establish houses of employment; open places of public worship; promote Sunday schools; and 'devise a plan by which all spontaneous charities may flow into one channel'.[70] Such ideas were viewed as fanciful by most citizens and when another dozen or so Societies with similar ideas followed over the years in the larger USA cities each failed to achieve their principal aim which was 'the promotion of co-operation between existing charitable societies'.[71]

One of the first American cities to attempt charity organization strictly along the lines theorized by London COS was Buffalo, NY, in December 1877 where the Rev. S. Humphreys Gurteen was the prime mover. Son of an English clergyman, he claimed both a personal association with Edward Denison in his East End Settlement and a hands-on knowledge of London COS procedures. Shortly after arriving in the USA, Gurteen had taken holy orders as an Episcopal clergyman at Hobart College before going to Buffalo as an assistant pastor.[72] He was quick to realize that after the Civil War private charity in the USA had specialized in target groups under the benevolence of remote patrons. Gurteen saw that in Buffalo there was a 'terrible chasm between rich and poor which was "becoming wider and wider"'. He developed the belief that the application of the COS concept of organization could rejuvenate earlier failed attempts to co-ordinate charities.

Gurteen's idea was to train investigators who would determine the reasons leading to an individual's destitution. Should an applicant be judged deserving, they would be provided with beneficial guidance but not material relief.[73] He wrestled with the same difficulty encountered by London COS in distinguishing between 'worthy and unworthy cases'. Gurteen became convinced that the key to solving the problem 'in all cases' was to let 'the labour axiom be the test, that is, whether or not the applicant is willing to do as much work as his condition will allow'.[74] It was decided that only men willing to chop wood or break stone and women ready to scrub clothes, for less than prevailing wages, deserved public assistance. Similar themes were developed by organizing groups in cities such as New York, Washington, DC and Philadelphia. The founders of New York COS warned citizens that they must recognize the danger of pauperism much as they would an epidemic threatening to leap the boundaries of the inner city. The threat was said to be best dealt with as 'we would a malarial swamp, draining and purifying it instead of walling it about, or its miasma will spread and taint neighbourhoods like the plague.[75] As in Britain, many charitable agencies turned a deaf ear to charity organization principles. In the city of New York alone there were 250 private charities in 1898, acting independently to relieve the poor and afflicted.[76]

Those attempting to organize charity in the USA believed that their new 'science' would inculcate a spirit of wholehearted support among the wider community once they accepted that the individual character of a destitute person possessed the innate power for them to regain the dignity of self-sufficiency. The charity organizer's intention was that each individual case would involve a conference between some of the many knowledgeable people confidently expected to be drawn towards helping the particular person. Their discussion would lead to advice on different aspects of the case and recommendations on various ways in which the applicant could improve himself. The organizing Society's salaried agent would collate this detailed advice and ask a volunteer colleague to visit the person or family to establish an enduring friendship.[77] It was intended that by precept and by the 'simple example of their own civilized and moral selves' the 'middle- and upper-class' visitors would naturally impart higher standards and knowledge to their client on how best they could rehabilitate themselves into society.[78] The slogan, 'not alms but a friend', used universally by would-be charity organizers, was adopted by USA practitioners in the belief that it admirably expressed their sentiments.

Although they found it exceedingly difficult to fulfil in practice, the theory of 'friendly visiting' was the topic about which early COS leaders in the United States wrote constantly and 'expended most thought and enthusiasm in the 1880s'.[79] They might have been expected to have been cautious following the unwelcome experiences of London COS and their provincial acolytes where, as we have discussed, visitor recruitment was burdensome and often unrewarding. London's explanation for their lack of public support was that most middle-class people in Britain had already moved their home and families away from the offensive city centre areas by the 1870s. Despite this awareness, USA charity organizers remained confident that population drift to suburbia had been delayed in most American cities compared with the transition in Britain. They were convinced that they could comfortably recruit well-to-do volunteers, willing and capable of investigating the needs of relief applicants and of proffering them advice.[80] In general this turned out to be a pipedream. There was great practical difficulty in effectively marketing the charity organization concept. Most American philanthropists chose to ignore the new 'science' of organization and continued along their traditional furrow. The consequence was that the original purpose of bringing the various aid-giving institutions into practical co-operation, to a large extent, remained unrealized.

Apart from a few cities, notably Boston, Baltimore and Indianapolis, American COS's were not even able to mount, let alone sustain, effective voluntary visiting campaigns. Like their counterparts in Europe,

COSs encountered indifference and considerable hostility among the middle orders of society. They found themselves with little alternative but to engage 'full-time agents' to do 'more and more of the work'.[81] When Miss A.H. Thwing of Boston visited London in 1893, she made no mention of the dearth of COS volunteers suffered in most USA cities. On the contrary, she claimed that in Boston there were 767 permanent COS visitors besides 140 part-time. Of these 75 per cent of them were said to be ladies recruited 'largely through personal influence'. Thwing described how the involvement of volunteers in the Boston experiment had been retained by the considerable skill of giving them just enough to do so 'that their interest may not flag, but not so much that they were weary of it'.[82] Other COSs in USA cities such as Buffalo and New York could, in practice, attract only a small fraction of the volunteers needed to form a comprehensive visitor network.[83] Although initially Baltimore seems to have recruited fairly successfully, by the twentieth century only about one in four COS visits in the city were being carried out by volunteers.[84] Organizers used a similar excuse to that aired by London COS some years earlier in blaming the accelerated segregation of social classes. As Leiby pointed out, whereas there might have been sense in attempting to develop friendly visiting where rich and poor grew up together, it was a much more uncomfortable experience for both giver and receiver where the visitor came from a different city neighbourhood separated along class lines.[85] Those attempting to organize poor relief in other USA conurbations encountered persistent recruitment difficulties. In some urban areas which had in excess of 250 000 inhabitants, they attracted only a few volunteers to their cause. Where visitors were recruited, the majority were apparently unable to grasp fundamental COS principles and 'seemed to feel that their only duty was to see their families through some immediate need'.[86]

Whereas American COSs accepted the inevitability of each Society employing at least one 'paid' agent, there was a clear difference with COS procedures in Britain in that salaried 'investigators' in the USA were not treated as second-class citizens.[87] On the contrary, American agents were to become precursors of the new breed of professional social worker. By the early twentieth century, in most cities, 'the important duties of investigation and relief' were performed by the official COS agent with 'friendly visitors' mainly working under their direction. In some localities the professionals and volunteers formed 'a consultative and advisory committee' aimed at furnishing 'moral advice and stimulus'. Even in Boston, where COS recruitment was claimed to be relatively easy, it was customary for the 'paid agent to make investigation and to organize relief'.[88] Not only was it expected that agents would confer closely with COS volunteers but also that they would provide advice as to appropriate action.[89] American charity organizers had to accept that the idealistic principle of having 'friendly visitors' allocated to specific families 'in practice fell far short of what had been hoped for'.[90] Michael Katz has described how when Buffalo COS decided to engage waged investigators, they also sent out a strong message that coercion was a necessary ingredient of charity organization by paying police to investigate the domestic circumstances of everyone on relief.[91] At the same time, the law officers distributed 30 000 questionnaires to be returned completed to the COS for compilation of a central register of the poor.[92]

Charity organizers in Britain were strongly critical that 'friendly visiting' in the USA had strayed a long way from the seminal role envisaged by the COS founding fathers. It was described as being, 'very generally limited to advisory and consultative work'. W. Grisewood, of Liverpool CRS, offered his unsolicited opinion that 'under such a plan' as practised in the USA, 'voluntary visitors lose their chief value'. He hoped that American charity organizers would attempt a 'nearer approach to Elberfeld methods' by entrusting the 'volunteer with the responsibility of dispensing the aid'.[93]

Although there was an early expansion of charity organization in the USA, it was limited geographically. Almost all nineteenth-century American COSs operated north of the Potomac and east of the Mississippi. Some organizational attempts had been short-lived. Margaret Rich believed this was because each had started with 'too great enthusiasm', an ignorance of the principles of charity organization, an unreasonably high expectation of early results and that they were to discover that 'the patience of fellow-workers was too little'.[94] The so-called 'negro problem' in the northern cities had been shelved by these early COS enthusiasts as being unrelated to poverty. Charity organizers decided it was wiser to 'concentrate on the problem of poverty among the whites, leaving that among the coloureds for the future'.[95] In Chicago, a detailed social survey around the turn of the century concluded that 'blacks had to form their own charitable organizations because they had been systematically excluded from mainstream charities'. Daniel Devine cynically remarked that American charity organizers were 'certainly' not in the forefront of those asking fellow countrymen to 'change their ways when it came to race relations'.[96] F.D. Watson concluded that the few sporadic COSs existing pre-1914 in the American West mainly had 'either no grip on the local situation or were charity organization societies in name only'.[97]

Even in Indianapolis, birthplace of one of the most successful American charity organization movements, their members were persistently attacked publicly. Critics roundly condemned COS methodology as a 'system of espionage'. Others claimed that the COS suppressed benevolence by their high investigative overheads. Allegedly, it had resulted in 'the poor – the deserving poor – get only 50 cents out of each dollar collected'. In Boston, often looked upon as a COS bastion, Katz claims that their efforts were irrelevant as regards remedying the problems of unemployed workers during economically depressed periods.[98] As early as the 1890s, John Boyle O'Reilly, the Irish-born poet and Editor of the Boston *Pilot*, had described organized charity as being a manifestation of the selfish values and tight-fisted policies of bankers and businessmen. O'Reilly deplored:

> The vulgar sham of the pompous feast
> Where the heaviest purse is the highest priest;
> The Organised Charity, scrimped and iced
> In the name of a cautious statistical Christ.[99]

One of the few female theoreticians of early charity organization in the USA was Josephine Shaw Lowell. She published her seminal work, *Public Relief and Private Charity*, in 1884. After being widowed during the Civil War, Lowell had helped found the New York COS in the early 1880s and served as its guiding spirit until her death in 1905, much of the time as Commissioner. In spite of the COS in the USA being male-dominated during the nineteenth century, Josephine Lowell's forceful character made her an indispensable asset. Her conviction that terms like 'worthy' and 'unworthy' were absurd in the social context might lead to the impression that her brand of charity organization was softer than most.[100] This notion would be misleading. Lowell had adopted her stance on this emotive issue because she believed it was politically advantageous to maintain total focus on the unsuitability of 'inadequate relief'. She was convinced that such a phrase described all relief unless the recipient could be expected to derive long-term benefit and used this argument in attempting to justify why the COS persistently discarded such a high proportion of distraught applicants.[101] Lowell maintained that it was preferable to concentrate the limited available funds on a smaller number of persons to ensure that 'relief given to them really relieved them'.[102] She was implacably opposed to public outdoor relief in the belief that it lacked the 'redeeming features of private charity, because there is nothing personal or softening in it'. For Lowell, outdoor relief was nothing but 'openly advocated communism'.

It encouraged the 'idle, improvident and even vicious man' to live in 'idleness and vice'. Lowell alleged that the 'riotous living' she detected among the poor meant that their 'innocent and helpless' dependants were invariably left to suffer 'far more than had the relief being denied'. In spite of Lowell's stringent views, William Grisewood summed up American charity organization as seen through British COS eyes when, in 1905, he described it as being 'both generous and sane, erring perhaps a little on the side of liberality'.[103]

Most of the first COSs in the United States were structured by a male hierarchy bent on confining 'women to the infantry in the war against pauperism'. In the early 1880s, S.H. Gurteen considered that friendly visiting should be enough to 'satisfy the ambition of any woman'. He was concerned in case women 'sought a more active, directing role than he felt they deserved' and wondered about what 'the ladies' may have the temerity to want next. He asked whether women might even expect, 'seats on the council and district committee?' Some might even want 'jobs as agents?' Gurteen's uneasiness was allegedly based on the belief that 'women were frivolous, unaware of their social responsibility'.[104] Nevertheless, his thoughts were not unchivalrous in all situations, as illustrated by his response to an anecdote he gleaned from London COS. Gurteen applauded their rescue of an impoverished English Viscountess who had been discovered, after the 'kindly intervention of Lord Beaconsfield', in 'scanty surroundings ... making shirts for four cents each'. Allegedly, the Lady had happily been 'finally and adequately relieved by the benevolent' members of the London COS. This image of the titled Lady fallen on hard times epitomized what Gurteen meant by a 'deserving' case.[105]

Regardless of the possible off-putting effects of his male chauvinism on the ladies, Gurteen confidently expected hundreds of women visitors from the 'educated and well-to-do classes' to materialize, all anxious to search out 'worthy' cases. He attempted to entice the ladies into the COS fold by reassuring them of his own confidence that coming as 'mothers and daughters' from 'bright and happy homes adorned by virtue and radiant with love ... every woman of education and household experience' had special personal virtues. Gurteen expected lady volunteers to impart these attributes to 'the cheerless tenement or the wretched hovel'. COS ladies could be confident that 'the gentlemen composing the committee' would be meeting together, 'after a day of business and toil, to decide what is the kindest and wisest thing to do in the various cases brought before them'. But Gurteen warned females that before forwarding cases to the male committee, they would need to be constantly on guard against the 'untruthfulness and imposition on the part of the poor'. His advice was that when confronted by the poor, COS ladies should 'always withhold gifts so as to avoid demoralising them'.[106]

The attendance, hierarchical structure and written contributions in NCCC reports, in which the concepts of charity organization had become increasingly apparent, confirm that endemic male-domination remained in most USA localities into the twentieth century. From 1910 onwards an attempt at gender balance in the hierarchical structure of the NCCC came with the appointment of Miss Jane Addams of Chicago as President. Subsequently, NCCC Presidential appointments followed a chronological pattern whereby a female was regularly given the position every four or five years, as instanced by: Mary Willcox Glenn in 1915; Julia C. Lathrop in 1919; and Grace Abbott in 1924. During the 1920s, socio-economic changes had forced the movement to accept that Gurteen's assumptions of 40 years earlier that personal ability was gender-based was no longer tenable. Women were now being accepted, in the USA, as having a naturally dominant role in some aspects of social work. A greater number of the papers presented to the annual Conference were delivered by females, as illustrated, for example, by the constructive presentations from Mary E. Richmond. The organized charity movement at Baltimore, Philadelphia and New York were each, in turn, served prominently by Richmond over a period of time. Like Lowell before her, Richmond's strong determination helped her brush aside attempts at male dominance. Between 1898–1904 she taught at the new Summer School of Applied Philanthropy in New York where she proved herself as equally capable of pursuing hard-line COS principles as any man. Richmond dismissed the idea that charity should be made available to the 'unworthy' poor. Even unemployment among the worthy was viewed suspiciously because it carried 'prima facie evidence of inefficiency or unwillingness to work'. She saw the goal of charity being to encourage independence. Consequently, personal aid under Richmond's regime was usually doled out 'one day's worth at a time, so that the job-seeking activities of the recipient could be scrutinised'. This persistent probing also ensured that the poor remained 'properly docile and faithful'.[107] Richmond accepted that 'many women in poor neighbourhoods lead starved, sordid lives and long for genuine friendliness and sympathy'. Even then, she was convinced that 'one of the few rules which it is safe to follow blindly' is that of never encouraging 'any woman to become the breadwinner who has an able-bodied, unemployed man in the house'.[108]

Mary Richmond was given full-time charge of the Russell Sage Foundation Field Department when it was established in 1909. She gave a 'famous series of summer institutes' attended by a diversity of people, from all over the country, anxious to develop skills as social workers.[109] Richmond's 1917 book, *Social Diagnosis*, provided a system for casework and became a basic text in the development of modern social work in the USA. As a professional social worker herself, she perceptively foresaw the danger that, regardless of gender, the 'opinionated and self-righteous attitude' of some professional workers would frighten away 'devoted volunteer workers'.[110] Richmond's clarity of vision about what she saw as the future of charity organization, eventually overcame all but the most extreme male supremacists. J.C. Pringle, who as a London COS representative attended the fiftieth anniversary of charity organization in Buffalo, NY, reported that 'the ovation to Miss Richmond, when she rose to read her paper, was the high point of the conference, long to be remembered'.[111]

A growing number of American COS leaders began to accept that external forces in a modern economy could have an overbearing influence in dictating the plight of the destitute. Edward T. Devine, of New York, was one such person. In his presidential address to the NCCC assembly at Philadelphia in 1906, Devine emphasized that, in the changing circumstances, there was need for open minds when considering 'Modern Philanthropy'. While confirming the basic desirability of investigating reasons why a poor person had reached his miserable condition, Devine argued that modern philanthropists should also be asking the more 'natural' question about 'who has exploited him for profit'. When this 'other party' had been found, Devine recommended that he should be dealt with by 'radical methods'.[112] The awakening acceptance and interest in the 'social control of economics' by clamping a 'rational democratic harness onto an expanding American industrialisation' manifested itself repeatedly in national conferences during the twentieth century.[113] In her 1910 NCCC Presidential address, Jane Addams wondered whether it was because 'modern industrialisation is so new that we have been slow to connect it with poverty around us?' She based her text on St Augustine's words, 'thou givest bread to the hungry, but better were it that none hungered and thou had'st no need to give to him'.[114] The sentiments expressed by Devine and Addams demonstrated a greater readiness among USA charity organizers than was generally admitted by their contemporaries in London COS Council, about recognizing that disparities in socio-economic structures could go a long way towards explaining the presence of impoverished people.

The federal authorities in the States, motivated by the 1930 slump, decided to re-define the support a man should expect for his family when thrown out of work through fractures in the national and local economies. The resulting Social Security Act signed by Roosevelt on 14 August 1935 was accepted with an acquiescent realism by most of those charities previously having pretensions about organizing relief themselves. For the first time in the USA, 'social work became an accepted function of government'.[115] Monsignor Keegan, Executive Director of Catholic Charities in New York City, believed that no realist could fail to perceive that the USA was destined to witness a far greater measure of intervention by public authority. He was convinced that future federal intervention would not, as in the past, focus entirely on the fostering of trade, production and commerce but on 'the protection of large social groups and for the maintenance of social peace'.[116] It would, of course, be wrong to imagine that COSs on either side of the Atlantic aimed 'to alter the existing social order'.[117]

When measured by the rapid growth in new outposts, the charity organization movement expanded swiftly across the USA during the 1920s. The movement encompassed much of the country with over 350 functioning Societies. Looked at cursorily, this suggests a strengthening of COS influence but reality was different. The surge in the numbers of organizing Societies furnished a misleading gloss. It arose after the American Association for Organizing Charities (founded in 1911) had decided to distribute their ideological message in less urban areas. COS representatives toured the country preaching 'the gospel of the paid trained Secretary on full time' in scores of small rural communities, some with a population 'as low as 5000 or even less'. This contrasted with the earlier COS policy when it had been argued that it was 'hardly desirable to create a charity organization society in a community of less than 40,000'. In spite of the numerical gains in smaller new organizing Societies and although there was more ideological flexibility adopted in America than in the United Kingdom, the charity organization concept turned sour. USA adherents discovered that memories of their forebears' rigorous actions had made them pariahs in most charitable circles. American organizing Societies post-World War One, whether they were new or old groups, large or small, feared the public association of the acronym COS so much that they adopted a discreet 'variety of titles, all alike in discarding the word "charity"'.[118]

The organization of charity, the detection of imposture, the judgement of individual worthiness, the suppression of vagrancy and the elimination of indiscriminate almsgiving had all featured prominently in early pronouncements of USA charity organizers. Like their peers in Britain, they had to suffer grievously from precisely the same intense public suspicion and hostility from other charitable bodies. On each concept, they were forced into strategic retreats from what had originally been registered as inviolable ethical positions and which were still theoretically being maintained as such by the London COS. According to Daniel Devine, the fact that emphasis had been shifted inter-war from these fundamentals with some of them actually being scorned from within was 'a measure of the change' that had taken place.[119] In spite of these ideological retreats and the greater flexibility they adopted towards modernizing social work, the disreputable aura around American organizing Societies frustrated their involvement in the crucial federal welfare decisions of the 1930s. Charity organizers were scarcely included in the evolving social welfare mainstream of the Roosevelt era. They had been left withering in the backwaters of extreme individualism. As a movement they announced in 1930 that henceforth their 'own special competence' would be limited to case-work with 'disorganised families'. Their institutional titles were commonly changed to include the words, 'Family Welfare Association', a name to be selected years later by their London counterparts in their own search for a more compatible public image.[120] In general confirmation of the post-war trend, there was now no room for either of the words 'charity' or 'organization'.

Germany, the birthplace of the Elberfeld system of poor relief discussed in the introductory chapter of this volume, saw a nineteenth-century expansion of charity organization to many cities. It was claimed by the London COS, with wishful enthusiasm, that charity organization in Germany was operating right 'across the fatherland'. When attending the fiftieth anniversary celebrations at Elberfeld in 1903, representatives from Liverpool CRS pointed regretfully to the difficulties there had been in applying the Elberfeld system in England. They mainly blamed the continuing 'multiplicity of disorganised charity and the reluctance of Poor Law guardians to participate' in the UK.[121]

But, laying aside the misleading euphoria arising from the anniversary celebrations, the application of Elberfeld methods had not been widely welcomed with open arms in Germany. In localities where the concept had been attempted, principles had been bent to make the methodology less demanding on middle-class townspeople. A basic hurdle was that, unlike Elberfeld, regulations in most German municipalities did not make service as a 'volunteer' visitor compulsory. Salaried organizing officers soon had to be employed to work alongside the few volunteers that could be recruited. In Berlin the paid officials were described as 'Town Sergeants', in Hamburg as 'Messengers' and in Bremen as 'District Superintendents'. In 1905, W. Grisewood observed that in these German towns and elsewhere, it had been found difficult 'to raise the work of the unpaid almoner to the required efficiency'. He explained that throughout the fatherland there had been the greatest difficulty in engaging interest from other charities. Grisewood noted that the city of Hamburg was still 'afflicted with over 400 charitable foundations' with the result that 'systematic Poor Law work has been greatly delayed'.[122] E. Aders, chairman of the Elberfeld Poor Law Administration accepted that, after 50 years, their system had still not been 'acknowledged' adequately and remained 'many times misunderstood'. It was 'these wearying' problems which Aders considered made the 'duty of the visitor' remain 'the most beautiful and honourable ornament with which the citizen can be adorned'.[123]

Elsewhere in Europe, attempts to organize charity remained stuck in a narrow individualist groove with little sign of their propaganda being heeded more widely by the public. As time progressed, there was broad public acceptance across the continent for more state involvement in social affairs. Those who remained tied to outdated COS concepts were left adrift from the main decision-making processes. In Holland, prior to the First World War, the state Poor Law had traditionally only provided public relief where help could not be found from the Church, charity or other private sources. It was an unsatisfactory formula in practice because lack of mutual contact between the different sources 'proved to be a hindrance to more satisfactory results'.[124] In 1912, discussion at the fifth annual meeting of the COS in Holland exposed 'how many difficulties of principle and practice' still remained in spite of repeated attempts to promote co-operation between relief agencies.[125] Some years later, Professor Gosta Bagge of Sweden, speaking in July 1932 at the Second International Conference of Social Work, delighted his COS audience in London with his opinion that the popular idea of the individual no longer being expected to bear the cost of his own upkeep had 'led to a state of indescribable confusion'. The London COS applauded Bagge's comments and reminded the world at large that they alone 'through the years' had broadcast his current warning. They found it 'startling to recall' that for many years their own voice had been the 'lone one crying in the wilderness'.[126] The Third International Social Work Conference held four years later and again organized in London by the COS, included contributions from Europe and the USA. The London COS Council's report of the conference was a far cry from their exalted pronouncements on the overall condition of British society half a century earlier. Then COS pronouncements had been shaped in order to influence the destiny of millions. Now they found it appropriate to record thanks formally to 'the friends who made it possible to give tea'.[127]

This chapter has shown how, like the COS in London, their counterparts in other parts of the world found it impossible to make much further progress after an early promising surge of interest. In the USA, where methods of supporting the poor had been considerably influences by the English Poor Laws, London COS's concept of organized charity was adopted enthusiastically by idealist groups. The convention of USA state charities, which had been initiated in the mid 1870s, formed the nucleus of the code of limited public social service until the Roosevelt reforms of the 1930s. By this time, much as had been the experience of the London COS a quarter century earlier, national government had recognized that in the industrial age, the support of innocent families socially marooned by economic decline, could not be left to voluntary whim. Charity organizers in America were relatively quick to recognize that the federal social welfare formulae adopted in the 1930s had largely side-streamed them. Even before the federal laws were instituted, many charity organizers had decided to withdraw from the wider arena to confine their attention to family welfare. It was to take their London COS counterparts, doggedly persisting in their truculent opposition to Whitehall involvement, a further ten painful years to follow the narrower family welfare route taken by charity organizers in the USA.

6
Reasons for COS Decline

A once established opinion, however delusive, can hold its own front from age to age.

Sir E.B. Tylor[1]

We have gathered from earlier chapters that the progress of the London Charity Organization Society (COS) was turbulent from their early days. Nevertheless, for 20 years or so the Society were able to present an impression of a seemingly impregnable brand of individualism conducted by superior people, each with impeccable social contacts. Even when it is accepted that towards the end of the nineteenth century the image of the COS in Britain did show signs of wear around the edges, there is a widely held impression that their stark philosophy continued to flourish undiminished overseas. In particular, there is the belief that COS concepts developed particularly strongly in the USA and had massive influence on American welfare changes of the twentieth century. Discussion in the previous chapter showed that COS involvement in governmental decision-making across the Atlantic waned badly in the 1930s. This was despite the fact that American COS leaders had shown a much greater willingness to soften primitive rigidities in response to contemporary social reality than had their counterparts in London.

In Britain, there were widening circles of criticism against the COS's rigid adherence to the doctrine that a strong individual character could gain personal achievement and self-reliance regardless of environmental condition. Adherence to these principles meant that eventually, during the twentieth century, the COS deteriorated into being a besieged idiosyncratic minority. This chapter brings together the various strands of hostility directed against the London COS and their provincial acolytes, discusses why early friends became enemies and why the Society found itself increasingly socially adrift from mainstream decision-making on improving the condition of the poor. It has become apparent that the abandonment of the COS by influential political allies lagged chronologically behind their demise from public esteem. This hiatus was undoubtedly helped by the efforts of redoubtable propagandists such as Charles Loch, the Bosanquets and Octavia Hill, who used the influential contacts of the prestigious COS Council to maximum effect.

An early mistake by the London COS was the decision to couple their supposed mission on the organization of other charities with a rigid individualistic doctrine. In fact, their most important contribution turned out to be their casework methodology. Because the COS believed that their social role committed them irrevocably to a specific political theory, they became joined in a 'long-drawn-out battle with the rival theory, socialism, from which they emerged years later with, so to speak, rather hardened arteries'.[2] The COS failed to recognize that there was no inherent incompatibility between casework methodology and the state. Had they been imaginative enough to disentangle their practical techniques from political ideology, the COS could have made it attractive for others to adopt the broader use of casework decades earlier than turned out to be the case. At the same time they could have engineered for themselves a dominant role in the changing social environment. Contributing to their regrettable pursuit along the wrong conceptual track was that around 1870, at the time of their formation, COS philosophy was symbiotic with the attitudes of the prevailing Establishment and government. The emergent COS drew a spurious sense of power from this realization and arrogantly instructed others that charity without rigorous investigation was mischievous and morally wrong. Many of the charitably minded individuals expected to digest this unsolicited COS instruction were themselves of independent mind and means. They were not prepared to be harangued by what they saw as unwelcome intruders to the world of charity, regardless of what prestigious sociopolitical contacts the COS might possess. Even when the COS were at the crest of their influence, the annoyance of well-to-do independents and middle-class factions, coupled with the irritation of many parish clergy, came together publicly as a barrage of virulent criticism. The Society itself had to admit that many of the vehement attacks against it came from thoroughly respectable persons who genuinely, if mistakenly, disapproved of COS fundamental principles.

It is now illuminating to survey how adverse early criticism of COS methodology gathered pace and how the inflexible COS response became a mantra to the inviolability of their principles. It was soon apparent that the seminal COS concept of combining the activities of other charities with those of the Poor Law had fallen on barren ground. As a consequence, COS 'Inquiry and Prosecution' work directed towards the applicants who did approach them contributed much to the Society's early public prominence. On the one hand it gained respect but on the other hate and dislike. At a meeting of the St Pancras COS District Committee in the early 1870s, Captain Peter Snow condemned members for pursuing a course that was 'not according to the true spirit of Christianity, nor the manly and generous character of Englishmen' which were opposed to judging whether the 'poor person in the gutter' was 'deserving or not'. The COS were furious when Snow added that the 'real causes of crime and poverty were not to be found among the poor but among the upper classes'. Other early critics adopted the line of attack that was to constantly plague the COS. It concerned what many described as their 'extravagant and expensive' administrative expenditure. The COS hoped in desperation that the 'extreme scurrility' of pamphlets directed against them, such as that published in March 1876 entitled *An Inquiry into the Scourge to Humanity, Phantom Charity and National Calamity, the Soulless, Heartless, Impertinent Charity Organisation Society*, would reflect adversely on the author(s) and 'elicit sympathy' for the Society.[3]

After functioning for some months wrapped in their own serene self-confidence, the London COS was jolted by a Mr Fleming speaking from the body of the hall at the Society's 1871–72 AGM. He complained bitterly about a recent case of 'genuine distress' which he had brought before a COS District Committee 'without effect'. The *Charity Organisation Reporter*, commenting on the incident, claimed that because the meeting had shown 'signs of impatience' at Fleming's revelations, he was 'stopped by the Chairman', Gathorne-Hardy, MP.[4] Another problem for the emergent COS was that some of their most prominent disciples seemed to have little grasp of their underlying philosophy. For example, the Rt Hon. W.E. Forster, MP, a prominent educationalist, when chairing the 1874 London COS annual meeting, attempted to placate doubters with the confusing assurance that the Society was 'not guided by strict and rigid principles of political economy'. Forster went further by informing his bewildered COS audience that in his opinion, 'if we restricted our charity entirely to deserving objects, we should restrict it far too much'.[5] But if such comments were intended to impress the public, they cut little ice. The barrage of complaints against the Society's harshness continued. So much so that the following year, the Rev. W.G. Lewis congratulated COS members on belonging to 'one of the best abused associations in existence' having heard them described as being 'composed of miserable *doctrinaires*'. Lewis told his audience that since the public announcement of his speaking at a COS meeting, he had received 'constant reminders that he was identifying himself with a very hard-hearted Society'.[6] In similar vein, Lord Shaftesbury, some years later, described how his early involvement with the COS had led to him receiving 'letters of protest' informing him that 'all his past fame had gone to the dogs and that he had become a shrivelled specimen of bygone benevolence'. Shaftesbury recounted how other COS Chairmen had received similar letters.[7] In 1900, at a London meeting, Lord Derby relished his own revelation that it would be an unusual year in which the COS did not receive a 'fair amount of criticism' from newspapers. It was, Derby believed, 'one of those healthy shower-baths' which seem to 'invigorate the Society'. He claimed that these encounters encouraged the COS to arise with 'fresh strength' and to 'thrive' on the 'sneers'.[8]

The Earl of Lichfield, the early financial bastion of the Society, confessed to being 'perfectly aware that one of the most damaging accusations made against' the COS was that it expended 'an enormous amount upon organisation and very little on relief'. Lichfield had accepted as early as 1872 that such accusations were 'only natural'. He fully expected that there would be some 'fears and jealousies excited in the minds of the members of charitable agencies already existing'.[9] When addressing the Society in 1876, Lichfield admitted there were 'objections' to the COS and set out 'to meet them'. He explained that one of the objections centred on 'what at first sight' appeared to be the hardship associated with the 'minuteness and closeness of which investigations were carried out'. Another was that the Society had 'acted harshly in its dealings with the poor'. A third objection was the Society's alleged insistence that if they could not relieve the poor 'effectually' they would not touch them. Sir Rutherford Alcock congratulated the Earl on what he described as his astute perception of some of the problems facing the Society. Alcock assured his COS audience that 'one of the easiest luxuries in the world was to give money' and issued the warning that he who stepped between the indiscriminate giver and his pleasure was sure to get small thanks for his pains. Alcock addressed head-on the criticism that COS investigation was excessively protracted by willingly accepting that 'extreme cases' could occur such as when persons unfortunately died 'before your inquiries are completed'. He was also alert to the occasional danger that the COS may do 'harm by inquiring about them – perhaps they owe a little rent, and an inquiry may set the landlord upon them'. Alcock conceded a certain sympathy for protests that COS 'cases have been pushed off so long they are urgent' but he remained resolute that the main consideration must always be of achieving 'the means of doing the greatest good to the greatest number'.[10] This type of platitude, drawing from broadly respected Utilitarian themes, did little to deflect public opinion from the widely held conviction that the COS were needlessly harsh in their dealings with the poor.

An impression of the simmering antagonism among the working class towards COS methods came, in 1876, from a letter to the 'Workmen's Club Journal'. Writing under the pseudonym 'Rasp', a workman raised the following seven objections about the COS activities:

- it wasted too much money on 'mere' administrative machinery;
- it did not restrain mendicity;
- it failed to reach cases most deserving of help;
- being a 'distant organisation', even its enquiry could not be as effective as that made by 'people nearer the spot';
- it made relief a 'mechanical thing';
- it offended the spirit of independence of the poor; and
- the work to be done would be 'better done by individual effort'.[11]

At this stage, the COS were still managing to create the general impression of being unfazed by the encircling criticism. They convinced themselves that any softening in their responses to the poor would weaken individual character and erode morals. J. Hornsby Wright, an influential COS member, argued that if men be 'but children of an older growth' it was logical that the birch should survive 'unto later years and be applied to older as well as younger juveniles'. In Hornsby Wright's opinion, what was needed was 'more penalty and less petting, more rods and less sugar-candy'.[12] These were exactly the type of unsympathetic comments which alerted the public about the COS agenda on how to deal with the poor. Consequently, when London COS offered the Lord Mayor 'the whole of their machinery' to help relieve the economic distress of 1878, a correspondent to *Social Notes*, advised the Lord Mayor to have the 'good taste to decline the assistance (?) so generously offered' by these 'organising busybodies'. The letter, signed WMT, asked that 'in the name of charity' the COS should not be given the chance of 'filtering' the funds now being 'poured into the Mansion House'. 'The enormous amount of money' which the COS were said to get 'by hook or by crook, and the infinitesimal portion that finds its way into the pockets of the poor' was said to be 'condemnation of the entire society'.[13] The Rev. H.R. Haweis wrote to *The Times* claiming that the COS had failed to win the confidence of 'the deserving poor, the clergy or the charitable public'.[14] In reply, Sir Charles Trevelyan blamed what others had described as COS short-comings on the lack of co-operation they had received from clergy, societies, visitors and corporations.[15] Haweis later claimed that within a month of his letter to *The Times*, the newspaper had received 12 letters and two reports relating to COS activities, most of them critical.[16]

In his paper, *The uncharitableness of inadequate relief*, read at Exeter Hall on 20 May 1879, Francis Peek refuted as 'foolish' the frequently repeated public criticism concerning the high cost of a COS administrative officer's salary compared with the small amount of relief provided to the poor. Peek claimed that such criticism forgot that the 'truest charity' was designed to prevent the demoralization of mendicancy, to compel the idle to become industrious and to make the improvident become provident. The poor must always be mindful that should they 'lavish their earnings upon self-indulgence, when hard times came there will be no indiscriminate relief to fall back on'.

A disillusioned COS 'worker', writing to the *Charity Organisation Reporter*, claimed that by 1882 there was nothing in common between the Society's principles and the 'experimental methods of this latter-day almsgiving'. The two were said to be 'mutually irreconcilable' with the COS Council, which admitted 'no compromise'. Their disenchanted colleague pointed to the danger of the COS having 'won a sort of spurious popularity among the "upper" classes', based on the 'utter misapprehension' that the 'detection of imposture' was at least '*a* primary object, if not *the* primary object' of the Society's existence.[17] At much the same time, London COS Council were themselves having to admit that partly because of limited financial and personal support, they were 'far from satisfied with the work of District Committees which in some districts were very inefficient'. The districts offered the defence that they were suffering from 'an extreme deficiency of organizing power'.[18] As a background to these comments, no reader of London COS publications could fail to recognize that the early inequalities between districts remained deeply entrenched. Even COS stalwart A.H. Hill challenged COS complacency on the disparities in the funding and operational procedures of districts. He asked the COS to address the basic question, 'whether or not poor districts should be served as well as, or better than, the richer districts'?[19]

The perennial waves of hostility towards the COS eventually eroded some of their stoicism. The Society acknowledged the attacks by creating a dossier endorsed 'Complaints, Criticisms and Abuse'. This was in 1884 when London COS District Committee data suggests that occasionally they were being confronted in total with over 2000 relief applicants per month. The COS Council could not conceal the fact that they lacked adequate resources to deal with such a number. They had to concede that from time to time the pressure on volunteers and staff gave rise to an 'oversight' whereby 'good' case families were not extricated from their difficulties. They also admitted that deserving families might well have been saved had the Society been able to offer 'greater energy and resourcefulness'.

Some of the unwelcome stories that appeared in the national press claiming the exposure of a malfunctioning of their operations, particularly jolted COS equilibrium. One report referred to the deaths from starvation and suicide said to be arising directly from COS refusal to provide assistance. This claim, 'and many like it', was a factor leading to the inauguration of the anti-COS 'Charity Protection League'. The League's pamphlet, *Humanity Outraged and Christian Civilisation Disgraced*, was published in March 1884. It presaged a meeting called in Bethnal Green to 'Memorialise the Queen to withdraw her name as Patron from the COS, whose heartless and cruel treatment of the sick and dying poor will be exposed'.[20] W.H.Y. Webber's letter to the London *Standard* on 21 February 1884 attacked the Camberwell COS Committee for their maltreatment of a case sent to them by the Wesleyan Society. Webber charged the COS with 'unnecessary harshness, needless delay and inadequate relief'. The COS had to admit that their facilities in Camberwell were over-extended and that Webber's example was but a 'typical instance of the difficult and perplexing cases that an ill-supported Committee, with a district of unmanageable size, were called upon to face'. They attempted to deflect blame from themselves back to the Wesleyans for not supplying 'every facility'. In any case, alleged the COS, the 'delay was not greater than the circumstances rendered inevitable'. This COS attempt to switch blame to another institution or individual typified its defence against attacks on its own shortcomings. An example is the case of 'Huggins' of Bethnal Green whose alleged heartless treatment by the COS and subsequent death was the subject of acrid public comment. The Society had no compunction in replying 'conclusively that the whole blame, if any' rested with the Charity Protection League, seen by the COS as the major force behind the accusations. The COS recounted how the funeral of 'the poor man Huggins' had been made the 'occasion of a most indecent display of hostility from the pulpit by Mr Brewin Grant' in a diatribe against the Society.[21] The COS claimed their own 'dignified self-control as compared with the blatant rowdyism of their opponents' had led to a recruit recently joining their ranks.

In an address to Kensington COS, the disillusioned Henrietta Barnett told members how her confidence in the Society had faded. She described its early days when the Society had been seen as 'a watchman set on a hill', likely to bring meaningful social reform to the benefit of all classes. Gradually the COS had lost public sympathy largely because of their ceaseless 'investigations, organisations, registrations, co-operations, applications, administrations, each and all done by multiplication'. Barnett challenged her COS audience with the question, 'What does 463 cases thrown aside as "undeserving and ineligible" mean in the previous month's returns of work?'[22] In similar vein, Margaret Sewell, another early COS supporter and friend of Octavia Hill, who became head worker at the Women's University Settlement in 1891, felt help should be offered to those assessed by the COS as being 'ineligible for relief'. Sewell was convinced that the COS lost public sympathy with their tendency to abandon to their own devices those who they judged to be unhelpable.[23]

Towards the end of 1884, a London COS meeting was loudly interrupted by protesters. They complained at having been prevented from joining the meeting despite being in possession of entrance tickets. The ensuing clamour prevented Charles Loch from reading the COS's traditional letters of apology for absence from the great and the good. The ensuing 'scene of confusion' required the 'assistance of the police' but even they could not prevent what remained of the meeting being repeatedly interrupted by belligerent objectors. The platform announcement about the formation of a COS Convalescent Committee prompted angry cries from the body of the hall of 'a sham'. The delusive COS claim that members were winning the 'hearty goodwill and cordial support of managers and superintendents of every establishment with which they had been in relation' prompted exasperated cries of 'that is rather too thick'. One of the objectors, the Rev. Dr Lee, complained of having been 'hindered and pummelled on presenting himself for admission to the meeting'. He recommended that the Charity Organization Society would be more appropriately called the Charity Abolition Society which better suited 'their pig and gutter philosophy'.[24]

The COS could not effectively pretend to disregard the accumulative effect of the avalanche of antagonistic criticism hurled against it. It continued sporadic attempts to soften its public image by camouflaging the rigidity of its processes without real intention of modifying its basic philosophy. COS investigators were encouraged in 1886 to substitute the mollifying phrase 'not likely to benefit from COS assistance' for applicants hitherto dismissed as being 'undeserving'. In practice, little changed.[25] In much the same way, Beatrice Webb attempted to persuade the COS into presenting a gentler image by merely deciding whether applicants were 'helpable' or 'unhelpable'. Few COS members acted upon either suggestion and for years continued to attach the 'undeserving' tag to those they sent packing empty handed.

COS Occasional Paper no. 15, read by Octavia Hill on 1 February 1889 at Fulham Palace, derided the popular fashion of calling the Society 'cold, and formal, and inquisitive, and slow, and fifty bad things'. She claimed that, on the contrary, each COS committee was replete with 'really wise, sufficient, helpful almsgiving'. Hill described how, at COS meetings, there was none of the 'contemptible and cruel pandering to the confused hopes of the poor ignorant people'. She claimed that there was only the thought of how things would really tell on their lives when the sharp test of experience separated the 'true and abiding from the specious and the temporary'. Miss Hill believed impatience to be the 'curse of the time' with even benevolence being distributed in a 'frantic haste'.[26]

While chairing the 1890 COS annual meeting, Mr E. North Buxton took a perverse pleasure from the realization that the Society lived under 'what might be called a bracing air of criticism'. He alleged that the public were incapable of recognizing that the COS did not want 'to limit the flow of charity' and that on the contrary they wished 'to purify the stream at its source'. The Rev. H.L. Paget, another COS advocate, dismissed the haphazard distribution of charitable relief as being 'rather like shooting, at a very long range, at a shifting target, on a very foggy morning'.[27] Charles Loch tackled the frequently occurring allegation that COS inquiry methods, by their rigidity, were themselves unwittingly impeding the individual 'enthusiasm and devotion' of budding recruits. Loch claimed that 'facts prove the opposite'. COS inquiry was said by Loch to 'startle the novice as a revelation of new knowledge' which eventually provided 'security in his work'. He explained that the 'many restrictions' placed by the Society on the new recruit demanded his 'perpetual thoughtfulness'. This allegedly led to an intellectual 'high road' compared with the 'fool's paradise in which he formerly walked boldly along'. Loch brushed aside the ideas of inexperienced volunteers who had thought mistakenly that 'people ought only to be asked to state their troubles privately'. He dismissed such ideas as being 'quite inapplicable'. This was because he believed it dangerous for such work to be delegated to a volunteer possessing too 'much kindness of heart' while lacking the COS instruction and experience to avoid being misled by an applicant's fictitious evidence. Loch elucidated how such a hazard to the untutored person arose because the 'stress of life in which vice plays a part creates an hypocrisy, the cunning simulation of which has an air of reality that deceives all but a very few'.[28]

Time and again the COS received public notice of their unpopularity and repeatedly comforted themselves with the delusion that every brickbat merely confirmed the validity of COS dogma. The Archbishop of Canterbury, the Most Reverend Edward White Benson, warned the 1891 COS annual meeting that, although he wholeheartedly supported the 'science' of charity organization, the Society must recognize that it was 'very often not very popular'. He instanced the frequent reproach levelled against the COS that it spent 'a guinea in order to give a shilling's worth of relief'. The Archbishop joined his audience in taking comfort from the knowledge that the Society was not required to 'appeal to the multitude' but only to 'wise and sensible persons'.[29] In the same year, Octavia Hill spoke of 'fits of popular displeasure' levelled against the Society when it had 'ventured to stem the tide of sudden and mistaken action'. She mentioned the widespread disregard of COS warnings about the public being misled by General Booth's Salvation Army distributing funds without adequate prior investigation. Miss Hill attempted to enlighten the public by claiming it was wrong to place in one pair of hands the 'despotic control of a machine so huge that it cannot be rightly watched and guided by one human being'. She was thankful that the COS had 'not fallen quite so low as to contract with the Salvation Army to right our social system for us'.[30]

Miss Hill defended the COS position in another recent case in which it had asked the 'benevolent to hold their hands' by not providing indiscriminately 'when children come hungry and neglected to school'. She accorded 'all honour to those whose hearts go out in pity for starving children' but could imagine no course 'so sure to increase' their number than the 'wholesale feeding of them by charity'. Hill's experience had allegedly shown her how irresponsible charity led directly to 'diminution of distinct responsibility', drunkenness, loss of steady work, the abandonment of work training and the omission of house-duties.[31] She felt personally 'honoured' in sharing any 'unpopularity or censure that may be heaped' upon the COS. The voices of COS leaders were claimed to have issued 'high and clear' warning of unwelcome repercussions from the 'hasty conclusions' of the ill-experienced. This COS wisdom was said to have arisen above the 'popular clamour' which erroneously supported 'sentimental and garrulous philanthropy, amid the hasty, violent or ignorant theories'.[32]

In the face of the dismissive attitudes depicted by such a leading COS advocate as Octavia Hill, it was hardly surprising that the Society found itself having to admit in the 1890s that it was 'still unpopular'. The COS Council made yet another attempt to correct public attitudes by raising and responding to a number of 'popular objections' against its own activities:

- *'We Inquire too much'*. 'If COS inquiries were impertinent or vexatious let us be condemned – but they are not'. COS inquiry was justified by the question 'is it right to subsidise vice and hypocrisy?'.
- *'We practice vexatious delay'*. The COS were comfortable in the knowledge that 'inquiry means some delay'. When the COS considered there was real urgency it was met by 'some temporary relief'.
- *'We spend the great bulk of our income on offices and salaries'*. Administration costs necessarily accompanied the need for 'adequate investigation'.
- *'We are cold-blooded and critical'*. The COS's enigmatic response was to ask another question, 'is the surgeon cold-blooded when he probes the wound of his patient that he may discover and remove the deadly bullet?'

The COS explained to their diminishing public that the validity of the foregoing unyielding responses stood on the 'rock of ancient experience' and on a COS awareness, not commonly recognized, of 'a large and increasing, though often silent support' for their principles.[33]

Charles Loch indefatigably attempted to allay public concerns about what many saw as COS uncaring attitudes towards the poor. His defence of COS principles often merely compounded the widening apprehension outside the Society's own tight circle. Loch refuted the claim that 'people starve' while COS enquiries were being made. He ridiculed the simple-minded folk who saw charity merely as shovelling on to trollies the 'desired stuff' – food, meals, clothes and 'what stands for everything else, money' – and then 'tip up the load at the proper place'. He explained that what most members of the public could not grasp was that such material wastefulness made social gaps larger because 'it smothers and chokes goodness, independence and exertion'. Loch also denied the perennial 'most damning objection' that the COS wasted money on officials and offices, the simple reason for public confusion allegedly being that critics had misinterpreted COS financial data. In any case, as Loch explained, even where there had been no misinterpretation, 'without the expenditure on organisation the whole fabric of efficient relief would fall to pieces'.[34] Bizarrely, against mounting evidence to the contrary, Loch professed himself to be confident that 'working men' were beginning to see that charity organizers were not the 'inhuman monsters that have been described'. While he considered that the future of charity 'lay in the hands of no single class', Loch was 'certain' that without the 'personal help of the best men and women – it will not grow'. By this Loch meant that without individuals possessing COS enlightenment, charity would remain 'a poor stunted thing'. He explained how, in contrast, with the Society's input, charity would become a well-meaning tree in a 'smoke-laden atmosphere of dirt and dolefulness whose fresh shoots wither before hardening into serviceable wood'.[35]

COS propagandists like Charles Loch and Bernard Bosanquet fashioned their responses to the persistent criticism of the Society so as to develop the impression of charity organization being central to the public domain. Even these hardened publicity campaigners were shaken by the undisguised attack from within the COS ranks of the Rev. Canon Samuel Barnett, the early COS supporter and respected long-term member of the London COS Council. In the 1870s, Barnett had endeavoured to abolish Poor Law outdoor relief in his Whitechapel parish but by the 1880s had concluded that 'scientific charity' had led to the creation of a 'working man too thrifty to pet his children and too respectable to be happy'. He discovered that the 'life of the thrifty is a sad life, limited both by the pressure of continuous toil and by the fear lest this pressure should cease and starvation ensue'.[36] On another occasion, while still a COS Vice-President, Barnett's 'friendly criticism' stung senior COS members. He accused the Society of having been 'inclined to fall in love with the form of words, the mechanisms' and of becoming 'idolators' unable to see 'a new fact or accept a new idea'. Barnett claimed that what had earlier been true 'in a world dominated by one set of ideas' was for the COS still true in a 'world dominated by quite another set of ideas'. He maintained that the COS Council condemned more than it organized and despised 'where it ought to woo'. Barnett saw the pity of the Society's failure to 'catch the goodwill and enthusiasm of the time' as being that, by 1895, the COS voice was now 'hardly heard'.[37]

Mr R. Barrington rejected Barnett's comments and attributed his 'ignorance' to his recent non-attendance at COS meetings. Barrington dismissed Barnett's accusation of 'hardness and dogmatism'. He defended the COS 'severity of principle' as being both 'natural and necessary'. When a Mr Cockran attempted to sympathize with Barnett's warning about thrifty people becoming 'the most hard-hearted and selfish', he was reminded by Mr C.E. Maurice that the first COS question to applicants was 'as to the help that relations were giving'. Maurice interpreted this COS query as confirmation that the Society invariably acted as 'an encouragement to unselfishness'. Charles Loch recognized Barnett's criticism of COS activities as being an 'attack upon himself personally'. Much of Loch's acerbic diatribe against Barnett was directed against his previously attributed opinions on free dinners, shelters and emigration. With typical COS indifference to other opinion, Loch concluded that Barnett's conversion to socialism meant that his charges against the COS could be safely 'disregarded'.[38]

Helen Bosanquet has recounted how between 1896–98 there was a prolonged 'systematic attack' on the COS by the Editor of *The Councillor and Guardian* alleging that the COS's main objective was to show, in as many cases as possible, how applicants were 'unworthy' of assistance. Bosanquet was annoyed at what she claimed to be the same 'vindictive message' re-echoing repeatedly through the press. Typical was what Bosanquet alleged to be the 'misleading' case of a 'respectable working man' to whom the COS were said to have refused help for his 'starving wife and children' because 20 years previously he had been convicted of stealing a loaf of bread.[39] Mrs Bosanquet chose not to dwell on what had been 'misleading' about the case. On another occasion, the Rev. C.L. Marson, leader of the High Church Christian Social Union, in joining the mounting condemnation of COS meanness, warned that its principles could so easily in practice be turned into a 'gospel of the buttoned pocket'.[40]

The COS were singularly unimpressed when the closing decades of the nineteenth century saw a progressive tendency in academia and politics to interpret T.H. Green's 'common good' concept as justification for appropriately limited state intervention. The Society remained deaf to the mounting chorus criticizing the COS and its 'archaic' ideas, including the assumption that it was natural for there to be lower orders in society.[41] A wider public audience now applauded the concept that it was not pre-ordained for the majority of people to inherit at birth the expectation of ceaseless badly paid work so as to provide a refined and cultured lifestyle for the few. Helen Bosanquet's curious response to these modern ideas was to argue that since the lowest-paid workers made goods suitable only for the poor, they were not involved in making luxury articles for the rich.[42] It was this kind of muddled COS interpretation of a changing world which, in the emerging twentieth century, rooted them intellectually in the 1860s and fuelled the growing public impression of their 'remoteness and imperviousness'.[43]

The nebulous character of T.H. Green's pronouncements provided fertile ground for continued debate among those claiming to bear his banner of Idealism. Essentially, the ideological tussle was about the 'priority and relative weight' of environmental factors in individual and social life and over the limits of state action. Conservative Idealists, as typified by the COS, held that 'character being an expression of individual will, could only be developed by exercising that will autonomously'. Therefore self-help and self-reliance were the natural means of building character.[44] In contrast, while the New Liberals retained belief in the virtue of individual self-sufficiency, personal exertion and the like, they increasingly became convinced that by 'the removal of hindrances', Green had intended that the state should endow every person with the power to make the best of their own abilities. Of course, the Liberals themselves remained far from being collectivists in the socialist sense and were abidingly suspicious of proposals likely to increase state power where there was not an overwhelming case in its favour.[45] State action should be confined strictly to those matters needed to produce conditions by which all men would be sufficiently liberated to accept and enjoy whatever positive rights and freedoms the market economy could create. New Liberals recognized each individual as a social being. Because they were free, rational and moral persons, each was ethically committed to participate in the larger 'common good' which itself supplied a criterion of the individual's rights.[46] Where mainstream Liberal Idealists increasingly departed from the entrenched COS was in their acceptance that for many poor people, inhibited as most were by negative constraints, aspects of the cherished freedoms were illusory with life providing little more than ceaseless drudgery. A.D. Lindsay argued that the good citizen, as envisaged by Green, would first consider what, in social and economic terms, were harming the conditions necessary for others to live the good life and 'ask whether the State's compulsion may not be so used in the removal of these harmful conditions as to produce an addition of real liberty'.[47] As early as the 1880s, Arnold Toynbee, a friend, colleague and disciple of T.H. Green, had famously remarked that 'freedom given (to the poor) was under ordinary circumstances only a liberty to starve'.[48]

The unstoppable march of industrialization and concomitant urbanization extended the physical boundaries of the squalid slums in London and other British towns. Middle-class fears about socioeconomic disequilibrium becoming a breeding ground for political disturbance worsened. There was apprehension about the possibility of the respectable working class becoming socially dissatisfied and merging with an unruly destabilizing residuum in large-scale rebellion. This daunting prospect hastened middle-class acceptance of the need to improve living standards generally. Lynd has commented that 'whatever the theory of individualism, health was not an individual matter'. Although it had been possible previously for the comfortably-off to overlook the occasional undernourished family, it was not so easy 'to overlook square miles of them'.[49] The COS Council remained obdurately opposed to changing public attitudes about such matters. They persisted with the argument that individual character could overcome environmental shortcomings and that it was sinful to shower undeserved benefit on the dissolute. Whereas the COS agreed that improved morals and better living standards could enhance the social good of the poor, it disagreed with a growing majority about which stage in the process of improvement the sacred tenets of individualism were being transgressed. Against the mounting tide of popular opinion, the COS stubbornly refused to entertain the broad concept that the dilution of social stress through environmental improvement may set 'some natures free to be better'.[50]

J.A. Hobson was quite prepared to applaud the COS endeavour to 'stamp out pernicious forms of almsgiving' and to 'order, direct and economise the charitable energy which comes from the moneyed classes' but ridiculed the COS claim that its organized charity was 'scientific'. Hobson argued that the COS possessed no ability to 'think straight against the pressure of class interests and class prejudices' and that this had prevented COS members from being the 'scientific people that they claim to be'. He described as 'almost unparalleled audacity' Bernard Bosanquet's claim that, on the one hand, 'a large pension or gift of property to a man not yet demoralised would probably do no harm' whereas, on the other hand, Poor Law relief was 'a payment of idleness' certain to destroy individual character. Hobson asked the COS why similar rules did not apply to gifts and bequests to the rich? He derided the COS condemnation of doles and its claim that, because they came 'miraculously', such 'windfalls' violated the rational order of life. He questioned whether anything could be more miraculous than that he should 'wake up tomorrow and find certain shares which today are worth £100 are then risen to £105?'.[51]

A marvellous opportunity for the COS to persuade a broad audience to its way of thinking arose in 1905 when the Conservative government turned to them for guidance when appointing members of the Royal Commission on the Poor Laws and the Relief of Distress. The result was a powerful majority of Commissioners representing the traditionalist elements of the Local Government Board's higher echelons and the COS, their voluntary sector ideological running mates. The minority on the Commission ranged against these conservative elements included George Lansbury and Beatrice Webb, both of whom had earlier gained practical COS experience but who, having become disillusioned, now came to represent the progressively minded minority of Commissioners.[52] Early evidence from J.S. Davy, the LGB Chief Inspector, and his Poor Law Division Inspectorate colleagues across the country, forcefully emphasized individualistic ideas. They preached the 1834 doctrine of 'less eligibility' and repeatedly spoke about the need to organize indiscriminate and overgenerous relief.[53] Their conventionalist contributions ensured that throughout the next four years friction simmered among Commissioners, with the temperature occasionally being raised through Beatrice Webb's outbursts.[54] By the time the opposing factions had published their separate Majority and Minority reports, the change in government following the landslide collapse in Conservative parliamentary support did nothing to encourage major implementation of new Poor Law legislation. As a consequence, the two reports bore little immediate fruit other than to prompt a rash of conferences nationwide on the prevention of destitution. At this point we will, however, consider some aspects of the Majority report's recommendations because they have been used subsequently by latterday historians as a model purporting to demonstrate significant change in COS principles.

A.W. Vincent has claimed that the COS contribution to the Majority report encapsulated a more complex social theory 'than did simple unadorned individualism'. He admits that the COS treatment of the poor was at times 'harsh and uncompromising and that some of their workers had rather crude notions of self-help and character deficiency' but argues that other aspects of COS activities presented 'a coherent, thoroughly articulated social vision' which 'some members of the COS' attempted 'to put it into practice'.[55] Vincent suggests such trends indicate that, between 1870 and 1909, the ideas of the COS underwent 'a series of almost imperceptible changes' arising from the 'very logic of the COS arguments'.[56] To support this theme, Vincent could reasonably call on the Majority recommendation that there should be a move from the 1834 'harshness and still more of hopelessness' to a new 'spirit of efficiency and hopefulness'. More specifically, there were (a) the Majority's wish to abandon the workhouse test; (b) their newly-fashioned suggestion that outdoor relief could provide an 'opportunity' rather than an enduring abomination; and (c) their recent ambivalent acceptance that a 'mixed workhouse' may have advantages for certain types of inmate over the time-honoured segregated version.[57] Karl de Schweinitz has described these trends as an indication that by 1909 the COS was becoming more prepared to advocate the substitution of 'treatment' for 'test' and that the deterrence of the 1834 Commission was now being replaced by a COS-inspired programme containing elements of change.[58] Few would disagree that some slight reforming drift in COS attitudes was being signalled. Indeed, it would be astonishing had not some modicum of ideological COS drift not taken place over a 40-year period during which seminal shifts had occurred in the generally accepted ideas of how best the condition of the poor should, could and must be improved. What failed to dissipate public suspicion about COS intentions and what remained its distinguishing characteristic was the grudging reservations invariably accompanying any small concession that the COS felt forced to yield. This obstructive COS niggardliness featured all too clearly even within the Majority's recommendations. Examples included the reservations hedging possible change in workhouse organization and the constraints attached to the recommendation that medical assistance should not necessarily lead to disenfranchisement.[59] The result was, as Vincent admits, a 'confusing and certainly not consistent' Majority report.[60] Sadly for the COS, although in the driving seat when choosing the discussion agenda and in conducting the Royal Commission's business, it had again demonstrated its ideological obstinacy by an inability to develop a socio-political consensus. More broadly, Edwardian intellectuals and most historians since that time would concur with Vincent's proposition that the principles propounded by Loch and Bosanquet were wrapped in an ethical individualism structured on philosophical Idealism. At the same time, they would also be likely to claim that the COS's Idealistic package was one that had been wrapped abnormally. COS eccentricity was most clearly exposed by its intransigence in persistently placing environmental issues secondary to those of individual character.

José Harris is also among those raising the possibility that COS 'individualism' may have been misunderstood and that Bernard Bosanquet was not simply antistatist. He was, she claims, supportive of 'a republic of free, equal, independent, ethically mature and public-spirited citizens'.[61] As a 'free' and 'independent' person himself, it is hardly surprising that Bosanquet did favour such a conceptual state. Where opponents have taken issue is in Bosanquet's apparent inability to recognize how the squalid plight of the physically and emotionally destitute often involved conditions so intolerable that any possibility of raising their miserable horizons towards individual enlightenment would require an injection of material support. To most observers it was unreasonable for Bosanquet to expect that social outcasts, who were neither economically 'free' nor 'independent', would become 'equal' members of society unaided other than by moral exhortation. It was this unrealistic nature of the COS expectation, and therefore its hypocrisy, to which objection was taken.

The differences between the expanding mainstream of social decision-makers and the COS were crystallized on other occasions by their contrasting responses to the gloomy environmental exposures of social investigators such as Charles Booth, Seebohm Rowntree and the like. A growing number of Edwardians came to accept their own lack of responsibility in allowing such shameful national deficiencies to develop. They shared an acknowledgement of the pressing need to improve the physical well-being of Booth's poverty-stricken third. Not so the COS: they chose to nit-pick about the validity of Booth's data and to preserve their 'moral regenerationist' belief that the fortitude of human character would prevail regardless of the circumstances surrounding destitution.[62] Lewis has pointed to how Helen Bosanquet felt that 'poverty lines' had a 'false air of definiteness' and that Charles Loch rejected both Booth's and Rowntree's results on the grounds that neither had attempted any analysis of 'social habit'.[63]

The 1905–9 Poor Laws Commission was to prove a wasted opportunity for the COS to convince Parliament and the broader public about the wisdom of the Society's way of thinking. From that time, fewer of the countless Commissions and Committees later deliberating on social issues for the Liberal government involved much in the way of COS membership. An article in the *Quarterly Review*, probably by COS supporter W.A. Bailward, described the mounting consequences of persistent public 'objections' raised against the Society. The article explained how; 'eminent clergy' preached 'violent sermons' in opposition to the Society, how with few exceptions the COS now had 'no friends in the press' and how public men of all 'parties and professions' treated the COS 'with marked coolness'. What worsened the situation was that those now coming up from Oxford and Cambridge considered COS teaching 'antiquated and obsolete'. Instead, as COS members themselves complained, golf and 'other amusements' monopolized the time of these gentlemen of leisure and the 'Society sees them no more'.[64]

A widely circulated Fabian Tract by Mrs Townshend claimed that COS schemes for bringing all charitable agencies and persons together in organized form had never got off the ground. She blamed the lack of success on the COS itself. Allegedly, it had 'stuck to the theory of individual independence and the danger of state interference' in a modern world where man-made laws were enabling the rich to grind the faces of the poor. Townshend claimed that the COS had remained 'habitually oblivious' to the value of any state action except 'the Poor Law' and then only after ensuring that every penny was stigmatized. She criticized COS concepts for providing self-satisfaction to the upper and middle classes in their easy and sheltered lives.[65] Lewis has recorded how W.A. Bailward 'commented sadly' in 1910 about how the COS's 'necessary advocacy of economic principles is distasteful to a large section of the charitable public'.[66]

Violet Markham, a Poor Law guardian and leader of Chesterfield's Civic Guild, blamed COS unpopularity on its failure to recognize that 'the best doctrines may turn into cruel dogmas if pressed too hard'. The Society, she claimed, had 'held aloof' and had shunned the 1911 'Conference on the prevention of destitution' which had been a 'genuine effort to bring all classes together'. Markham described how when the COS had occasionally deigned to involve itself in state ventures it had always been half-heartedly, followed by a prolonged phase of groaning and an apparent lack of sympathy which together 'creates so much prejudice'.[67] Mowat has described how any legislation involving even the hint of unstigmatized state provision was condemned by the COS as 'harmful'.[68]

What had rubbed salt in the wound for the COS was that while much of its heavy artillery was engaged in the rebuttal of Webb-inspired Fabian attacks within the Commission, the parliamentary Liberals had introduced legislation on matters against which the COS had long fought. In 1906, Local Authorities were allowed to provide free meals for poverty-stricken schoolchildren and, a couple of years later, people over 70 years old with incomes less than £31 10s could claim a state pension of 5s per week. The COS was especially piqued that neither of these 'handouts' carried the stigma of pauperism and were, to them, but thinly disguised methods of outdoor relief. As discussed in Chapter 4, the old age pensions proposals were considered by the COS as thoughtlessly introduced, taken without adequate discussion, and devoid of the planning preceding a similar scheme in Germany. Hobson ridiculed the COS refusal 'to recognize the social economic forces which cause poverty' and that it had adopted 'that dangerous position which is known as "sitting on the safety-valve" '.[69]

In spite of the deepening opposition to the Society's conservatism, the years immediately prior to 1910 appear to show a revival in COS fortunes when measured by the increase in the number of new COSs emerging around the country. Dismayed by what it saw as Liberal collectivist reforms, some provincial traditionalist middle-class groups reacted by attempting to organize the voluntary sector within their own localities and chose to operate under the COS banner. However, the emergence of these new provincial Societies was overshadowed by the simultaneous creation and the faster expansion of groups like the Guilds of Help who shared allegiance to the principals of investigation and organized charitable provision but who projected a more sympathetic image. Another major difference that transpired, as discussed above, was that these alternative groups were more willing to accept the inevitability of increasing state involvement. They shrewdly recognized their role as being an attempt to stem the institutionalized welfare tide by harmoniously maximizing efficiency in the voluntary sector. After the First World War, the Guilds of Help, and similar groups, displayed a pragmatic acceptance that they would be required to work in a framework combining statutory and voluntary provision. Not so the COS. Inability to interpret the inevitable implications of the mounting social legislation prevented the COS from consolidating what became little more than its ephemeral pre-war revival. Faced with the reality of a more rapid growth in basically similar organizing groups, a COS Special Committee summarized what it saw as the main reasons for the continued unpopularity of the Society as follows:

- many COS workers came from outside the district in which they served;
- non-conformists disliked the society;
- borough councillors were prejudiced against it;
- the Society's name was disliked;
- it did not give enough;
- its pronouncements invariably favoured individualism and opposed socialism;
- it was looked upon by the working class as largely representative of a class which they feel to be injuring them and doing them great injustice.[70]

Eventually it dawned on some COS leaders that if they were to retain any meaningful involvement in social matters, they must at least provide an impression that they were willing to participate in the societal restructuring currently being statutorily imposed. Although COS members truculently attempted to justify their previous criticism of each successive wave of state intervention, there was a reluctant acknowledgement that the weight of opposing social forces was mounting. The COS even went so far as to imply that in future they would become more co-operative with others.[71] But it was just not part of the COS composition for its members to eat humble-pie or to lose debates gracefully. At every turn, they continued to chunter on unyieldingly to succeeding governments about the moral dangers of state intervention.

Typical of COS persistence in publishing half-truths – to cocoon loyal supporters within a specious sense of well-being while blinding themselves from cold reality – came with one of its pre-war annual reports. It referred misleadingly to the COS's 'continuous progress in the organisation of charity' alleging that its efforts had resulted in 'closer and more intimate relations with many societies and agencies'. As ever, the London COS Council could not miss the temptation of attempting to inflict their principles on a government by now left with little alternative but to turn its back to them. Even though few politicians were listening, the COS informed Whitehall of its deep concern about where state policies would lead. The COS detected with dismay that among the public at large, there was a diminished 'fear of the moral injury which state dependence may cause'. This wide acceptance allegedly carried the consequential danger that the poor would cease to dislike being in receipt of 'state aid'. The COS saw it as its 'duty' to keep the 'true principles of social advance clearly in mind'. At the same time it informed its own members that, because of the wayward public trend to socialism, believers in COS maxims would require, 'faith, unselfishness, patience, constant thoughtfulness and wholehearted devotion'.[72] The COS persisted perennially with delusory propaganda aimed at lulling its members into the fallacy that, as a Society, it was 'gaining more and more the confidence of the public'.[73]

During the inter-war period, there was no pause in the COS policy of niggardly sniping at any further legislation that included even a hint of state provision for the type of individual the COS judged to be 'undeserving'. The Society attracted public bitterness by opposing the 1918 Child and Maternal Welfare Act which obliged local authorities to provide support for poor mothers and their children. Then the COS compounded the widespread contempt for its attitudes with the unpopular opinion that Addison's 'out-of-work donation' to the 'demobilised soldier' was a 'desperate remedy'. The COS claimed to possess evidence of how such assistance 'encouraged idleness and undermined self-reliance'. These ill-considered and woefully mistimed outbursts consolidated the COS's social isolation. It became 'clear' even to the COS Council that they could not 'expect in the future the steady supply of volunteers, whether whole-time or part-time', that they had 'counted upon in the past'.[74]

When the Rev. J.C. Pringle returned again to be General Secretary of the COS in 1925 he was determined to reverse negative public attitudes about the Society's activities. Pringle's optimism, determination, scholarship and eccentricity were stamped indelibly on succeeding London COS reports. Each was copiously littered with esoteric biblical, literary or folklore references woven into flowery innuendoes. The Society's 1926 report typified Pringle's delusion that the COS had been blessed with a social mission and should continue the fight against intrusive falsehoods. Allegedly, the 'revulsion from an over-development of State aid was leading thoughtful people of all classes to return to COS ideals'. The report mysteriously extracted great comfort from the 'superficial unpopularity of the COS' with the claim that influential people were 'breathlessly interrupting each other' to vociferate COS maxims, while protesting with the vehemence of St Peter 'we know not the name'. According to the London COS, there were 'a million or more cases' that should be investigated. They claimed that instead, in the prevailing intellectual vacuum, state provision was 'dangerously being granted' with a 'packet of relief tickets and a place on the out-relief list'. The COS explanation for the changed social climate in which the COS found itself between the wars was that 'politics reign and science is nowhere'.[75] Pringle dismissed collectivism as 'an aberration' which would eventually disappear. Rooff has described his analogy on the subject in the 1931 London COS report as 'pathetic in its naiveté. Pringle had used Barrie's *Wintry Tale* to conclude that: "Collectivism was a phantasm … which, like Miss Julie Logan … has vanished" '.[76] A good number of COS members were both aghast and embarrassed by Pringle's prose. Some were made to feel uneasy about their own literary inadequacies while others considered it a serious misjudgement on behalf of the London COS Council in believing that Pringle's contrived verbosity could possibly attract other than middle-class eccentrics towards the Society's principles. It was even less likely bait for latent recruits from among the working classes who, the COS continued to claim, were welcome to its deliberations.

The enduring failure of the London COS to empathize with what was happening socially around it was constantly confirmed during the inter-war years by the ornamental prose of its annual reports. Under the title, 'Who killed Cock Robin? Who saw him die?', the 1934 London COS report attempted to augment the Society's moral crusade with the folklore belief that nothing would bring a heavier curse than the killing of a robin because of its 'unselfish devotion to humanity and especially to children'. Robin Redbreast was used as a synonym for the COS because it too was 'the revealer and the symbol of the truth we most need to know'. Another parallel with contemporary society detected by the COS was that Robin's excellent manner of association 'blithe, trusting, unafraid' was, like the Society's own, mortally threatened by the Devil's 'active forces of social disintegration'. The sparrow, Robin's fairytale slayer, was symbolized by the 'urbanised industrial population'. The fly, which saw Robin die, was cast by the COS as the 'most disreputable being in existence – poisoner of baby's milk, poisoner of the athlete's meat'. Namely, any person willing to witness the 'destruction of the spirit without which a good social life is impossible'. Interwoven within their Cock Robin satire was open contempt for the recent 1933 Unemployment Bill. This had allegedly permitted the government to substitute for the 'principle of limitation', as enunciated by G.J. Goschen in 1869, a worthless socialist formula whereby an applicant's need was to be determined by a set of regulations.[77] The COS went on to question 'the *quality* of a sample of the population which we are maintaining out of public funds' and cited studies on the 'pedigree of families' dependent on Poor Law relief. They were claimed to show that 'there was no way of avoiding the conclusion that England is suffering a frightful loss of the best hereditary strains'. The Society expressed the hope that the British people 'may be stirred to do something really effective toward reducing their burden of defective humanity' instead of drifting along doing everything they could 'to increase it'.[78] A résumé by the COS's Rev. H.J. Marshall of his 'remarkable statistical analysis' of Public Assistance administration between 1934–37 described the need for a 'drastic and ruthless elimination of inefficiency' and gave 'short shrift to that cruel and wicked idea' on the part of the public that '**the more extravagant it is the better**!!!'.[79] A year later Marshall continued his vitriol against Family Allowances using the argument that 'want is a personal matter'. He questioned whether Britain's overseas competitors would pay the inflated prices sufficient to meet Britain's 'high wages and the 500 million pounds' spent on social services.[80]

Ministers of State and their civil servants received little pleasure from the constant COS sniping at legislation which they themselves perceived as being far from political collectivism. The inter-war Whitehall generation no longer had the inclination to placate a group of fusty reactionaries. Unyielding COS postures meant that members were unable to share common ground with elected government representatives at either local or national level. For similar reasons, peer group friends abandoned them while, at the other end of the social scale, the poor continued to view the COS as mean, scrimping and cruelly judgmental. Even then, in spite of the relentless friction sparked by the Society, social workers did respect the sincerity of many COS individuals in the field and remained genuinely appreciative of their administrative methodology during the formative years of the emergent social worker profession.

The atmosphere of national emergency created by the impending Second World War was one last opportunity for the COS to conjure wider recognition of their worth to the national well-being. As illustrated in Chapter 4, authorities charged with mobilizing national resources recalled COS organizational abilities at previous times of emergency and recruited the Society's involvement when preparing for war. In the climate of crisis, patriotism allowed the COS to mothball their most hide-bound individualistic principles and to join others in defeat of the common enemy. The skill of marshalling people and material resources exercised by the COS whenever it was able in the past, often in a self-constructed vacuum, were called into play. Financial constraints that had shackled COS administrators for generations, were temporarily lifted by wartime grants from the Ministry of Health, the Red Cross and other War Relief agencies. The outdated principles of the COS created less friction when their efforts were sensibly adjusted by the lubricating balm of national endeavour. Archaic individualistic theories were laid aside during the wartime emergency with the COS finding it possible to temporarily subjugate some of its cherished principles. The COS advised and motivated others so effectively on the best use of public services in wartime that the scars of its verbal battles with a succession of, what it had described as, 'collectivising' governments showed surface healing. Had it taken the opportunity, the relatively harmonious wartime scenario may have belatedly allowed the Society to construct a central place for itself in the brave new world of welfare administration that was to follow.

When Benjamin Astbury accepted the reins from the ailing J.C. Pringle a year or so prior to the Second World War, the COS at last acquired a Secretary with the practical experience and social background to move the moribund Society towards contemporary social thinking. Unfortunately, the COS had already dug itself into such a deeply entrenched isolationism that even Astbury's ameliorating personal qualities could not overcome widespread suspicions about the COS's long-term agenda. His task was made no easier by the continued presence and interference, during the war years, of influential hard-core COS members still resolutely opposed to dilution of their Victorian individualism. Once the war was won, this entrenched attitude surfaced again. The result was that even with the superficial bonding throughout the voluntary sector welded by wartime social activities, there were many outside the COS portals who retained the opinion that the Society's pre-war assumption of superiority would return with peacetime normality. This caution among wartime colleagues was reinforced by the realization that, within the London COS Council, there remained the conviction that the Society's founding precepts were inviolable. Consequently, when peace loosened the emergency bonds, COS co-operation with other bodies disintegrated. As an institution, the COS lacked the emotional motivation to embrace social activities that it had shunned pre-war, especially as they realized that a more intense form of state involvement was inescapable. The COS decision to change its title to the Family Welfare Association (FWA) confirmed the inevitable. Driven by their parlous financial situation, the London COS had been forced to accept that the Society, long established to organize the activities of all other charities, would in future attempt to organize none but themselves.[81] By the time of this awareness, the 40 London COS District Committees formed across London with such a flourish during the 1870s had dwindled to a mere 21.

How do we explain COS failure to sustain its early dominance on social issues? Apart from its cold aloofness guaranteeing its isolation, the COS made the error of unnecessarily associating its methodology with a particular brand of political economy. The Society had been formed in 1869 on the basis of a philosophy already approaching its sell-by date. These thought patterns became unsustainable when former allies abandoned it for what had become the commonly accepted dominant ideology. London COS's unwillingness to associate itself with contemporary procedures were not eased by the repeated decision to engage senior salaried administrators who lacked the social background or requisite imagination to translate COS traditional principles to the needs of the modern world. Successive officers of the Society mistakenly interpreted their social role as being that of showering the diminishing number of acolytes prepared to listen, with the occasional marginal repackaging of outdated ideas. At the same time, this impolitic attitude sustained elitist COS Councils in the delusory belief that their own social pedigree remained the dominating factor dictating the well-being of the nation. Charles Loch, Bernard Bosanquet and John Christian Pringle were among COS leaders who devoted themselves to the impossible task of interpreting and construing every nuance in an ever-developing social scene as validation for COS individualism. These full-time administrators, and the part-time Council they served, perversely claimed to draw strength from the realization that more and more people detested them. As the years passed, any early public respect for the COS translated to disregard, then to distaste and eventually to ridicule. Would things have been different had the dominant class-conscious COS publicists possessed a more realistic outlook and an ability to direct the Society into contemporaneously acceptable philosophical routes? Might this have permitted the retention of certain principles which in turn would have maximized their effect on a changed world? By the time Bernard Astbury the person most likely to be equipped with the necessary attributes, appeared, it was too late.

This volume's exposé of how the prestigious London COS maintained a façade that screened its own problems and presented a misleadingly glowing impression of its own efficacy contributes fundamentally to present-day sociopolitical debates. Conservative writers still contrast what they allege to be the moral erosion of state welfare handouts and the apparent ability of an admirable Victorian middle class to shield the poor from potentially disruptive factors. Towards the end of the twentieth century, the American social authoritarian Lawrence Mead echoed the London COS caution that the work obligation must necessarily be attached to all poor assistance.[82] Claims by Charles Murray that modern welfare programmes were themselves culprits in eroding stable family life fuelled the socioeconomic policies of Ronald Reagan and Margaret Thatcher.[83] Similarly, under the banner 'The New Victorians and the New Rabble', Murray has argued that despite modern temptations 'the affluent, well educated part' of British society, who allegedly had not been so badly tainted by the Welfare State, would edge back towards what he contended was the commendable morality of Victorian society. He warns that in contrast, 'a large portion of what used to be the British working class', whose morals have been eroded by state handouts, 'will continue to degenerate' into crime, addiction, single parenthood, child neglect, work dropouts and homelessness. Murray brushes aside suggestions that in a fast-moving modern society, Victorian ethics cannot exist. He claims that in nineteenth-century England, industrialization and urbanization was just as fast, sweeping and 'wrenching' as now. Even then, Murray alleges, 'the middle class was superbly efficient at propagating its values throughout society, and its success overcame the naturally disruptive forces of modernisation'.[84]

The London COS was very much to the fore in generating this deceptive aura of Victorian efficiency revered by Murray, Mead *et al.* This volume has looked behind COS propaganda and, using the Society's own data, exposed the reality that the very name 'Charity Organization Society' was a sham, built as it was on the commendable but erroneous assumption that it would be able to 'organize' the many dozens of charities scattering alms haphazardly across the metropolis. The abject failure to achieve this primary aim followed COS inability to engage with other relief agencies and its subsequent cold-shouldering by most charitable bodies, Poor Law guardians, clergy and by the poor themselves. The many inconsistencies that then became endemic in COS operations have also been discussed. The COS's reluctant acceptance that to remain functional it had to become yet another provider of alms was itself an affront to its own founding principles. Having been pushed into this bizarre situation, the COS allowed inexcusable incompatibilities to develop. The basic flaw in its 'scientifically' designed methodology was that it created the situation whereby the poor in rich districts of London could expect to receive distinctly more support from the COS than might their peers in poorer districts. Overall, analysis of COS data has shown how the value of its own alms was often no greater than were the Poor Law doles it derided as being shamefully inadequate. The book has also shown the hollowness of COS claims that its unique investigative methodology equipped its members alone to introduce a viable system of loans. Originally, the Society alleged that repayment of the loans by the poor had the inestimable therapeutic value of inspiring within them feelings of self-reliance and independence.[85] When defaulting on COS loans became so financially crippling as to expose basic flaws in their investigative procedures, COS lending had to be largely abandoned.[86] They were replaced by the introduction of pensions, a form of relief shunned by COS founders, because of their allegedly character-sapping likeness to the Poor Law outdoor relief they so despised. The change in COS attitudes to loans and pensions illustrates that unwelcome external pressure did occasionally influence COS policy. Unfortunately, COS determination to maintain a façade of permanence regarding their founding principles, made it nigh impossible for it to concede that it had succumbed to enforced change.

Charles Loch's dynamic involvement in the introduction of trained hospital almoners and his attempts to organize what he saw as the confused administration of medical charities, provident dispensaries and voluntary hospitals, ensured a succession of invitations to membership of Select Committees and Commissions. In addition, as discussed in Chapter 3, Loch's well publicized opinions on the behavioural boundaries for assisting the condition of poor school children and for the caring of epileptics, the homeless, mentally defective and physically disabled, contributed to keeping the COS's name in the public domain throughout the last quarter of the nineteenth century. Unfortunately, although Loch's input helped to make these pressing social problems more widely known, the rigidity of COS solutions in practice eventually exposed the hardness of their eccentricity in a softening world. There was always COS insistence that case investigation was paramount and that benevolence should be granted only to those who 'deserved' it. It was the apparent ease with which COS members averted their gaze from heart-rending cases of destitution simply because the individual(s) had not previously fulfilled the COS's behavioural code that ensured the Society's isolation from mainstream reformers. Charitable outsiders were disturbed by the pride with which the COS repeatedly claimed that it was only by using their unique investigative methodology that the plight of some pathetic destitute individual had been exposed as being entirely of their own feckless making.

Even then, the COS concept that investigation by knowledgeable persons should determine the validity of an applicant's need is justifiably acknowledged as being a significant contribution to casework methodology as practised by modern social workers. Unfortunately, the COS was soon constrained by its inability to apply this commendable idea in practice so that it was socially acceptable. This COS failure was compounded by the Society's accompanying conviction that the middle and upper classes were inherently knowledgeable about matters concerning the poor and were morally superior to them. A limited amount of COS procedural training, usually centring on how not to be fooled by cunning indigents, was considered sufficient to equip volunteers on how to pontificate on the needs of their poorer neighbours. Evidence from COS sources has exposed the deep-rooted inconsistencies and the frequent value inadequacies in what relief the COS did provide. These fundamental COS flaws were usually accompanied by the regrettable harshness characterized by COS 'scientific' rigour constantly being taken to hold precedence over the weakness of confused compassion allegedly suffered by the charitable majority.

It has also been recognized that the COS attempt to co-ordinate activities of disparate charities in 1860s London with the statutory Poor Law was, in itself, an admirable idea. It was largely devised by knowledgeable, sympathetic individuals like Edward Denison and

Henry Solly, each with personal experience of living as neighbours to the desperately poor. Again, the COS soon veered from the conceptual track through the unnecessarily hard-hearted interpretation by a remote elitist COS Council determined to defend individualistic principles at all costs. Support which the COS may have engendered initially from other charities was quickly dissipated by what others saw as their uncaring, inflexible harshness. In time, the COS lacked either the will or the means to refine its founding ideas to account for the changing modern world. During the twentieth century, its largely self-created isolation led to widespread scorn and to the forced COS abandonment of all pretence at occupying the over-arching philanthropic role it had once been convinced was essential for the stability of the national exchequer. A temporary reprieve came with the Second World War when the London COS were asked to help create a network of advice centres and emergency schemes across the capital. The demands of national unity bound the COS to operate effectively with various socially supportive groups. Even before the end of hostilities, the emergency bonding with other social agencies was becoming frayed. Towards the end of 1944, the London COS Council intimated that at some future early date it would change its name to The Family Welfare Association and so signalled its intention to focus on a more limited, singular path.

It had become apparent that the London Charity Organisation Society, founded with such brilliant aspirations three-quarters of a century earlier, was now hopelessly out of touch with its contemporaries. It was but a distorted mirror of a bygone age. In the public's eyes it reflected the image of hard-hearted, mean, pitiless, inflexible, class-biased elderly fogies, judgemental of others. In its over-bearing confidence, the COS had misinterpreted for too long that public revulsion merely confirmed the validity of its own archaic principles.

Notes

1 Beginnings of the London Charity Organization Society

1. Keith Feiling, *A History of England* (1970 edn), pp. 780–4.
2. Adam Smith, *The Wealth of Nations* (1776).
3. John Stuart Mill, *Utilitarianism* (1863, 12th edn 1895), pp. 118–19. Italics in original.
4. Samuel Smiles, *Self-Help* (1859, IEA edn 1996), pp. 2, 3 and 211.
5. John Ruskin, *Unto This Last and other writings* (1862 Penguin edn 1985), p. 189.
6. Calvin Woodard, 'The COS and the Rise of the Welfare State' (PhD thesis, University of Cambridge, 1961), p. 180.
7. George Crabbe, *The Village* (Norton Anthology; English Literature, Vol. 1, 6th edn 1993), p. 2498.
8. M. Dorothy George, *London Life in the Eighteenth Century* (1925, Peregrine edn, 1966), p. 173.
9. G.W. Oxley, *Poor Relief in England and Wales 1601–1834* (1974), pp. 109–19; M. Blaug, 'The Myth of the Old Poor Law and the Making of the New', *Journal of Economic History*, 23, 2 (1963), pp. 151–84; J.D. Marshall, *The Old Poor Law 1795–1834* (1973 reprint), pp. 12–45.
10. J.D. Marshall, op. cit., pp. 26–7.
11. W. Chance, *The Better Administration of the Poor Law*, Charity Organisation Series (1895), p. 1. Total poor relief expenditure in 1829 was £6.83 m, it peaked in 1831 at £7.04 m and dropped by 1833 to £6.32 m. These were all lower costs nationally than earlier in the century when they had peaked in 1817 at £7.87 m; J.D. Marshall, op. cit., p. 26.
12. *The Poor Law Report of 1834*, re-published with introduction by S.G. and E.O.A. Checkland (1974), p. 334.
13. *The Poor Law Report of 1834*, op. cit., p. 429. K. de Schweinitz, *England's Road to Social Security* (South Brunswick, 1975 edn), p. 131. Lynn Hollen Lees, *The Solidarities of Strangers*: the English Poor Laws and the People, 1700–1948, (Cambridge, 1998), pp. 115–52.
14. *Second Annual Report of Poor Law Commissioners*, PP 1836 [c595], XXIX, p. 43.
15. *Sixth Annual Report of Poor Law Commissioners*, PP 1840 [c245], XVII, pp. 16–18.
16. *Report of the Royal Commission on the Poor Laws and the Relief of Distress*, PP 1909 [c4499], XXXVII, p. 141.
17. Karel Williams, *From Pauperism to Poverty* (1981), pp. 64–5.
18. T. Mackay, *A History of the English Poor Law from 1834 to the Present Time*, Vol. III (New York 1900), p. 355.
19. *Twenty-second Annual Report of Poor Law Board* PP 1870, [c123], XXXV.1, p. 9.
20. Gareth Stedman Jones, *Outcast London* (Peregrine edn 1984), pp. 101–5.
21. *Twenty second Annual Report of Poor Law Board*, op. cit., p. 11.
22. William Davis, *Hints to Philanthropists or A Collective View of Practical Means for Improving the Condition of the Poor and Labouring Classes of Society* (IUP 1971 facsimile of 1821 Bath edn), p. iii.

23. *The Philanthropist*, 7 (1819), p. 319.
24. Donna T. Andrew, *Philanthropy and the Police, London Charity in the eighteenth century* (Princetown University Press 1989), pp. 175–7.
25. *Annual Report of Brighton Provident and District Society* (1831), p. 13.
26. Ibid., Rule 12. There are also indications that at least one Provident Society in suburban London was even more generous to investors during the 1830s in certain circumstances. *Provident Societies Recommended* (publisher J.G. Rivington, 1833, p. 10).
27. Margaret Simey, *Charitable Effort in Liverpool in the Nineteenth Century* (Liverpool, 1951).
28. Joan Gaddum, *Family Welfare Association of Manchester and Salford, A Short History, 1833–1974* (Manchester 1974).
29. *Report, Society for Relief of Distressed Travellers and Others* (Oxford, 1814).
30. M.J.D. Roberts, 'Reshaping the Gift Relationship', *International Review of Social History*, XXXVI (1991), pp. 216, 219, 217, 208 and 226. Concerning Bodkin's appointment, it is fascinating to note the similarities with the Rev. Henry Solly's claims to the Earl of Lichfield for a salaried position in the early days of the London COS; refer to the Solly papers, LSE archives, Miscellaneous 154, 10 (b), accession number M226, especially draft letter 20 July 1869.
31. C.L. Mowat, *The Charity Organisation Society, 1869–1913* (1961), p. 7.
32. Quoted by Lord Shaftesbury, *COR*, 26 June 1872, No. 23, p. 120.
33. Thomas Chalmers, *On the Sufficiency of the Parochial System Without a Poor Rate for the Right Management of the Poor* (Glasgow, 1841), p. 11.
34. In particular; Thomas Chalmers, *The Christian and Civic Economy of Large Towns*, 3 vols (Glasgow, 1821–6).
35. Sir Charles Trevelyan, *Charity Organisation Reporter*, 27 March 1872, p. 61.
36. Stewart J. Brown, *Thomas Chalmers and the Godly Commonwealth in Scotland* (Oxford, 1982), p. 140–1.
37. B. Kirkham Gray, *Philanthropy and the State, or Social Politics* (1908), p. 88.
38. Olive Checkland, *Philanthropy in Victorian Scotland* (1980), p. 300.
39. M.T. Furgol, 'Thomas Chalmers' poor relief theories and their implementation in the early nineteenth century' (PhD thesis, Edinburgh University, 1987), pp. 403, 406 and 410.
40. W. Grisewood, *The Relief of the Poor in Germany* (1905 Liverpool), p. 4.
41. M.E. Rose, 'Poor Relief and Scientific Charity', unpublished paper (Manchester, c1986).
42. G. Browne, 'The Elberfeld System of Poor Relief', *West Midland Poor Law Conference* (May 1889), p. 36.
43. J.R. Green, *Stray Studies*, 2nd Series (1904), p. 170. Also, the Municipality of Elberfeld Poor Law Regulations stated, 'Under the law, service as an Overseer or Almoner is compulsory', W. Grisewood, op. cit. (1905 Liverpool), pp. 6–8.
44. W. Chance, 'The Elberfeld and English Poor Law Systems: a Comparison', *Economic Journal*, 7 (1897), p. 332.
45. *First Annual Report of the Local Government Board*, Appendix 35, PP 1872 [c516], XXVIII, pp. 63–8.
46. W. Grisewood and A.F. Hanewinkel, *Jubilee Celebrations of the Elberfeld Poor Law* (Liverpool 1903), p. 6.
47. *Charity Organisation Reporter* (27 March 1872), p. 63.

48. *Charity Organisation Reporter* (13 November 1872), p. 167.
49. *Charity Organisation Reporter* (11 December 1872), p. 188.
50. C.L. Mowat, op. cit., p. 11.
51. Baldwyn Leighton (ed.), *Letters and Other Writings of the Late Edward Denison, M.P. for Newark* (1872).
52. Henry Solly, *How to Deal with the Unemployed Poor of London and with its 'Roughs' and Criminal Classes*, paper to the Society of Arts (22 June 1868), and Thomas Hawksley, *Charities of London and Some Errors of their Administration, with some Suggestions for an Improved System of Private and Official Charitable Relief*, paper to the Society of Arts (17 December 1868).
53. William Beveridge, *Voluntary Action* (1948), pp. 168–70.
54. C.L. Mowat, op. cit., (1961), p. 16 (fn).
55. Thomas Hawksley, op. cit. p. 16.
56. A 'highly arrogant plan'; B. Rodgers, *The Battle against Poverty*, Vol. 1, *From Pauperism to Human Rights* (1968), p. 45.
57. Cited by Helen Bosanquet, *Social Work in London, 1869–1912* (1912), p. 23.
58. LSE archive collection of Solly papers, classification: Miscellaneous 154, 10(b); accession number: M226.
59. LSE Solly collection, op. cit., J 121 and onwards.
60. C.B.P. Bosanquet was the half brother of the philosopher Bernard Bosanquet who, as discussed in Chapter 6, became such a prominent advocate of COS principles later in the century. A barrister by profession, he was a member of a well-known wealthy Northumberland land-owning family. C.B.P. Bosanquet studied and published tracts about historical methods of charitable effort, being particularly influenced by the claims of Thomas Chalmers. During his time in London in the 1860s he gave time to the friendly visiting of the poor. Bosanquet's decision in 1875 to return to manage his North-east estates led to the appointment of C.S. Loch, his successor as London COS Secretary. It is also interesting to note that Bosanquet was related to Samuel Richard Bosanquet, treasurer of the London Mendicity Society, 1843–1882; M.J.D. Roberts, op. cit., fn. 88, p. 229.
61. C.B.P. Bosanquet, *London, some Account of its Growth, Charitable Agencies, and Wants* (1868), p. 205.
62. This is a useful reflective summary by E.C. Price, COS Assistant Secretary. Even then, more than 20 years after the events there were those, such Hawksley, Solly and Dare, who still believed passionately that insufficient accord was being given by those attempting a history of the COS to the pioneering efforts of the 'Society for the Prevention of Pauperism and Crime'. Price's article concludes with an extract from a letter dated 22 October 1892 from Thomas Hawksley to the Editor of the *Review*, in which he expresses the 'earnest hope' that the COS delay in publishing the history of their origin indicated an intention to revise it so that the facts were stated in 'logical and chronological order'. He continues doggedly, 'The movement began with Mr Solly and the Association for Prevention of Pauperism and Crime...'.
63. After receipt of a letter from Solly, it is conceded that 'under these circumstances it seems not unreasonable inference that this particular Sub-committee on Charities (which included Hawksley and Solly) formed a link in whatever historical connection existed between the "Committee on the Destitute Poor and Criminal Classes" and the "Society for the Organisation

of Charitable Relief and Repression of Mendicity"'.

64. They include: Helen Bosanquet, op. cit. (1912); C.L. Mowat, op. cit. (1961); David Owen, *English Philanthropy, 1660–1960* (1965), pp. 211–46; K. de Schweinitz, op. cit. (1975), pp. 140–53; Madeline Rooff, *A Hundred Years of Family Welfare* (1972), pp. 22–63; A.F. Young and E.T. Ashton, *British Social Work in the Nineteenth Century* (1956), pp. 92–114; K. Woodroofe, *From Charity to Social Work* (1968), pp. 25–55; and Judith Fido, 'The COS and Social Casework in London, 1869–1900', in A.P. Donajgrodzki (ed.), *Social Control in Nineteenth Century Britain* (1977), pp. 207–30.

2   The First Five Years

1. See hand-written notes passed between the Rev. Henry Solly and others (including the Earl of Lichfield) from November 1868 onwards in LSE archive collection of Solly papers, classification: Miscellaneous 154, 10(b); accession number: M226 (30 November 1868).
2. In his obituary it was mentioned that 'Lord Lichfield was at the time guaranteeing the rent of the office and all other expenses of the Council', *COReview* (February 1892), p. 45.
3. *Twenty-second Annual Report of Poor Law Board*, PP 1870 [c123], XXXV.1, pp. 9–11.
4. LSE Solly collection; miscellaneous 154, 10(b) 3; J 279, pp. 4–5.
5. Charles Loch Mowat, *The Charity Organisation Society, 1869–1913* (1961), p. 24.
6. *Fourth Annual Report of COS Council* (1873), pp. 3–4. This attitude became a source of dissent within the COS movement because of its implication that the poorer districts, which by definition suffered the most poverty, did not need the good offices of the COS so urgently simply because there were so few charitable funds available for them to organize.
7. Helen Bosanquet, *Social Work in London, 1869–1912* (1912), p. 38.
8. *Charity Organisation Reporter*, 27 March 1872, p. 63.
9. Helen Bosanquet, op. cit., pp. 46–7.
10. Ibid., pp. 5–11.
11. *COR* (12 June 1872), p. 109.
12. *COR* (24 January 1872), No. 2, p. 7.
13. For a diagrammatic impression of COS investigative procedures, see R. Humphreys, *Sin, Organized Charity and the Poor Law in Victorian England* (1995), p. 113.
14. *First Report of the COS Council* (1870).
15. *COR* (5 November 1873), p. 150.
16. Cited by Helen Bosanquet, op. cit., p. 42.
17. *Third Annual Report, St Saviour's, Southwark COS Committee* (1873–4), p. 4.
18. *COR* (24 June 1874), p. 276.
19. For example, *Fifth Annual Report of Paddington COS District Committee* (1874) shows only their Clerk, Inquiry Officers and Collector being referred to as 'Mr'.
20. Debate on 'Co-operation with the Industrial Classes', reported in *COR* (15 March 1876), pp. 54–5.
21. Helen Bosanquet, op. cit., pp. 35–6.

22. *COR* (17 January 1872), pp. 1 and 2.
23. *COR* (27 March 1872), p. 57.
24. *COR* (24 January 1872), No. 2, p. 7. Another example was provided by Paddington Committee which had spent £489 15s 3d on overheads to distribute £755 1s 10d relief. They, too, were proud of their relief record, pointing to how by the nature of things, an undeserving case must cost 'much more' to investigate than a deserving one; *Fourth Annual Report of COS Council* (1873), pp. 12–13.
25. *COR* (28 February 1872), pp. 30–1.
26. *Fourth Annual Report of COS Council* (1873), pp. 4 and 8.
27. *COR* (28 February 1872), p. 31.
28. *COR* (27 March 1872), p. 59.
29. Ibid.
30. *Sixth Annual Report of COS Council* (1874), p. 4 'great need of more working members' and pp. 12–13, 'need of volunteers'.
31. *COR* (27 March 1872), p. 57.
32. The Marquis's father had been President of the London Mendicity Society from 1847 until his death in 1869; M.J.D. Roberts, 'Reshaping the Gift Relationship', *International Review of Social History*, XXXVI (1991), fn. 88, p. 229.
33. *COR* (27 March 1872), pp. 56–7.
34. *COR* (26 June 1872), p. 119.
35. Charles Loch Mowat, op. cit., p. 20.
36. *COR* (17 March 1875), p. 47. On this occasion the annual meeting was presided over by the Right Hon. Lord Hatherley and the large attendance included Lord Napier and Ettrick, the Right Hon. J. Stansfeld, MP, Kay-Shuttleworth, MP, the Dean of Winchester and three retired Generals.
37. *COR* (26 June 1872), p. 119.
38. *Fourth Annual report of Charity Organisation Society* (1873), p. 21, includes Table of population, area inhabited, houses, rateable value and the poor-rate for each metropolitan Poor Law District; see also the *First report of the Local Government Board*, BPP 1872 [c516], XXV111.
39. *COR* (24 April 1872), p. 76.
40. *COR* (8 May 1872), p. 87.
41. *COR* (12 June 1872), p. 109; for Sir William Bodkin's similar views, *COR* (10 July 1872), p. 126.
42. For some while after the resignation of the Rev. H. Solly as Secretary on 28 February 1869, the COS had themselves been victims of two assistant secretaries who misappropriated funds in a lax system of accounting; M. Rooff, *A Hundred Years of Family Welfare* (1972), p. 306.
43. *COR* (24 April 1872), p. 73.
44. *COR* (1 March 1876), p. 45.
45. *Fourth Annual Report of COS Council* (1873), pp. 10–11.
46. *COR* (26 March 1873), p. 52.
47. *Fourth Annual Report of COS Council* (1873), p. 4.
48. Helen Bosanquet, op. cit., p. 31.
49. *Fourth Annual Report of COS Council* (1873), p. 3.
50. *COR* (12 June 1872), pp. 105–6.

51. Eighteen months later, C.B.P. Bosanquet, on the same subject, informed Council members that Eltham 'very seldom had any resident cases to return', Hackney 'did not send returns', Bethnal Green sent its returns fortnightly, and he could not say why there were no returns from the Islington, Strand, and City Committees; *COR* (21 January 1874), p. 191.
52. *COR* (24 January 1872), p. 7.
53. *COR* (10 July 1872), p. 126.
54. *COR* (1 May 1872), p. 77.
55. Ibid., pp. 77–8.
56. *COR* (16 October 1872), p. 149.
57. *COR* (23 October 1872), pp. 153–4.
58. *COR* (12 June 1872), p. 109; see also the Marquis of Westminster's views, *COR* (26 June 1872), p. 118.
59. *COR* (18 December 1872), p. 190; and *Third Annual Report, Bethnal Green COS Committee* (1872–3), p. 7.
60. *COR* (28 May 1873), p. 92.
61. *COR* (20 May 1874), p. 260.
62. *COR* (1873), pp. 17, 31, 41, 157, 161 and 175.
63. *COR* (25 March 1874), p. 231.
64. *COR* (17 March 1875), p. 45.
65. The Strand District Committee included the Duke of Northumberland as Chairman, W.H. Gladstone Esq., MP, as a Vice-Chairman, 34 other Committee members and 21 'Associates'. Many were prestigious, all were male. *Second Annual Report of the Strand COS District Committee* (1872–3), p. 2.
66. *COR* (17 July 1872), p. 133.
67. *COR* (20 November 1872), p. 170.
68. *COR* (16 October 1872), p. 150.
69. *Fourth Annual Report of the COS* (1872), p. 6. Refer to the discussion in Chapter 1 of this volume.
70. *Sixth Annual Report of the COS* (1874), pp. 14–15.
71. *COR* (13 January 1875), p. 6.
72. *COR* (11 February 1874), p. 205.
73. *COR* (13 January 1875), p. 6.
74. Helen Bosanquet, op. cit., p. 43.
75. *COR* (16 October 1872), p. 150.
76. *COR* (4 December 1872), p. 181.
77. *COR* (26 March 1873), p. 53.
78. *Fifth Annual Report of the St Marylebone COS District Committee* (1874), p. 10; *First Annual Report of the Stepney COS District Committee* (1873–4), p. 5; and *Second Annual Report of the Shoreditch COS District Committee* (1873), p. 3.
79. *COR* (3 November 1875), p. 131.
80. We learn from Table 2.3 that a total of 81 grants were provided by Fulham and Hammersmith COS District Committee during the same financial year 1872–3. From Table 2.6 it can be calculated that 107 of the 191 applications that year involved married couples, that is, a ratio of 56:100. Applying this ratio to the 81 grants suggests that 45 of them went to married couples and therefore that 126 adults were expected to share them. To get an impression of how many children were also expected to benefit from the grants; note from Table 2.6 that 556 children were associated with the 191 applications.

Now, by applying the ratio of 81:191, that is, grants:applications, to the number of children, there is the suggestion that around 236 children also benefited from the grants. Adding this number of children to the 126 adults likely to have been involved, there is the implication that around 362 adults or children shared the grants. Another approximation, based on the number of children shown in Table 2.6 as parented by married couples, would suggest rather more children participated in the grants and therefore their unit value would be less.

81. *First Annual Report of City COS Committee* (1873), p. 6.
82. Ibid., p. 7.
83. Ibid., p. 8.
84. *Second Annual Report of City COS Committee* (1874), p. 6.
85. Ibid., p. 8.
86. *Fifth Annual Report of Paddington COS Committee* (1874), p. 21.
87. Ibid., p. 25 (italics in original).
88. *Second Annual Report of Strand COS Committee* (1872–3), p. 6.
89. Ibid., p. 8.
90. *Third Annual Report of Strand COS Committee* (1873–4), pp. 7–8.
91. *Third Annual Report of Bethnal Green COS Committee* (1872–3), p. 2.
92. Ibid., p. 3.
93. Ibid., p. 4.
94. *Fourth Annual Report of Bethnal Green COS Committee* (1873–4), p. 8.
95. Ibid., p. 7 (italics in original).
96. Ibid., p. 8.
97. *Fifth Annual Report of St Marylebone COS Committee* (1874), p. 11.
98. *First Annual Report of Poplar, Bow and Bromley COS Committee* (1874), p. 26.
99. Ibid.
100. *First Annual Report of Stepney and Mile End Old Town COS Committee* (1873–4), p. 9.
101. *Fifth Annual Report of Paddington COS District Committee* (1874), p. 13.
102. *COR* (20 May 1874), p. 261.
103. *COR* (3 May 1876), p. 81.
104. *COR* (17 May 1876), p. 90.
105. *COR* (24 May 1876), p. 94.
106. *COR* (31 May 1876), pp. 97–9.
107. *COR* (21 June 1876), p. 107.
108. *COR* (28 June 1876), p. 111.
109. *COR* (5 July 1876), p. 117.
110. *COReview* (February 1892), p. 47.
111. *COR* (12 July 1876), p. 119.

3   Developments by the Turn of the Century

1. Sections of this chapter have been extracted from the author's LSE Working Paper in Economic History, No. 14, *Scientific Charity in Victorian London* (July 1993).
2. *COR* (24 February 1881), p. 50.
3. Jennifer Hart, 'Sir Charles Trevelyan at the Treasury', *English Historical Review*, Vol LXXV (January 1960), p. 99.

4. *COR* (5 July 1876), p. 116.
5. *Charity Organisation Review* (December 1890), p. 518.
6. *16th Annual Report of COS Council* (1883–4), p. 60. For similar comments from St Pancras (South), refer to p. 87 of the COS Report and for St Saviour's, Southwark COS being able to collect locally only £41 7s of their expenditure of £473, see p. 137 of the St Saviour's Report.
7. *8th Annual Report of COS Council* (1876), p. 12.
8. *COReview* (December 1890), p. 519.
9. *Twenty Second Annual Report of COS Council* (1889–90), pp. xvi and xvii.
10. Charles Loch Mowat, *The Charity Organisation Society 1869–1913* (1961), p. 22.
11. *Twenty-second Annual Report of the COS Council* (1889–90).
12. Refer to note (g), Table 3.7.
13. *Co-operation of District Committees of the COS with Boards of Guardians,* COS pamphlet (1879), pp. 15–64.
14. *Third Annual Report of the LGB,* PP 1874 [c1071], XXV.1, Report number 12, pp. 127–35. From 1875 the level of co-operation appears to have waned sharply with subsequent St Marylebone Committee reports merely indicating co-operation in general terms. Other District Committees achieving some degree of empathy with their local Poor Law Union in the crusade against outdoor relief were those at St George's-in-the-East and Whitechapel. Contact was eased by two COS stalwarts in Albert Pell and A.G. Crowder who doubled up as guardians. The Rev. Samuel Barnett, vicar of St Jude's Whitechapel, was also a driving force towards co-operation with local Poor Law authorities. Barnett's growing awareness from around 1883 that his involvement in reducing pauperism in the parish had done nothing to reduce poverty is discussed later in this volume.
15. *Twenty-second Report of the COS Council* (1889–90), p. xxi (brackets and italics in original).
16. Ibid., p. xxiii.
17. *COReview*, November 1900, No. 47, pp. 312–23.
18. *Twenty Seventh Annual Report of COS Council* (1894–5), p. 29.
19. *Sixteenth Annual Report of COS Council* (December 1884), p. 96 (brackets in original).
20. For further COS cases see: Lynn H. Lees, *The solidarities of Strangers: the English poor laws and the people, 1700–1948* (Cambridge 1998), pp. 168–74. For an assessment of the COS's case-work approach see: Pat Thane, *Foundations of the Welfare State* (2nd edn, 1996), pp. 21–4.
21. Report of St George's (Hanover Square) COS District Committee, *Sixteenth Annual Report of COS Council* (December 1884), p. 69.
22. Report of Clerkenwell and St Luke's COS District Committee, *Sixteenth Annual Report, COS Council* (December 1884), p. 108.
23. Report of City of London COS District Committee, *Sixteenth Annual Report of COS Council* (December 1884), p. 111.
24. Shoreditch COS District Committee, *Sixteenth Annual Report of COS Council* (December 1884), p. 116.
25. *COR* (24 January 1884), p. 35
26. *COR* (19 July 1884), p. 240.
27. *Sixteenth Annual Report of the COS Council* (December 1884), p. 106.
28. *COR* (29 March 1876), p. 64.

29. *Seventh Annual Report of COS Council* (1876), p. 13 (italics and brackets in original).
30. *Fifth Annual Report, Kensington COS District Committee* (1874), p. 8 (italics in original).
31. *Charity Organisation Paper* No. 1 (1871), p. 5.
32. *Royal Commission on the Aged Poor*, BPP 1895 [c7684], XIV, 2066–9, p. 125 and 2099, p. 126. Also S. and B. Webb (eds), *The Break up of the Poor Law; being Part One of the Minority Report of the poor Law Commission* (1909), pp. 28–42.
33. *Twenty-third Annual Report of Poor Law Board*, BPP 1871 (c396), XXVII, p. 38.
34. *Twentieth Annual Report, LGB*, BPP 1891 [c6460], XXXIII, pp. lxxxi–ii and BPP 1900, LXXIII.743 [c137].
35. *COR* (August 1900), Supplement, p. 1.
36. Shoreditch COS District Committee, *Sixteenth Annual Report of COS Council* (December 1884), p. 117.
37. *Sixteenth Annual Report of COS Council* (December 1884), p. 96.
38. Ibid., p. 160.
39. Ibid., p. 174.
40. *COReview* (26 March 1873), p. 52.
41. C.S. Loch, 'Loans', *Charity Organisation Paper* No. 6 (1875), p. 1.
42. *COR* (26 March 1873), p. 52.
43. *Fifth Annual Report of COS Council* (1873), p. 5. Also see 'Loans', *Charity Organisation Paper* No. 6 (revised February 1876).
44. *Fourth Annual Report of COS Council* (1872), p. 6.
45. *Sixteenth Annual Report of COS Council* (December 1884), p. 142. As early as 1874 the COS Kensington Committee admitted that there had been 18 defaulters out of their total of 59 loans; *Fifth Annual Report of the Kensington COS District Committee* (1874), pp. 38–9.
46. *Sixteenth Annual Report of COS Council* (December 1884), p. 136.
47. Ibid., including extracts from district Committees, pp. 127, 137 and 125.
48. *Fifteenth Annual Report of COS Council* (May, 1884), p. 38.
49. Ibid.
50. *First Report of the COS Council* (1870) and the accompanying 'Rough sketch of Proposed Plan'.
51. K. Woodroofe, *From Charity to Social Work* (1968), p. 39.
52. *Twenty-second Annual Report of Poor Law Board*, Appendix 4, BPP 1870 [c123], XXXV.I, pp. 9–11. *First Annual Report of the Local Government Board*, Appendix 20, BPP 1872 [c516], XXVIII, pp. 63–8.
53. Beatrice Webb, *My Apprenticeship* (1979 edn), pp. 198–9.
54. *Seventh Annual Report of London COS Council* (1876), pp. 13–14.
55. *Third Annual Report of the Local Government Board*, PP 1874 [c1071], XXV, p. 133; *First Annual Report of Poplar, Bow and Bromley COS District Committee* (1873), p. 8.
56. *Annual Report of the Paddington District Committee; Sixteenth Annual Report of the COS Council* (December 1884), pp. 62–3.
57. *Twenty-seventh Annual Report of London COS Council* (1894–5), p. 8.
58. *Sixteenth Annual Report, COS Council* (December 1884), p. 86.
59. Ibid, pp. 126–30.
60. *Sixteenth Annual Report, COS Council* (December 1884), p. 140.

61. *COReview* (November 1900), No. 47, p. 319.
62. *COReview* (June 1893), No. 101, p. 222.
63. *Twenty seventh Annual Report of COS Council* (1894–5), pp. 8 and 9.
64. C.S. Loch, *The Charities Register and Digest* (1890), p. clv.
65. Ibid. (1890), p. clv.
66. *Sixteenth Annual Report of COS Council* (December 1884), including summary Accounts of district Committees, p. 221. It is appreciated that at least one of these pensions may not have been spread over a full twelve-month period, but the COS report provides no support for this supposition.
67. *Annual Report, St James, Soho, and West Strand COS District Committee* (1887), p. 13.
68. *Twenty-fourth Annual Report of COS Council* (1891–2), pp. 29–31.
69. That is, 188 pensioners shared a total of £1955 during the twelve-month period.
70. *Twenty-seventh Annual Report of COS Council* (1894–5), pp. 8 and 95.
71. *COReview* (February 1885), p. 76.
72. *COReview* (March 1885), p. 139.
73. Ibid. p. 139.
74. *COReview* (April 1885), p. 188.
75. Ibid.
76. Howard Newby, 'The Deferential Dialectic', *Comparative Studies in Society and History*, Vol. 17, No. 2, (1975), p. 161.
77. *COReview* (March 1887), p. 121.
78. *Third Annual Report of LGB*, BPP 1874 [c1071], XXV.I, Appendix B, p. 145.
79. C.L. Mowat, op. cit., p. 98; and the *Twenty-fourth Annual Report of COS Council* (1893), pp. 29–30.
80. *Sixteenth Annual Report of COS Council* (December 1884), p. 103.
81. *Annual Report of Kensington COS District Committee* (1887), pp. 10–11.
82. *COReview* (1885), p. 283.
83. Ibid., p. 404.
84. *COReview* (1886), p. 515. (italics in original).
85. *COReview* (1888), p. 168.
86. *COReview* (1889), p. 352.
87. *Annual Report of St Olave's COS District Committee* (1887), pp. 6–7.
88. Council Annual Reports regularly included a list of COS 'Publications and Papers'.
89. C.L. Mowat, op. cit., p. 73.
90. For example, refer to *COS Report on Soup Kitchens or Dinner-tables of the Metropolis* (1871).
91. *Twenty-first Annual Report of the COS Council* (1888–9), pp. 12–13.
92. C.L. Mowat, op. cit., p. 75.
93. *COReview* No. 81 (September 1891), pp. 367–8 and No. 88, also (April 1892), pp. 158–60.
94. C.L. Mowat, op. cit, pp. 75–6.
95. *COReview* July 1895, p. 328.
96. Helen Bosanquet, *Social Work in London, 1869–1912* (1912), pp. 219–22.
97. A.F. Young and E.T. Ashton, *British Social Work in the Nineteenth Century*, (1956), pp. 108–9.
98. Helen Bosanquet, op. cit., pp. 206–7.

99. Report of COS Special Committee of the Accounts of Charitable Institutions, (1890); *Thirty-first Annual Report of the COS Council* (1898–9), pp. 24–6.
100. *Thirty-second Annual Report of the COS Council* (1899–1900), p. 12.
101. *Twenty-ninth Annual Report of the COS Council* (1896–7), p. 26; *Thirty-second Annual Report of the COS Council* (1899–1900), p. 24; *Nineteenth Annual Report of the COS Council* (1886–7), p. 9.
102. *COR* (14 June 1883), pp. 199, 205–7, 218 and 222; *COReview* (November 1890), pp. 430–1.
103. C.L. Mowat, op. cit., p. 90.
104. Report of Emigration Sub-Committee, *Thirty-second Annual Report of the COS Council* (1899–1900), p. 39; Dudley Baines, 'Population, migration and the regions', R. Floud and D. McCloskey (eds), *The Economic History of Britain since 1700*, Vol. 2, (2nd edn, Cambridge 1994), p. 49.
105. *COReview* (November 1900), No. 47, p. 320.
106. *COR* (27 March 1872), p. 60.
107. *Thirty-second Annual Report of the COS Council* (1899–1900), pp. 80–3.
108. Frank K. Prochaska, *Women and Philanthropy in Nineteenth-century England* (Oxford 1980), pp. 109–10.
109. *Twenty-third Annual Report, COS Council* (1890–1), p. 1.
110. *Seventh Annual Report of the COS Council* (1875), pp. 55–6; *Thirty-second Annual Report of the COS Council* (1899–1900), pp. 80 and 82.
111. *Thirty-second Annual Report of the COS Council* (1899–1900), p. 9.
112. *COReview* (June 1897), p. 298.
113. Helen Bosanquet, *Strength of the People* (1903 edn), pp. 208–9. (italics in the original).
114. *Thirty-second Annual Report of the COS Council* (1899–1900), pp. 2–3.

4 1900 Onwards – a Half-Century of Change and General COS Decline

1. *Sixtieth Annual Report of COS Council* (1927–8), p. 12.
2. *Sixty-seventh Annual Report of COS Council* (1934–5), p. 16.
3. *Sixtieth Annual Report of COS Council* (1927–8), p. 12.
4. James Leiby, *The History of Social Welfare and Social Work in the United States* (New York 1978), p. 114.
5. *Sixty-seventh Annual Report of COS Council* (1934–5), p. 16.
6. *Sixteenth Annual report of the LGB*, PP 1887, [c5131], XXXVI.1.
7. *Twenty-fourth Annual report of COS Council* (1892), p. 2.
8. *Fortieth Annual Report of COS Council* (1907–8), pp. 10–11.
9. A.F. Young and E.T. Ashton, *British Social Work in the Nineteenth Century* (1956), p. 107.
10. C.L. Mowat, *The Charity Orgaisation Society 1869–1913* (1961), p. 147.
11. *Thirty-fifth Annual Report of COS Council* (1902–3), pp. 2–3.
12. The Cautionary Card was a register of persons and organizations judged, by the COS, to be fraudulently requesting money. It was regularly updated and made available throughout the COS movement and to other *bona fide* interested parties.
13. *Sixty-fifth Annual Report of COS Council* (1932–3), pp. 23–4.

14. H. Bosanquet, *Social Work in London, 1869–1912* (1914), pp. 198, 202–3, 275 and 293. Other Commission members were Mrs Helen Bosanquet, Miss Octavia Hill, Rev. L.R. Phelps, Rev. T.G. Gardiner and T. Hancock Nunn, Esq. Chairman of the Commission was an ex-Cabinet Minister and long-time COS Council member, Lord George Hamilton. Frictional discussion and competing reports between the COS contingent and opposing factions on the Commission are discussed in Chapter 6.

15. Beatrice Webb, another member of the Poor Laws Commission, noted in her diary signs of Loch being stressed, rude and 'evidently very ill' during the protracted deliberations. Beatrice Webb, *Our Partnership* (1948), pp. 389–90, 343, 377. Helen Bosanquet, who herself had contributed greatly to the authorship of the 1905–9 Royal Commission Majority report, also found her health deteriorating. She, together with her none-too-robust husband Bernard, partly retired from the public spotlight to settle in Oxshott, Surrey during the pre-war years.

16. *Forty-first Annual Report of COS Council* (1908–9), p. 6.

17. *Fifty-ninth Annual Report of COS Council* (1926–7), p. 6.

18. Madeline Rooff, *A Hundred Years of Family Welfare* (1972), pp. 123–4 and p. 133.

19. Competing interpretations of Green's principles are discussed in Chapter 6.

20. J.C. Pringle, *Social Work of the London Churches* (1937), pp. 212–15 and 221.

21. *COReview*, No. 281 (May 1920), Supplement, p. 142.

22. J.B. Hurry, *Poverty and its Vicious Circles* (2nd edn 1921), p. 362.

23. R. Saunderson, 'The Relief of the Unemployed', *COReview*, No. 290 (February 1921), p. 119.

24. *COReview*, No. 294 (June 1921), pp. 232–3.

25. *Fifty-ninth Annual Report of COS Council* (1926–7), p. 1.

26. Ibid., p. 1.

27. Ibid., p. 12.

28. Ibid., p. 12 (brackets and italics in the original).

29. *Sixty-second Annual Report of COS Council* (1929–30), p. 17.

30. *Sixty-ninth Annual Report of COS Council* (1936–7), p. 15.

31. Kathleen Woodroofe, *From Charity to Social Work* (1968), p. 54.

32. Cited by Jane Lewis, *The Voluntary Sector, the State and Social Work in Britain* (1997), p. 85.

33. *Sixty-eighth Annual Report of COS Council* (1935–6), pp. 15–8.

34. *Fifty-ninth Annual Report of COS Council* (1926–7), p. 3.

35. *Thirty-fourth Annual Report of COS Council* (1901–2), pp. 17–8, refer to Table 4.9 for an overall influence of this funding source.

36. *Thirty-sixth Annual Report of COS Council* (1903–4), p. 23.

37. Ibid., p. 24.

38. *Fifty-eighth Annual Report of COS Council* (1925–6), p. 4.

39. L.V. Shairp, 'Industrial Disputes and the Relief of Distress', *COReview*, Vol. XXXV (January 1914), pp. 30–7.

40. *Thirty-seventh Annual Report of COS Council* (1904–5), p. 17.

41. *Fifty-ninth Annual Report of COS Council* (1926–7), pp. 11–2.

42. *Seventieth Annual Report of COS Council* (1937–8), p. 7.

43. Ibid., pp. 7–8.

44. M.E. Brasnett, *The Story of the Citizens' Advice Bureaux* (1964).

45. *Seventy-seventh Annual Report of Family Welfare Association (formerly the Charity Organisation Society)* (1944–5), p. 3.
46. R.H. Titmuss, *Problems of Social Policy* (1950), pp. 261–2.
47. *Seventy-sixth Annual Report of COS Council* (1943–4), p. 12.
48. *Seventy-seventh Annual Report of Family Welfare Association* (1944–5), pp. 7–8.
49. Ibid., pp. 8–9.
50. *Fifty-seventh Annual Report of COS Council* (1924–5), p. 9.
51. *Fortieth Annual Report of the COS Council* (1907–8), p. 6.
52. Flora Thompson, *Lark Rise* (1939), p. 100.
53. *COReview* (September 1908).
54. *Forty-first Annual Report of COS Council* (1908–9), pp. 42–3.
55. *Seventy-first Annual Report of COS Council* (1938–9), p. 15.
56. O. Newman and A. Foster, *The Value of the Pound* (1995), p. 305.
57. *COQuarterly* (April 1928), Vol. II, No. 2, pp. 52–8.
58. *Thirty-fourth Annual Report of the COS Council* (1901–2), p. 82.
59. E.C. Ramsbottom, 'The course of wage rates in the UK', *Journal of Royal Statistical Society*, Vol. 98 (1935).
60. *Thirty-ninth Annual Report of COS Council* (1906–7), pp. 25–9.
61. *Fortieth Annual Report of COS Council* (1907–8), pp. 37–9.
62. *Thirty-ninth Annual Report of COS Council* (1906–7), p. 27.
63. See Table 4.6 for 1901–2 comparison.
64. *Seventieth Annual Report of COS Council* (1937–8), p. 73.
65. *Sixty-seventh Annual Report of COS Council* (1934–5), p. 21.
66. *Sixtieth Annual Report of the COS Council* (1927–8), p. 14.
67. *Sixty-seventh Annual Report of the COS Council* (1934–5), p. 17.
68. *COQuarterly* (October 1927), Vol. 1, No. 3, pp. 151–7 (italics in original).
69. *COQuarterly* (July 1932), Vol. VI, No. 3, p. 100.
70. *COQuarterly* No. 206, (1907), pp. 74–6. See also Chapter 6 of this volume.
71. Madeline Rooff, *A Hundred Years of Family Welfare* (1972), p. 278.
72. *Sixty-seventh Annual Report of COS Council* (1935), p. 17. (bold print as in the original).
73. Ibid., pp. 84–5.
74. *Sixty-third Annual Report of the COS Council* (1930–1), p. 2.
75. *Seventy-first Annual Report of the COS Council* (1938–9), p. 13.
76. *COQuarterly* (October 1931), Vol. V, No. 4, p. 157.
77. J.C. Pringle, op. cit., p. 233. (Capitals and italics in the original).
78. *Social Work* (July 1943), Vol. 2, No. 9, pp. 357–9.
79. Madeline Rooff, *A Hundred Years of Family Welfare* (1972), pp. 169–85.
80. On 4 December 1944 it was announced that the name would change to 'The Family Welfare Association', to come into effect at some later date. *Seventy-sixth Annual report of the COS Council* (1943–4), p. 5.
81. *Social Work* (October 1943), Vol. 2, No. 10, pp. 385–7.
82. Seventy-third Annual Report of COS Council (1940–1), pp. 3, 8, 12–5 and 22; and *Seventy-second Annual Report of COS Council* (1939–40), p. 24. The annual subscription of King George VI increased from £10 to £20.
83. *Seventy-sixth Annual Report of COS Council* (1943–4), p. 14.
84. *Seventy-eighth Annual Report of Family Welfare Association* (1945–6), p. 14.
85. *Eightieth Annual Report of Family Welfare Association* (1947–8), p. 4.
86. *Eighty-first Annual Report of Family Welfare Association* (1948–9), pp. 4, 15–6.

87. *Seventy-sixth Annual Report of COS Council* (1943–4), p. 4.

5 Charity Organization outside London

1. *COR*, 54 (9 April 1873), p. 67.
2. *Fourth Annual Report of London COS Council* (1873), p. 6.
3. Charles Loch Mowat, *The Charity Organisation Society 1869–1913* (1961), pp. 91–2.
4. E.W. Wakefield, *COReview*, 139 (1908), p. 40. Early indications were that COS invitations for the Guilds to enlist as corresponding Societies were declined; *Thirty-ninth Annual report of London COS Council* (1907), p. 32.
5. Robert Humphreys, *Sin, Organized Charity and the Poor Law in Victorian England* (1995), p. 96.
6. *Twenty-second Annual Report of COS Council* (1889–90), pp. v–vii.
7. There are indications that some of the units included by the COS in their data were flattered by the appellation 'Society'. For example, one of those listed by the COS, from 1880–82, was the Dorking Mendicity Society having as honorary secretary W.W. Clark of the High Street. Clark was the proprietor of a chemist's shop, 97 High Street, Dorking and a member of the local Poor Law Board. Whether Clark ever had much success in organizing charities is doubtful as his Mendicity Society seems to have had slight impact. It was not mentioned in the local Kelly's Directory (1882).
8. *Thirty-second Annual Report of London COS Council* (1900), pp. v–viii.
9. Charles Loch Mowat, op. cit., p. 93.
10. *COReview*, No. 101 (June 1893), p. 223.
11. Ibid., pp. 223 and 233.
12. *COReview*, No. 121 (February 1895), p. 59.
13. *COReview*, No. 101 (June 1893), p. 236. It was also reported on p. 233 of the same issue that Mr J.W. Pennyman, Chair of the Provincial Sub-Committee, when visiting COSs in the country, had 'frequently been met with the objection that it was impossible to get volunteer workers'.
14. *Twelfth Annual Report of COS Council* (1880), pp. 4–7; and *Forty-sixth Annual Report of COS Council* (1914), pp. vi–x.
15. *Forty-first Annual Report of COS Council* (1909), pp. 67–8.
16. *Sixty-seventh Annual Report of COS Council* (1935), p. 84.
17. Alan Kidd, 'Charity Organisation and the Manchester Unemployed, c1870–1914', *Social History*, 9, (1984), pp. 57–8.
18. *Report of Interdepartmental Committee on Physical Deterioration*, PP XXXII, (1904) [c2175]; Dudley Baines, 'Population, migration and regional development', in R. Floud and D. McCloskey, *The Economic History of Britain since 1700*, Vol. 2 (Cambridge 1994), pp. 36–8; B.S. Rowntree, *Poverty: a Study of Town Life* (1901) and C. Booth, *Life and Labour of the People in London*, 17 Vols (1889–1903). For discussion of negative COS responses to the Booth and the Rowntree surveys, refer to Chapter 6 of this volume.
19. Alan Kidd, op. cit., pp. 55–6.
20. Of the 80 or so Guilds of Help operating across Britain in 1914, the COS felt comfortable about claiming only two of them in their data summarized in Figure 6.1. They were at Falmouth and at Middlesbrough.

21. Pat Thane, *Foundations of the Welfare State* (2nd edn 1996), p. 161.
22. Margaret Brasnett, *Voluntary Social Action* (1969), pp. 5–6.
23. Dorothy C. Keeling, *The Crowded Stairs* (Plymouth 1961), p. 19.
24. M. Cahill and Tony Jowitt, 'The New Philanthropy', *Journal of Social Policy*, 9 (3 July 1980), p. 368.
25. G.R. Snowdon, 'Report on the Guilds of Help...', PP 1911 (XXXII) [c5664], p. 16. Some Guilds which adopted names such as 'Civic League', 'League of Help' and 'City Aid' are included in this number; L.V. Shairp, *COReview*, Vol. XXXII, New Series, No. 187 (July 1912), p. 73.
26. Keith Laybourn, *The Guild of Help and the Changing Face of Edwardian Philanthropy* (Lampeter, 1994), pp. 83 and 205–7.
27. See Chapter 1 of this volume reference the activities at Elberfeld and their influence on the London COS.
28. W. Milledge, *COReview*, Vol. XXXI, New series, 185 (May 1912), p. 243.
29. W. Milledge, *COReview*, 115 (July 1906), pp. 48 and 46.
30. *COReview*, 115 (July 1906), p. 56. This concurs with Kidd's opinion that the theoretical persistent and influential model of charity organization was one of class relations and remained fundamentally unaltered as practised by COSs in the provinces; Alan Kidd, op. cit., p. 61.
31. Elizabeth Macadam, *The New Philanthropy* (1934), p. 33.
32. This contrasted with the network of COSs outside the capital where, despite London's claim that provincial Societies were independent, each could expect acerbic public criticism and even excommunication should they stray from the authoritarian edicts despatched from the central Council.
33. Keith Laybourn, *The Evolution of British Social Policy...*, (Keele 1995), pp. 156–7.
34. G.R. Snowdon, op. cit., p. 4.
35. Anon, *Guilds of Help* (June 1911), p. 3.
36. *COReview*, 139 (1908), p. 52.
37. R.A. Leach, 'Guilds of Help...', *Thirty-sixth Poor Law Conference for North Western Districts* (1910), p. 424.
38. Keith Laybourn, op. cit. (1994), pp. 3 and 13–27.
39. *Thirty-sixth Poor Law Conference for North Western Districts* (1910), p. 440.
40. C.S. Loch, 'The Policy of Voluntary Aid...', *COReview* (February 1912), pp. 82–3.
41. *COReview*, 115 (July 1906), p. 55.
42. W. Grisewood, *The Relief of the Poor in Germany* (Liverpool, 1905), pp. 24–5.
43. Dorothy C. Keeling, *The Crowded Stairs* (Plymouth 1961), pp. 23, 38–9.
44. *COReview*, 134 (February 1908), p. 80.
45. Keith Laybourn, op. cit. (1994), pp. 165 and 168.
46. The NCSS was to become the National Council of Voluntary Organisations (NCVO).
47. M. Cahill and Tony Jowitt, 'The New Philanthropy', *Journal of Social Policy*, 9, 3 (July 1980), page 382. Note that some Guilds elected to operate under their founding name even after the Second World War.
48. *Forty-ninth Annual Report of COS Council*, Appendix II (1916–17), pp. 16–17.
49. Margaret Brasnett, *Voluntary Social Action* (1969), p. 17.
50. *Fifty-second Annual Report of COS Council* (1919–20), p. 20.
51. Madeline Rooff, *A Hundred Years of Family Welfare* (1972), p. 118.

52. Henry A. Mess, *Voluntary Social Services since 1918* (1947), p. 14.
53. Between the world wars, the annual reports of the London COS ceased the formal inclusion of details of other organization. Instead, they provided similar information in the *Annual Charities Register and Digest*.
54. *Seventieth Annual Report of London COS Council* (1937–8), p. 29.
55. Ibid.
56. Madeline Rooff, op. cit., p. 118.
57. *Fifty-second Annual Report of COS Council* (1919–20), Appendix II, p. 13.
58. *Fifty-seventh Annual Report of COS Council* (1924–5), Appendix II, p. 21.
59. *Sixty-first Annual Report of COS Council* (1928–9), Appendix II, p. 35.
60. *Sixty-second Annual Report of COS Council* (1929–30), Appendix II, p. 27.
61. *Seventy-first Annual Report of COS Council* (1938–9), p. 12.
62. *Sixty-ninth Annual Report of the COS Council* (1936–7), pp. 28–9.
63. For example; attending the 1900 conference there were delegates from USA, Greece and Sweden. Papers were presented on different aspects of poverty in Canada and the USA; *COReview*, 44 (August 1900), pp. 57–190.
64. For example, Daniel C. Gilman (ed.), *The Organisation of Charities*, Chicago (June 1893), pp. 135–384.
65. Kathleen Woodroofe, *From Charity to Social Work in England and the United States* (1962), p. 84.
66. W. Grisewood, *The Relief of the Poor in America* (Liverpool 1905), p. 4.
67. R.T. Davis, 'Pauperism in the City of New York', *Proceedings of the First Conference of Charities and Correction*, New York (May 1874), pp. 24–6.
68. For example, *Fifth Annual Conference of Charities*, Cincinnati (May 1878), pp. 32–79 and *Eighth Annual Conference of Charities*, Boston (July 1881), pp. 144–67.
69. David Ward, *Poverty, Ethnicity and the American City*, 1840–1925 (Cambridge 1989), pp. 22–3. See Chapter 1 of this volume for discussion on Chalmers' activities.
70. W. Grisewood ..., *Poor in America*, op. cit., p. 10
71. Charles Loch Mowat, op. cit., p. 94.
72. Michael B. Katz, *In the Shadow of the Poorhouse* (New York, 1986) p. 72.
73. F.D. Watson, *The Charity Organisation Movement in the USA* (New York 1922), pp. 177–90.
74. S.H. Gurteen, *Handbook of Charitable Organisation* (Buffalo, NY, 1882), pp. 38 and 141.
75. Cited by Michael B. Katz, *The 'Underclass' Debate* (Princetown, 1993) p. 9.
76. W. Grisewood ..., *Poor in America*, op. cit., p. 16.
77. James Leiby, *A History of Social Welfare and Social Work in the United States*, (New York 1978), p. 115.
78. John H. Ehrenreich, *The Altruistic Imagination* (Cornell 1985), p. 62.
79. Daniel Devine, *Poverty and Society* (1988), p. 29.
80. Thomas J. Sugrue, 'The Structures of Urban Poverty: the Reorganisation of Space and Work in Three Periods of American History', in Michael B. Katz, op. cit. (1993), pp. 85–117.
81. Michael B. Katz, *In the Shadow of the Poor House* (New York 1986), pp. 80–4; David Ward, *Poverty, Ethnicity and the American City*, 1840–1925 (Cambridge 1989), p. 57.
82. *Charity Organisation Review*, No. 101, June 1893, pp. 234–5.

83. W. Grisewood..., Poor in America, op. cit., p. 35.
84. Daniel Devine, *Poverty and Society* (1988), p. 29.
85. James Leiby, op. cit., p. 116.
86. F.D. Watson, op. cit., p. 272.
87. Refer to Chapter 3 of this volume for discussion on how the COS in Britain signified the perceived class differences between their salaried agent and COS volunteers.
88. W. Grisewood..., *Poor in America*, op. cit., pp. 34–5.
89. O.C. McCulloch, 'Associated Charities, Report of the Committee on Charitable Organisation in Cities', *Proceedings NCCC* (1880), p. 3.
90. Margaret E. Rich, *The Belief in People* (New York 1956), p. 33.
91. Michael B. Katz, op. cit., (1986), pp. 76–7.
92. S.H. Gurteen, op. cit., p. 126.
93. W. Grisewood ..., *Poor in America*, op. cit., p. 28.
94. Margaret E. Rich, op. cit., p. 10.
95. F.D. Watson, op. cit., p. 358.
96. Daniel Devine, op. cit., p. 31.
97. F.D. Watson, op. cit., p. 359.
98. Michael B. Katz, op. cit. (1986), pp. 80–3.
99. John Boyle O'Reilly, 'Bohemia and Society', in Katherine E. Conway (ed.), *Watchwords* (Boston 1891), pp. 18–19.
100. Lowell's comments were influenced by adverse prevailing public attitudes. In 1896 the New York COS decided to strike out the word 'deserving' from its Constitution. A.F.C. Bourdillon, *Voluntary Social Services* (1945), p. 101.
101. Ward has noted that comparisons, not only among American cities but also among West European cities, 'were assumed to reveal that approximately a third of requests for relief were justifiable and that the remainder were caused by unemployment or misconduct'. David Ward, op. cit., p. 59.
102. Mary E. Richmond, *The Long View* (1930), p. 582.
103. W. Grisewood..., *Poor in America*, op. cit., p. 31.
104. Michael B. Katz, op. cit., (1986), p. 79.
105. S.H. Gurteen, op. cit., pp. 106–7.
106. Ibid., pp. 115–16.
107. John H. Ehrenreich, *The Altruistic Imagination* (Cornell 1985), p. 61.
108. Mary E. Richmond, *Friendly Visiting among the Poor* (1899), pp. 71 and 73.
109. James Leiby, op. cit., pp. 121–2.
110. Mary E. Richmond, op. cit., p. 345.
111. Margaret E. Rich, op. cit., p. 156.
112. E.T. Devine, 'The Dominant Note of the Modern Philanthropy', *Thirty-third Annual National Conference of Charities and Correction*, Philadelphia (May 1906), pp. 8–9.
113. Kathleen Woodroofe, op. cit., p. 95.
114. Jane Addams, Charity and Social Justice', *Thirty-seventh National Conference of Charities and Correction*, St Louis (May 1910), p. 17.
115. Kathleen Woodroofe, op. cit., pp. 146 and 175.
116. Very Rev. Robert F. Keegan, 'Democracy at the Cross-roads', *Sixty-third Annual National Conference of Social Work*, New Jersey (May 1936), pp. 7 and 21.
117. Kathleen Woodroofe, op. cit., p. 96.

118. F.D. Watson, op. cit., pp. 363, 442. For comparison of USA organizing Society titles, *Forty-second Annual Report of London COS Council* (1910), pp. xiv–xix and *Annual Charities Register and Digest* (1930), pp. 10–6.
119. Daniel Devine, op. cit., p. 34.
120. James Leiby, op. cit., p. 126.
121. W. Grisewood and A.F. Hanewinkel, *Jubilee Celebrations of the Elberfeld Poor Law* (Liverpool 1903), p. 12.
122. W. Grisewood, *The Relief of the Poor in Germany* (1905 Liverpool), pp. 17–18.
123. W. Grisewood and A.F. Hanewinkel, op. cit. (1903), p. 7.
124. A.J.L. van Beeck Calkoen, *COReview*, Vol. XXXI, New series, No. 182 (February 1912), p. 85.
125. A.J.L. van Beeck Calkoen, *COReview*, Vol. XXXII, New Series, No. 190 (October 1912), p. 240.
126. *Sixty-fourth Annual Report of London COS Council* (1932), pp. 18–19.
127. *COQuarterly*, Vol. X, October 1936, No. 4, pp. 183–98; and *Sixty-eighth Annual Report of London COS Council* (1935–6), p. 40.

6 Reasons for COS Decline

1. E.B. Tylor, *Primitive Culture* (1913 edn).
2. Una Cormack and Kay McDougall, 'Case-work in social service', Cherry Morris (ed.), *Social Casework* (1950), p. 28.
3. Helen Bosanquet, *Social work in London, 1869–1912* (1914), pp. 121–4.
4. *COR* (27 March 1872), p. 57.
5. *COR* (25 March 1874), p. 230.
6. *COR* (17 March 1875), p. 45.
7. *The Quarterly Review*, No. 410 (January 1907), pp. 73–4.
8. *COReview* No. 40, New Series (April 1900), pp. 209–10.
9. *COR* (27 March 1872), pp. 57–8.
10. *COR* (29 March 1876), pp. 66–7.
11. *COR* (19 July 1876), p. 126.
12. J. Hornsby Wright, *Thoughts and Experiences of a Charity Organizationist* (1878), p. 147.
13. *Social Notes*, No. 29 (21 September 1878), pp. 461–2.
14. *The Times* (11 March 1879).
15. *COR* (20 March 1879), pp. 79–80.
16. *COR* (1 May 1879), pp. 116–17
17. *COR* (1 June 1882), p. 167 (italics in original).
18. Helen Bosanquet, *Social Work in London 1869–1912* (1914), p. 65.
19. Ibid., pp. 64–5.
20. Ibid., pp. 134–6.
21. *COR* (20 March 1884), p. 94.
22. Henrietta Barnett, 'What has the Charity Organisation Society to do with Social Reform?' in S. and H. Barnett, *Practicable Socialism* (1895 edn), pp. 210–11.
23. M. Sewell, 'Some Aspects of Charity Organisation' (29 November 1897); cited by Jane Lewis, *The Voluntary Sector, the State and Social Work in Britain* (1996), p. 56.

24. *COR* (27 December 1884), pp. 425–6 and 428.
25. Robert Humphreys, *Sin, Organised Charity and the Poor Law 1870–90* (1995), pp. 162–3.
26. Octavia Hill, 'The Charity Organisation Society', *COS Occasional paper* No. 15, (1889). p. 4.
27. *COR* (April 1890), pp. 155 and 163.
28. Charles S. Loch, *Charities Register and Digest* (1890), pp. ix–x.
29. E.W. Benson, 'The Science of Charity', *COS Occasional Paper* No. 19 (1891).
30. Octavia Hill, 'The Charity Organisation Society', *COS Occasional paper* No. 20 (1891), pp. 2–3.
31. Ibid., pp. 3–4.
32. Ibid., p. 1.
33. *Twenty-third Annual Report of COS Council* (1891), pp. 1 and 4–6.
34. Charles Loch, 'Charity Organisation', *COS Occasional paper* No. 40 (1893), pp. 3–4.
35. Ibid., p. 4.
36. Samuel Barnett, 'University Settlements', reprinted in his *Practicable Socialism* (1895 edn), p. 165.
37. *COReview* (August 1895), pp. 338–44.
38. Ibid., pp. 361–72.
39. Helen Bosanquet, op. cit. (1903), pp. 142–4.
40. C.L. Marson, *Charity Organisation and Jesus Christ* (1897), p. 33.
41. Alfred Marshall, *Principles of Economics* (1891 edn), p. 3.
42. Helen Bosanquet, *The Strength of the People* (1903 edn), pp. 70–1.
43. Gareth Stedman Jones, *Outcast London* (Penguin 1984 edn), p. 147.
44. Michael Freeden, *The New Liberalism: an Ideology of Social Reform* (Oxford, 1978), p. 172.
45. G. Williams, *The State and the Standard of Living* (1936), p. 20.
46. G. Sabine, *A History of Political Theory* (New York 1963), p. 732.
47. A.D. Lindsay, Introduction to T.H. Green, *Political Obligation* (1941 reprint), p. xviii.
48. A. Toynbee, *Lectures on the Industrial Revolution* (1887), p. xi.
49. Helen Lynd, *England in the Eighteen-eighties* (1968), p. 147.
50. B. Kirkham Gray, *Philanthropy and the State, or Social Politics* (1908), p. 116.
51. John A. Hobson, 'The Social Philosophy of Charity Organisation', *Contemporary Review* LXX (1896), pp. 710–14 and 727. A similar stance was adopted by Mrs Townshend in Fabian Tract No. 15, *The Case against the Charity Organisation Society* (1911), p. 6.
52. George Lansbury, Leader of the Labour Party, 1931–5, was attracted towards helping the poor and as a young man worked with Whitechapel COS. He later described COS policy as 'heartless and brutal in its effects on the life of the poor'; G. Lansbury, *My Life* (1928), p. 130. Beatrice Webb had also been a front-line COS worker when young. She became critical of the COS's 'calm assumption' of 'social and mental superiority' and of its 'self-complacent mental harshness'. Eventually she described COS doctrine as being 'repellent' with members lacking the 'faintest glimmer' of what Webb signally called 'the consciousness of collective sin'. Immediately prior to the announcement of the Commissioners' names, the Prime Minister, A.J. Balfour lunched with the Webbs before joining them at a matinée performance of G.B.S.'s new

play *Major Barbara*; refer to B. Webb, *My Apprenticeship* (Cambridge edn, 1979), pp. 195, 202, 206, and 313–14.

53. Derek Foster, *The Evolution of the British Welfare State* (2nd edn, 1986), p. 159.

54. For an impression of the verbal tussles within the Commission: A.M. McBriar, *An Edwardian Mixed Doubles; The Bosanquets v. The Webbs* (Oxford, 1987), pp. 175–250.

55. A.W. Vincent, 'The Poor Law Reports of 1909 and the Social Theory of the Charity Organisation Society', *Victorian Studies* 27 (1983–4), p. 345.

56. Ibid., p. 361.

57. *The Majority Report of the Royal Commission on the Poor Laws and Relief of Distress* PP 1909 [c4499], XXXVII, Part IV, pp. 96, 159 and 140.

58. Karl de Schweinitz, *England's Road to Social Security* (New York, 1975 edn), pp. 189–91.

59. *The Majority Report of the Royal Commission on the Poor Laws and Relief of Distress* op. cit., pp. 140 and 445. Also, Octavia Hill's personal Memorandum on the need for a greater deterrence regarding disenfranchisement limits which is attached to the *Majority Report*, p. 678.

60. A.W. Vincent, op. cit. (1983–4), pp. 362–3.

61. José Harris, 'Political Thought and the Welfare State 1870–1940', *Past and Present*, 135 (May 1992), p. 132.

62. Peter Clarke, *Liberals and Social Democrats* (Cambridge, 1978), pp. 121 and 15.

63. Jane Lewis, op. cit., p. 40.

64. *The Quarterly Review* No. 410, (January 1907), pp. 55–76.

65. Mrs Townshend, op. cit., p. 6.

66. Jane Lewis, op. cit., p. 76.

67. *COReview* XXXI–XXXII, (1912), pp. 131–2.

68. C.L. Mowat, *The Charity Organisation Society – 1869–1913* (1961), pp. 156–9.

69. John A. Hobson, op. cit., p. 717.

70. Madeline Rooff, *A Hundred Years of Family Welfare* (1972), p. 323.

71. Jane Lewis, op. cit., p. 85.

72. *Forty-third Annual Report of COS Council* (17 June 1912), pp. 1–4.

73. *Forty-fifth Annual Report of COS Council* (25 May 1914), p. 2.

74. *Fifty-first Annual Report of COS Council* (19 May 1920), pp. 1 and 3.

75. *Fifty-seventh Annual Report of COS Council* (17 May 1926), pp. 1, 4 and 8.

76. Madeline Roof, op. cit., p. 357.

77. *Sixty-fifth Annual Report of COS Council* (25 April 1934), pp. 1–5.

78. Ibid., p. 11 (italics in original).

79. *COQuarterly*, Vol. XI, No. 3 (July 1937), pp. 193–4. Words in bold and the 3 exclamation marks are in the original.

80. *COQuarterly*, Vol. XII, No. 4, (October 1938), pp. 206–10.

81. Madeline Rooff, op. cit., pp. 169–85.

82. Lawrence Mead, *The Social Obligation of Citizenship* (New York 1986).

83. Charles Murray, *Losing Ground: American Social Policy 1950–1980* (New York 1984).

84. Charles Murray, *Underclass: the Crisis Deepens* (1994).

85. C.S. Loch, 'Loans', *Charity Organisation Paper* No. 6 (1875), p. 1.

86. Table 4.6 indicates the relatively small scale of COS 'returnable grants', as loans became known, by the end of the nineteenth century.

Bibliography

Parliamentary Papers: chronologically listed

Second Annual Report of Poor Law Commissioners, PP1836 [c595], XXIX, p. 43.

Sixth Annual Report of Poor Law Commissioners, PP 1840 [c245], XVII, pp. 16–18.

Twenty-second Annual Report of Poor Law Board, PP 1870 [c123], XXXV.1.

First Annual Report of the Local Government Board, PP 1872 [c516], XXVIII.

Third Annual Report of the Local Government Board, PP 1874 [c1071], XXV.1.

Reports to the Local Government Board by H.M. Secretary of State for Foreign Affairs, 'Poor Laws in Foreign Countries', Introduction, PP 1875 [1255], LXV.I.

Affairs, 'Poor Laws in Foreign Countries', Intrduction, PP 1875 [1255], LXV.1.

Twenty-third Annual Report of Poor Law Board, BPP 1871 (c396), XXVII.

Sixteenth Annual report of Local Government Board, PP 1887 [c5131], XXXVI.1.

Twentieth Annual Report of Local Government Board, PP 1891 [c6460], XXXIII, and PP 1900, LXXIII.743 [c137].

Report of Royal Commission on the Aged Poor, BPP 1895 [c7684], XIV, 2066–9 and 2099.

Report of Interdepartmental Committee on Physical Deterioration, PP 1904 [c2175], XXXII.

Majority Report of the Royal Commission on the Poor Laws and the Relief of Distress, PP 1909 [c4499], XXXVII.

S. and B. Webb (eds), *The Break up of the Poor Law; being Part One of the Minority Report of the poor Law Commission* (1909).

G.R. Snowdon, 'Report on the Guilds of Help ...', PP 1911 [c5664], XXXII.

Unpublished theses and archival material

M.T. Furgol, 'Thomas Chalmers' poor relief theories and their implementation in the early nineteenth century' (PhD thesis, Edinburgh University, 1987).

Gillian Wagner, 'Dr Barnardo and the COS', PhD thesis (LSE, 1977).

Calvin Woodard, 'The COS and the Rise of the Welfare State', PhD thesis (University of Cambridge, 1961).

M.E. Rose, 'Poor Relief and Scientific Charity', unpublished paper (Manchester, c1986).

The Solly papers, LSE archives, miscellaneous 154, 10(b), accession number M226, J 121-J 279 and onwards.

Publications of the Charity Organization Society (COS); from 1944–45, 'The Family Welfare Association'

Annual Reports of the (London) Charity Organisation Society Council, the Society for Organising Charitable Relief and Repressing Mendicity, COS (1870–1944).

Annual Reports of the Family Welfare Association, ('Seventy-seventh' annual report, 1944–5–).

Annual Reports of COS District Committees in London (1870–1944).

Charity Organisation Reporter (COR) weekly publication, Vol. 1, 17 January 1872 to Vol. 13, 24 December 1884.

Charity Organisation Review (COReview) monthly publication, Vol. 1, January 1885 to Vol. 297, new series, September 1921.

Charity Organisation Quarterly (COQuarterly) from Vol. 1, April 1927–October 1938.

Charities Register and Digest annual (1890).

Manual of Society for Organising Charitable Relief and Repressing Mendicity (1870).

COS Report on Soup Kitchens or Dinner-tables of the Metropolis (1871).

Co-operation of District Committees of the COS with Boards of Guardians, COS pamphlet (1879).

Report of London COS Special Committee of the Accounts of Charitable Institutions (1890).

Charity Organisation Paper No. 1 (1871).

C.S. Loch, 'Loans', *Charity Organisation Paper* No. 6 (1875, also revised 1876).

Octavia Hill, 'The Charity Organisation Society', *COS Occasional Paper* No. 15 (1889).

E.W. Benson, 'The Science of Charity', *COS Occasional Paper* No. 19 (1891).

Octavia Hill, 'The Charity Organisation Society', *COS Occasional Paper* No. 20 (1891).

'Church Charity', *COS Occasional Paper* No. 37 (1892).

C.S. Loch, 'Charity Organisation', *COS Occasional Paper* No. 40 (1893).

W. Chance, 'The Better Administration of the Poor Law, *Charity Organisation Series* (1895).

Other reports, pamphlets, learned journals and papers

Report of Society for Relief of Distressed Travellers and Others (Oxford, 1814).

The Philanthropist.

Reports of Brighton Provident and District Society.

Provident Societies Recommended.

Reports of Poor Law Conferences.

Social Notes.

Social Service and Social Justice (National Council of Social Service, April 1949).

Social Work.

Reports of Annual Conferences of Charities and Correction (USA).

Social Service and Social Justice (NCSS, April 1949).

Annual Conferences of Charities (USA).

Publications: alphabetically listed by author

Jane Addams, Charity and Social Justice', *Thirty-seventh National Conference of Charities and Correction*, St Louis (May 1910).

Donna T. Andrew, *Philanthropy and the Police, London Charity in the eighteenth century* (Princetown U.P. 1989).

Anon, *Guilds of Help* (June 1911).

W.A. Bailward, *The Slippery Slope* (1920).

Dudley Baines, 'Population, migration and the regions', R. Floud and D. McCloskey (eds), *The Economic History of Britain since 1700*, Vol. 2 (2nd edn, Cambridge 1994).

Henrietta Barnett, 'What has the Charity Organisation Society to do with Social Reform?' in S. and H. Barnett, *Practicable Socialism* (1895 edn).

Samuel Barnett, 'University Settlements', ibid. (1895).

William Beveridge, *Voluntary Action* (1948).

M. Blaug, 'The Myth of the Old Poor Law and the Making of the New', *Journal of Economic History*, 23, 2 (1963).

Charles Booth, *Life and Labour of the People in London*, 17 Vols (1889–1903).

William Booth, *In Darkest England and the Way Out* (1890).

Bernard Bosanquet, *Knowledge and Reality* (1885).

Bernard Bosanquet, *The Civilisation of Christendom* (1895).

Bernard Bosanquet, (ed.), *Aspects of the Social Problem* (1895).

Bernard Bosanquet, *Philosophical Theory of the State* (1899).

C.B.P. Bosanquet, *London, some Account of its Growth, Charitable Agencies and Wants* (1868).

Helen Bosanquet, *Rich and Poor* (1899).

Helen Bosanquet, *Strength of the People* (1903 edn).

Helen Bosanquet, *Social Work in London, 1869–1912*, (1912).

A.F.C. Bourdillon, *Voluntary Social Services* (1945).

George Bourne, *The Bettesworth Book* (1920 reprint).

Margaret E. Brasnett, *Voluntary Social Action* (1969).

Margaret E. Brasnett, *The Story of the Citizens' Advice Bureaux* (1964).

Stewart J. Brown, *Thomas Chalmers and the Godly Commonwealth in Scotland* (Oxford, 1982).

G. Browne, 'The Elberfeld System of Poor Relief', *West Midland Poor Law Conference* (May 1889).

Maurice Bruce, *The Coming of the Welfare State* (1961).

M. Cahill and Tony Jowitt, 'The New Philanthropy', *Journal of Social Policy*, 9 (3 July 1980).

Thomas Chalmers, *The Christian and Civic Economy of Large Towns*, 3 volumes (Glasgow, 1821–6).

Thomas Chalmers, *On the Sufficiency of the Parochial System Without a Poor Rate for the Right Management of the Poor* (Glasgow, 1841).

W. Chance, 'The Elberfeld and English Poor Law Systems: a Comparison, *Economic Journal*, 7 (1897).

S.G. and E.O.A. Checkland, *The Poor Law Report of 1834*, re-published with introduction (1974).

Olive Checkland, *Philanthropy in Victorian Scotland* (1980).

Peter Clarke, *Liberals and Social Democrats* (Cambridge, 1978).

Una Cormack and Kay McDougall, 'Case-work in Social Service', in Cherry Morris (ed.), *Social Casework* (1950).

George Crabbe, *The Village* (Norton Anthology; English Literature, Vol. 1, (6th edn 1993).

R.T. Davis, 'Pauperism in the City of New York', *Proceedings of the First Conference of Charities and Correction*, New York (May 1874), pp. 24–6.

William Davis, *Hints to Philanthropists or A Collective View of Practical Means for Improving the Condition of the Poor and Labouring Classes of Society* (IUP 1971 facsimile of 1821 Bath edn).

Helen Dendy (later Bosanquet), *Thorough Charity* (1893).

Daniel Devine, *Poverty and Society* (1988).

E.T. Devine, 'The Dominant Note of the Modern Philanthropy', *Thirty-third Annual National Conference of Charities and Correction*, Philadelphia (May 1906).

J. Theodore Dodd, *Infantile Mortality in London Unions* (Oxford, 1906).

John H. Ehrenreich, *The Altruistic Imagination* (Cornell, 1985).

Keith Feiling, *A History of England* (1970 edn).

Judith Fido, 'The COS and Social Casework in London, 1869–1900', in A.P. Donajgrodzki (ed.), *Social Control in Nineteenth Century Britain* (1977).

Derek Foster, *The Evolution of the British Welfare State* (1986 edn).

Michael Freeden, *The New Liberalism: an Ideology of Social Reform* (Oxford, 1978).

Joan Gaddum, *Family Welfare Association of Manchester and Salford, a Short History, 1833–1974* (Manchester 1974).

M. Dorothy George, *London Life in the Eighteenth Century* (1925, Peregrine edn, 1966).

Daniel C. Gilman (ed.), *The Organisation of Charities* (Chicago, 1893).

B. Kirkham Gray, *Philanthropy and the State, or Social Politics* (1908).

Keith Gregson, 'Poor Law and organised charity:…', in Michael E. Rose, *The Poor and the City: the English Poor Law in its Urban Context, 1834–1914* (Leicester 1985), pp. 93–127.

W. Grisewood and A.F. Hanewinkel, *Jubilee Celebrations of the Elberfeld Poor Law* (Liverpool 1903).

W. Grisewood, *The Relief of the Poor in America* (Liverpool, 1905).

W. Grisewood, *The Relief of the Poor in Germany* (Liverpool, 1905).

Edward Grubb, *The Problem of Poverty and the Work of the Christian Church* (1887).

S.H. Gurteen, *Handbook of Charitable Organisation* (Buffalo, NY, 1882).

José Harris, 'Political Thought and the Welfare State 1870–1940', *Past and Present*, 135 (May 1992).

Jennifer Hart, 'Sir Charles Trevelyan at the Treasury', *English Historical Review*, Vol. LXXV (January 1960), p. 99.

Thomas Hawksley, *Charities of London and Some Errors of their Administration, with some Suggestions for an Improved System of Private and Official Charitable Relief*, paper to the Society of Arts (17 December 1868).

Kathleen Heaseman, *Evangelicals in Action* (1962).

Kathleen Heasman, *Christians and Social Work* (1965), LSE 'pamphlet' collection; B/c268.

John A. Hobson, 'The Social Philosophy of Charity Organisation', *Contemporary Review* LXX (1896).

Glenn K. Horridge, *The Salvation Army* (1993).

Robert Humphreys, *LSE Working Paper in Economic History*, No. 14, *Scientific Charity in Victorian London* (July 1993).

Robert Humphreys, *Sin, Organized Charity and the Poor Law in Victorian England* (1995).

J.B. Hurry, *Poverty and its Vicious Circles* (2nd edn 1921).

Gareth Stedman Jones, *Outcast London* (Peregrine edn 1984).

Michael B. Katz, *In the Shadow of the Poor House* (New York, 1986).

Michael B. Katz, *The Underclass Debate* (Princeton, 1993).

Robert F. Keegan, 'Democracy at the Cross-roads', *Sixty-third Annual National Conference of Social Work*, New Jersey (May 1936).

Dorothy C. Keeling, The Crowded Stairs (Plymouth, 1961).

H.J. Kellard, 'The Burial of Bumble', *Social Work*, Vol. 5, No. 2, April 1948, p.169.

Alan Kidd, 'Charity Organisation and the Manchester Unemployed, c1870–1914', *Social History*, 9 (1984).

G. Lansbury, *My Life* (1928).

Keith Laybourn, *The Guild of Help and the Changing Face of Edwardian Philanthropy* (Lampeter, 1994).

Keith Laybourn, *The Evolution of British Social Policy…* (Keele, 1995).

Helen Hollen Less, *The Solidarities of Strangers: the English Poor Laws and the People, 1700–1948* (Cambridge, 1998).

James Leiby, *The History of Social Welfare and Social Work in the United States* (New York, 1978).

Baldwyn Leighton, (ed.), *Letters and Other Writings of the Late Edward Denison, M.P. for Newark* (1872).

Jane Lewis, *The Voluntary Sector, the State and Social Work in Britain* (1996).

D. Lindsay, 'Introduction' to T.H. Green, *Political Obligation* (1941 reprint).

C.S. Loch, *The National Insurance Bill* (1911).

Helen Lynd, *England in the Eighteen-eighties* (1968).

Elizabeth Macadam, *The New Philanthropy* (1934).

A.M. McBriar, *An Edwardian Mixed Doubles; the Bosanquets v. The Webbs* (Oxford, 1987).

O.C. McCulloch, 'Associated Charities, Report of the Committee on Charitable Organisation in Cities', *Proceedings of the National Council of Charities and Correction* (1880).

Thomas Mackay, *Co-operation of Charitable Agencies with the Poor Law* (1893).

Thomas Mackay, *A History of the English Poor Law from 1834 to the Present Time* (1899).

Alfred Marshall, *Principles of Economics* (1891 edn).

J.D. Marshall, *The Old Poor Law 1795–1834* (1973 reprint).

C.L. Marson, *Charity Organisation and Jesus Christ* (1897).

Lawrence Mead, *The Social Obligation of Citizenship* (New York, 1986).

Henry A. Mess, *Voluntary Social Services since 1918* (1947).

John Stuart Mill, *Utilitarianism* (1863, 12th edn 1895).

C.L. Mowat, *The Charity Organisation Society, 1869–1913* (1961).

Charles Murray, *Losing Ground: American Social Policy, 1950–1980* (New York 1984).

Charles Murray, *Underclass: the Crisis Deepens* (1994).

Howard Newby, 'The Deferential Dialectic', *Comparative Studies in Society and History*, Vol. 17, No. 2 (1975), p. 161.

O. Newman and A. Foster, *The Value of the Pound* (1995).

John Boyle O'Reilly, 'Bohemia and Society', in Katherine E. Conway (ed.), *Watchwords* (Boston, 1891).

David Owen, *English Philanthropy, 1660–1960* (1965).

G.W. Oxley, *Poor Relief in England and Wales 1601–1834* (1974).

E.A. Pearson, 'Some elements of hope from the War', *COR*, No. 216 (October 1915), pp. 337–8.

George C. Peden, *British Economic and Social Ploicy: Llyod George to Margaret Thatcher* (Oxford 1985).

J.C. Pringle, *Social Work of the London Churches* (1937).

Frank K. Prochaska, *Women and Philanthropy in Nineteenth Century England* (Oxford, 1980).

E.C. Ramsbottom, 'The course of wage rates in the UK', *Journal of Royal Statistical Society*, Vol. 98 (1935).

Margaret E. Rich, *The Belief in People* (New York, 1956).

Mary E. Richmond, *Friendly Visiting among the Poor* (1899).

Mary E. Richmond, *The Long View* (1930).

M.J.D. Roberts, 'Reshaping the Gift Relationship', *International Review of Social History*, XXXVI (1991).

B. Rodgers, *The Battle against Poverty*, Vol. 1, *From Pauperism to Human Rights* (1968).

Madeline Rooff, *A Hundred Years of Family Welfare* (1972).

Seebohm Rowntree, *Poverty: a Study of Town Life* (1922 edition).

John Ruskin, *Unto This Last and other writings* (1862, Penguin edn 1985).

G. Sabine, *A History of Political Theory* (New York, 1963).

A.A. Toynbee, *Lectures on the Industrial Revolution* (1887).

G. Sabine, *A History of Political Theory* (New York, 1963).

Robert Sandall, *The History of the Salvation Army* Vol. III (1953).

R. Saunderson, 'The Relief of the Unemployed', *COReview*, No. 290 (February 1921), p. 119

K. de Schweinitz, *England's Road to Social Security* (South Brunswick, 1975 edn).

M. Sewell, 'Some Aspects of Charity Organisation' (29 November 1897); cited by Jane Lewis, op. cit. (1996).

L.V. Shairp, 'Industrial Disputes and the Relief of Distress', *COReview*, Vol. XXXV (January 1914), pp. 30–7.

Margaret Simey, *Charitable Effort in Liverpool in the Nineteenth Century*, (Liverpool, 1951).

Samuel Smiles, *Self-Help* (1859, IEA edn 1996).

Adam Smith, *The Wealth of Nations* (1776).

Samuel Smith, *The Economics of Charity* (1888).

Henry Solly, *How to Deal with the Unemployed Poor of London and with its 'Roughs' and Criminal Classes*, paper to the Society of Arts (22 June 1868).

Thomas J. Sugrue, 'The Structures of Urban Poverty: the Reorganisation of Space and Work in Three Periods of American History', in Michael B. Katz, op. cit. (1993).

Pat Thame, *Foundations of the Welfare State* (2nd edn 1996).

Flora Thompson, *Lark rise to Candleford* (1939).

Richard Titmuss, *Problems of Social Policy* (1950).

Richard Titmuss, *Commitment to Welfare* (1968).

Mrs Townshend, 'The Case against the COS', *Fabian Tract* No. 158 (1911).

A.A. Toynbee, *Lectures on the Industrial Revolution* (1887).

E.B. Tylor, *Primitive Culture* (1913 edn).

A.W. Vincent, 'The Poor Law Reports of 1909 and the Social Theory of the Charity Organisation Society', *Victorian Studies*, 27 (1983–4).

Andrew Vincent and Raymond Plant, *Philosophy, Politics and Citizenship* (1984).

David Ward, *Poverty, Ethnicity and the American City, 1840–1925* (Cambridge 1989).

F.D. Watson, *The Charity Organisation Movement in the USA* (New York 1922).

Robert Wearmouth, The Social and Political Influence of Methodism ... (1957).

Beatrice Webb, *My Apprenticeship* (1979 edn).

Karel Williams, *From Pauperism to Poverty* (1981).

Kathleen Woodroofe, *From Charity to Social Work in England and the United States* (1962).

J. Hornsby Wright, *Thoughts and Experiences of a Charity Organizationist* (1878).

Norman Wymer, *Father of Nobody's Children* (1954).

A.F. Young and E.T. Ashton, *British Social Work in the Nineteenth Century* (1956).

G. Williams, *The State and the Standard of Living* (1936).

Index

volunteers – *continued*
  leisured classes, 178
  matching with applicants, 28, 91,
    98, 104, 129
  overseas, 128
  recruitment, 25, 31–3, 37–9, 43, 63,
    65, 91, 98, 104, 127–31, 137,
    150, 169–70, 178, 182
  social status, 30, 33, 63, 66, 128,
    178, 185
  sympathies misplaced, 28, 81–2, 86,
    136, 169–70
  training, 66, 91, 103–4, 124,
    128–31, 136–7, 169–70
  unreliable, 82, 86, 128, 136, 170

Wages, 76, 79–80, 106, 173, 183
War
  American War of Independence, 2
  Boer, 137
  Civil War (USA), 149
  First World, 96, 100, 108, 137, 142,
    159, 180
  Hundred Years, 2
  Napoleonic, 2
  Second World, 110–11, 131, 184
  widows, 102, 120, 181
Washington, DC, 149
Waterloo, Battle of, 2
Watson, F.D., 152
Watt, James, 2
wealthy public
Webb, Beatrice, 176, 179
Webber, W.H.Y., 167
Webster, Thomas, 23
welfare system, 26, 97, 127, 184

Wellington, Duke of, 2
West Ham, 120, 122
West, Col, 33–4
Westminster, 46, 128
  Marquis of, 33–4
Wharncliffe, Lord, 49
Whatley, Archbishop, 14
Whitechapel, 24, 37, 46, 49–50, 65,
  81, 84, 107–8, 172
Whitehall, 87, 99–101, 104, 110, 137,
  181, 183
Wilberforce, William, 13
Wilkinson, W.M., 20, 22, 26, 57
Wilson, Lady, 136
Wiltshire, 14
Wimbledon, 142
Winchester, 133
Wodehouse, Rev. A.P., 136
Wood Street Mission, Manchester, 137
Woollcombe, H.L., 99, 101
Worcestershire, 14
work, 7, 67, 80–1, 97, 138, 170
  'chronically slack', 80
  irregular, 170
  odd jobs, 110
  part-time, 110
  'test', 56, 176
Work Centres, 108
worker mobility
workers, industrial, 97, 106
Working Men's Club and Institute, 19
Workmen's Club Journal, 165
Wright, Hornsby, 32, 165

York, 146
Yorkshire, 135